THE LIVING EARTH BOOK OF

WIND &
WEATHER

THE LIVING EARTH BOOK OF

WIND & WEATHER

CARL A. POSEY

Reader's Digest

THE READER'S DIGEST ASSOCIATION, INC.
Pleasantville, New York / Montreal

The Living Earth Book of Wind & Weather

A Reader's Digest Living Earth Book

Produced for The Reader's Digest Association, Inc.,
by Redefinition, Inc.

The credits that appear on pages 222-223 are hereby made a part of
this copyright page.

Library of Congress Cataloging in Publication Data

Posey, Carl A., 1933–
        The living earth book of wind & weather / Carl A. Posey.
            p.   cm.—(Reader's Digest living earth)
        Includes index.
        ISBN 0-89577-625-1 (alk. paper)
        1. Winds.   2. Air.   3. Weather.   I. Title.   II. Series:
QC931.P77 1994
551.5'1—dc20   94-16264

Printed on recycled paper

Printed in the United States of America

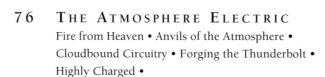

An Ocean
of Air

All life, as far as anyone has been able to discover, occurs in the lower depths of an invisible ocean of air and in the denser sea of water it enfolds. This transparent wrapper may be the unique abode of life. Nothing spends its whole life very far above the bottom of this atmosphere, except for the odd bacterium adrift on invisible currents—not even the soaring bird, certainly not the human borne aloft on improvised wings.

We rarely notice much of this shallow ocean of air. The motions, the life-pervading events, that endlessly unfold there concern us mainly as they alarm or threaten the safety of our benthic home. For the atmosphere to seize our attention, it must offer a roaring gale, a wall of water, lightning flickering like rage in a band of black thunderclouds, or an apocalyptic tale of what harm the human hand can do to this life-sustaining sea of air. We perceive, without quite seeing, the atmosphere's invisible hand—the shiver of leaves caused by a passing breeze, the shift in wind direction that means that some aspect of life will subtly change.

But if we think about such things at all, we tend to do so only perfunctorily; most of us are not much drawn to trace the more subtle currents of the atmosphere—there are professional weather people who do that for a living. Farmers and mariners and aviators, whose lives are linked to the air, still find significance in a red sunset or the sharp reversal of a blast of wind. Fewer and fewer among us, however, have more than a passing interest in what transpires in the more distant reaches of our vast, gaseous enclosure. We are as complacent about our comfortably furnished capsule of wind and air as goldfish are about their bowl of water.

It should go just the other way. Our ocean of air should be as vivid to us as the water ocean seems to be to the canny cetaceans who plumb it, who seem to know where the great, globe-circling currents flow, what food they carry, what threats and benefits. After all, our bodies and senses have evolved for life in a transparent sea, a world where air, not water, is the medium of scent and sound—where it is life itself. Like our ocean-going cousins, we feed on the atmosphere, filtering out its oxygen to fuel our vital internal fires, and give back a carbon-rich exhaust that plants breathe—and exhale more oxygen into the atmosphere.

The wind and air speak to us, but in a language that we seem less and less able to comprehend. If we were like elephants, which are believed to communicate at sound frequencies too low for humans to hear, we might discern the soft, infrasonic messages of storms a thousand miles away or detect the atmospheric ripples that fan out from any heavy weather. Lightning might appear not as celestial bolts but as a cleaving of the ambient electromagnetic field.

Our sea of air would then clamor for and hold our attention, not merely because it makes our homeland warm or cold, moist or dry, dangerous or safe, but because it would be perceived whole and fully interwoven. We would possess a keen awareness that weather is ever-changing news of the lower atmosphere and would perceive in the longer sweeps that mark climatic change an airy counterpart to human history. The thunderclouds and lightning, the winds and whirlwinds that populate the planet's old mythologies, would intertwine with the fabric of our lives.

This province, now rendered ordinary, can easily be restored to something rare—we just strap on a pair of wings and, like an immature albatross learning, as someone once wrote, to be an albatross, feel the rush of wind and air across an outstretched wing. Every pilot knows that inspiring touch of air upon the borrowed wings of airplanes—small craft whose wings, instructors like to nag, are your wings. And so they are. Upon their surface you feel the air, the fluid medium of flight, as you would a rush of water. To fly through the cool, stable, dense atmosphere of autumn is like diving through a cold, crystal-clear sea. The aircraft shudders each time currents of differing velocities brush against one another in a zone of turbulent shear. One's kinesthetic sense discerns the movement of the buoyant gas as it floods downward into canyons, where these once-placid currents, were they water, would go white with foam.

But the firm stroke of the atmosphere upon those wings also puts you in touch with something much larger. The whole mantle seems to become as transparently visible as a clear sea, the currents moving along surfaces defined by the density and temperature of air. From this immediate and discernible scale you can infer whole continents of atmospheric activity. A little imagination is all that is needed to sense that today's uplifting currents first spooled off a body of dense air and then descended, dry and clear, to boom across the land until the barrier of mountains cams them upward for thousands of feet, where they rise and cool—and, if you are in the right place at the right time, send you soaring on your borrowed wings. At such moments, the mind can almost grasp the shifting patterns of the web of global winds, the pulses that bring today's weather from a mountain range or desert or ocean half a world away. It is a rare moment, to see our vast, complicated envelope of air suddenly whole; alas, it is seldom nowadays that we look up with anything like wonder. But wonder still awaits us there. ☁

THINNER THAN AN ONION SKIN

Held up against the fiery face of the middle-sized star we call the Sun, our planet is barely a freckle; and the airy domain of all life, relative to this tiny sphere, is thinner than the skin of an onion.

Seen small, the atmosphere is easier to comprehend. A laboratory demonstration might begin with a perfectly smooth sphere the size of a basketball, covered by an invisible shell of air. This shell has a dense lower stratum that is nearly as thin as a sheet of paper near the surface and then diminishes outward until it vanishes into the space beyond our model. If the ball is then made to spin from west to east, this shell would begin to move with it, but in a slippery fashion, so that east-west winds begin to circle with the toy planet. And even at this elementary stage, the orderly bands may show signs that they are prone to riot.

The Winds of a Spinning Planet

Although these planet-girdling winds move in a straight line through space, their imprint along the planet's turning surface is curved. In a sense, every wind is a whirlwind. These twists are produced by the *Coriolis effect*, named for Gustave-Gaspard Coriolis, the 19th-century French physics professor who first applied theory to what had been observed but not understood: A body—a parcel of air, an artillery projectile, a fallen tree drifting on an ocean current—traveling in a straight line over a rotating Earth describes a curved path on the ground. He translated that idea into a force acting at a 90° angle to the direction of motion, one that becomes more pronounced with increasing wind speed.

On our spinning laboratory model of the Earth, the Coriolis effect merely adds some scallops along the edges where currents of different velocities shear and eddy against one another. Later, this effect will twist poleward-moving air into the familiar swirling spirals of cyclones and storms.

Held loosely to the planet by gravity, the gaseous envelope is strongly inclined to stratify horizontally, with the lower layers compressed by the weight of the upper layers. If gravity were the only force at work, the air would be more compressed in its lower layers than it is. But its gradual thinning with altitude and the decrease in atmospheric pressure with height generate an upward counterforce. In this way, the air remains suspended, neither rising nor sinking very much at all. The resulting poise is what scientists call *hydrostatic balance*, and, because it operates most of the time—the competing forces of gravity and expansion are never more than slightly and temporarily unequal—the more

or less horizontal impulse of the atmosphere is regarded as its normal behavior.

Strong vertical movement—*convection*, as it is called—is the anomaly. Indeed, the atmosphere's inclination to move forcefully upward is equated with instability. As in structures and human personalities, the word suggests that you should be prepared for the worst. In fact, almost all of the real heart-stopping drama in the atmosphere comes from vertical motion, up or down, of air from its proper stratum to a higher or lower one—remarkable, when you think that this convective motion occurs in something relatively thinner than an onion skin.

LET THERE BE LIGHT

Until now, our model has been spinning in a uniform twilight, with its surface and the air swirling over it both at a constant temperature. Now change the lighting so that a beam of hot illumination comes only from the right; half the spinning ball is now always in darkness. Where the gas is heated, it expands; where it is cold, it remains dense and heavy. But these differences are not merely those between day and night: The sphere receives more illumination at its equator than at its poles. Thus, the laboratory Sun has created an equatorial zone of relatively light, warm air, flanked by polar zones of relatively heavy, cold air.

In the process, this inequality of heating has sculpted an invisible terrain defined by the relative weight of the atmosphere. Humans have almost certainly known for millennia that wind was a force—it filled ancient sails and propelled the blades of antique windmills, after all. Evangelista Torricelli, incumbent in Galileo's chair of mathematics in Florence, demonstrated that air also had weight. He invented an instrument to measure atmospheric weight—a *barometer*—in 1643, after discovering that if you stand an evacuated glass tube vertically in a pot of water, *something* presses on the water's surface, squeezing it up almost 34 feet (10 m) in the glass tube. By substituting a much denser fluid—mercury—for water, he could reckon that force in inches of mercury; 29.92 inches

A strong breeze fills the sails of the four-masted barkentine *Sea Cloud* in the Pacific Ocean off Baja California. From earliest times, coastal inhabitants around the world have found ways to harness the inexhaustible force of the winds, creating one of the earliest forms of long-distance transportation.

(0.76 m) of mercury is the nominal value at sea level. Torricelli correctly inferred the *something* to be the weight of the atmosphere—*atmospheric pressure*.

From his work came the means of observing the air by measuring its weight and seeing how the weight varies with time and place and with altitude. At sea level the weight of the atmosphere is about 14.7 pounds per square inch, often expressed in another unit, the *bar*—a name, like that of Torricelli's barometer, derived from the Greek word for weight—in the metric system of measurement. But the unit used most often today is the *millibar,* one thousandth of a bar. If pressure is contoured into a topographic map of the imaginary terrain of air—the weightier portions being portrayed as hills, the lighter ones as valleys and sinks—millibars provide a counterpart to meters and feet. Standard sea-level pressure is 1,013.2 millibars, a weight that is said to equal one atmosphere. Most of the time the contours of this terrain are gentle, rarely reaching highs above 1,050 millibars or lows below 960 millibars.

The flow of the air becomes more chaotic as the gas flows from dense to less dense, from the mounds of high pressure to the valleys of low pressure. Its impulse is to rush straight down the steepest slopes of high pressure into the valleys of low; instead, deflected by the force that Coriolis noticed, the air moves like a conservative skier, following the contours of this invisible terrain. Air does not go screaming into the deep low-pressure center of a storm; rather, it glides in around it.

North of the Equator, the air flows clockwise around high pressure, counterclockwise around low; south of the Equator, these flows reverse. The winds spiraling toward and away from these unseen features seem in other respects to be random and restless; in fact, they are deliberate currents of a gas that perpetually seeks, but can never find, equilibrium. In the fluid dynamic game, there is no rest for the windy.

There is, however, a kind of latent equilibrium that may be detected on a long airplane flight along an east-west course. If the pilot merely plots a compass heading between the point of departure and some distant destination, the atmosphere's tendency to compensate will usually maintain the craft on its course, at least according to one expert. Max Conrad, a famous flyer of light airplanes over vast distances—he flew a Piper Aztec around the world in 1961 and left another on the Antarctic ice trying to fly a north-south great circle around the Earth 9 years later—maintained that on a long flight you need only hold a steady compass course

because the winds, spinning now north, now south, now from ahead, now from behind, tend to cancel one another out. In the resulting more or less straight line of your flight, the atmosphere's hidden equilibrium can be read.

Now, looking more closely at our model, it seems that something else is going on. The air, which began as parallel strands of prevailing currents in our first model and later became scalloped and illuminated in the next two models, now develops a strong impulse north and south from the Equator. Hot air between the tropics shuttles toward the poles, where, sinking and cooling, it turns back toward the equatorial heat. Aided by the tendency of the global ocean of water to change temperature slowly, the air keeps moving in its efforts to moderate its extremes. The atmosphere begins to look like a simple heat engine, no more complicated than the circulation in a pot of heated water.

The swirls, or cells, created by this thermal motion—tiny on a basketball-sized model, immense in the real atmosphere—are named for George Hadley, the British physicist who first explained the existence of the westward-moving winds of the tropics. Using data from the *trade winds*, as these are called, he created a model of this flow of air between the Equator and the poles. Hadley thought one great cell would do for each hemisphere. But, hypothesizing all this a century before Coriolis came along, he missed the effect of the planet's rotation, which transforms his simple north-south circulation into the more horizontal spirals of a strong high-pressure area. For example, winds blowing around the Azores–Bermuda High, a fixture over the North Atlantic, move east to west in this part of their clockwise flow from the tropics toward the Arctic, where they give up their heat energy, cool, and sink back toward the Equator.

But these easterly winds are found mainly at the lowest depths of the atmosphere. Farther up, the winds are mostly

HIGH AND LOW PRESSURE

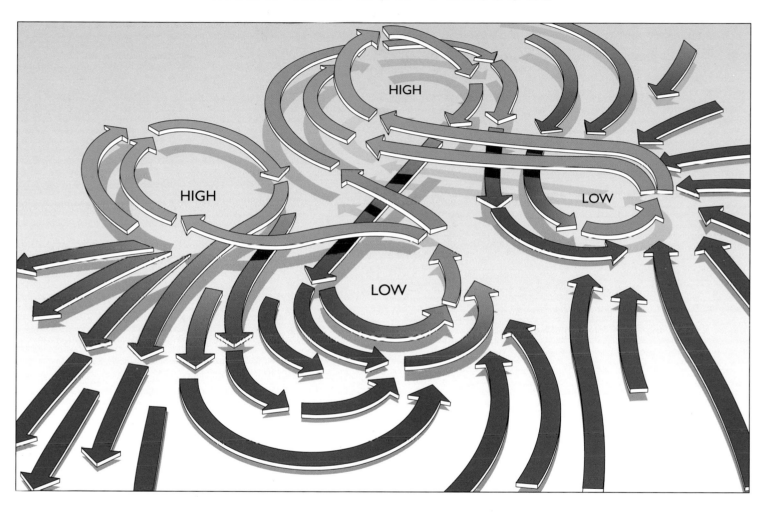

A search for equilibrium drives winds from areas of relatively higher atmospheric pressure toward centers of lower atmospheric pressure, portrayed here as a kind of invisible freeway system. Twisted by Coriolis effects, surface air (*red*) converges toward low pressure. In the northern hemisphere air moves around low pressure in a counterclockwise cyclonic sweep as it rises (*purple*). Behind it, more surface air converges.

As the uplifted air (*blue*) spools off the top of the low pressure system, however, it descends clockwise, or *anticyclonically*, around the slopes of a high pressure area—like a skier following the contours of a slope. Diverging at the surface, the air renews it quest for low pressure in an unending series of airy figure eights.

- ■ **Cool air**
- ■ **Sinking or rising air**
- ■ **Warm air**

the winds of a spinning planet, girdling the Earth from west to east in the same way that the high-level winds of Jupiter and Saturn band their giant planets. Chaos, like pressure and density, decreases with height.

A PLANET FOR ALL SEASONS

A final touch is needed to make the laboratory globe more like the real world. So far, the sphere has rotated on a vertical axis, with the light striking it at right angles. Now tilt this axis 23.45°—the exact angle wobbles very slightly over time—so that the illumination strikes the sphere obliquely, exacerbating the chaotic surface flow already introduced by uneven heating. Finally, set the model in orbit around our powerful light source, so that the strongest rays strike different parts of the planet at different points in the orbit. This creates changes that occur at longer intervals than those of days and nights— changes we experience in the real world as seasons.

The Sun illuminates one face of the planet, bringing the dawn to eastern Africa. The terminator—the constantly moving division between day and night—shows up clearly.

We trace this progress through an illusion: the Sun seems to move across the sky each day and to shift position north or south—relative to us—during the year. It only appears to rise in the east because the Earth rotates us toward it, and the illusion that it moves north and south across the Equator comes from the changing vantage points along our year-long orbit.

The two extremes in this illusory creeping of the Sun across the sky—the northernmost and southernmost lines on the globe to catch a perpendicular solar ray—are parallels of latitude called *tropics*, named for constellations that are in the sky when the Sun appears to be directly overhead: Capricorn in the south, Cancer in the north. They are as far from the Equator—23.45 degrees of latitude—angularly speaking, as the Earth is tilted on its axis. When the Sun's rays strike these parallels straight on, the event is called a *solstice*. When the perpendicular solar ray strikes the Equator—it happens twice each year—the event is called an *equinox*.

During the December solstice, the planet is closest to the Sun, but the Northern Hemisphere is tilted away from it; everything there grows cold, and the chilled atmosphere flows southward. Approaching the June solstice, the Earth is farthest from its star, but the Northern Hemisphere tilts toward the light. The north's atmosphere warms along with its land and sea; it carries summer to the Arctic.

MIDNIGHT SUN

Some summer evenings go on and on. From the time the Sun strikes the equator—the equinox—about March 21, the frozen land above the Arctic Circle sees more and more sunlight until the Sun ceases setting. The closer to the pole, the longer the period of the midnight sun. At 71° north latitude, the parallel of Barrow, Alaska, the Sun does not set from May 10 to August 2. At the North Pole itself, there is no sunset for about six months. Summer becomes a short-lived paradise of eternal light for plants and insects. The long growing season produces pansies and petunias the size of dinner plates, fills the air with hardy mosquitos and blackflies, and creates fruits and vegetables on the grand scale.

The reason for this plethora of sunlight is the 23.5° tilt of the Earth's axis of rotation, which presents the northern or southern polar regions to the Sun during part of the planet's year-long orbit. During those intervals between equinox and solstice, the Sun stays in the Arctic or Antarctic polar sky, skirting the horizon without setting.

These events are etched on the Earth's surface by four imaginary circles parallel to the equator: the Tropic of Cancer at 23.5° north, the Tropic of Capricorn at 23.5° south, and the Arctic and Antarctic Circles at 66.5° latitude. The Tropics mark the Sun's closest approach to the poles—the solstice—during its illusory passage north and south. The Circles mark the lower limits of summer's midnight sun.

Setting only far enough to brush the mountain tops before rising again, the summer sun moves across the sky of the Arctic North in this multiple-exposure photograph (above). At the North Pole this phenomenon occurs every night for a full six months.

Their faces painted crimson by the midnight sun, tourists photograph a colorful view in Kotzebue, Alaska (above), where there is a full day of continuous sunlight during the June solstice. Because the low-flying midnight sun stays close to the horizon, its light—like the light of a setting sun—follows a long path through the stratosphere, which scatters and absorbs light at the blue end of the color spectrum, and reddens the sky. The long hours of daylight during the growing season also affect plants, producing monsters such as this 98-pound (44.5-kg) cabbage (right) grown in Palmer, Alaska, in 1990.

New Alaska State Fair record 98 LBS. Alaska GROWN LESLY DINKEL

DAVE INGALLS

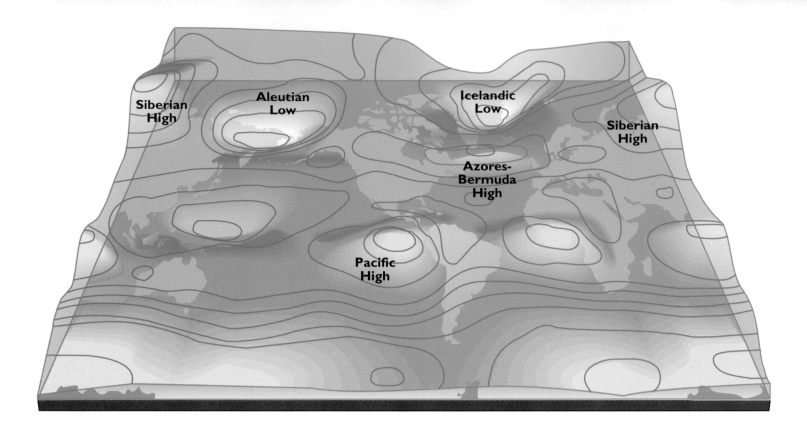

The invisible terrain of atmospheric pressure over the planet's surface in January appears in this "topographic" treatment, in which lines of equal pressure—isobars—averaged for January have been used as contour lines to define the wrinkled surface followed by the winds.

PREVAILING WESTERLIES

All of this geography is written in the atmosphere, albeit less neatly than on a map. Like the planet it enfolds, the atmosphere too has a kind of equator, a shifting, wriggling zone where the tropics of the Northern and Southern Hemispheres meet—weatherfolk call this the *Intertropical Convergence Zone.* Lying generally a few degrees north of the geographic equator, it holds the bands of easterly winds set up by cold air returning to be revitalized by the sun.

North of the tropics, again, is a wavy zone that ebbs and intensifies—an invisible terrain of mountains and valleys that alters seasonally. In winter, the dominant features in this endlessly changing topography are huge centers of high pressure—there is nothing else on earth like the dome of cold air that creates the Siberian High, poised over eastern Central Asia. Next to it is a declivity of pressure, the Aleutian Low. Farther east, winter brings the Icelandic Low, a large crater of low pressure sitting over the North Atlantic at about the latitude of Hudson Bay. The tracks of the world's great northern storms braid through the valleys between this high and low terrain. Farther south, the Azores–Bermuda High takes the winter form of a long saddle of high pressure stretching from

JANUARY PRESSURE SURFACE MAP

The invisible terrain of atmospheric pressure over the planet's surface in January appears in this "topographic" treatment, in which lines of equal pressure—isobars—averaged for January have been used as contour lines to define the wrinkled surface followed by the winds. Major features are the frigid "mountain" of the *Siberian High* in the north, where it is winter, and deep, storm-breeding lows over *Iceland and the Aleutians.* The *Azores-Bermuda High* is elongated into a long ridge. Below the equator, the major feature is the persistent *Pacific High*; south of the Pacific High is a "cliff" of low pressure—the region called the Roaring Forties for its ferocious winds.

the mid-Atlantic almost all the way across the United States.

South of the Equator, the terrain takes a different form in winter. A parade of weak and poorly defined highs—rounded foothills—drifts over the equatorial oceans. But even farther south, one sees why the region is known as the Roaring Forties. The isobars—pressure-map equivalents of topographic contour lines—stream around the planet, packed close together; like topographic contours, they suggest a cliff. The conservative-skier metaphor we used earlier to describe the

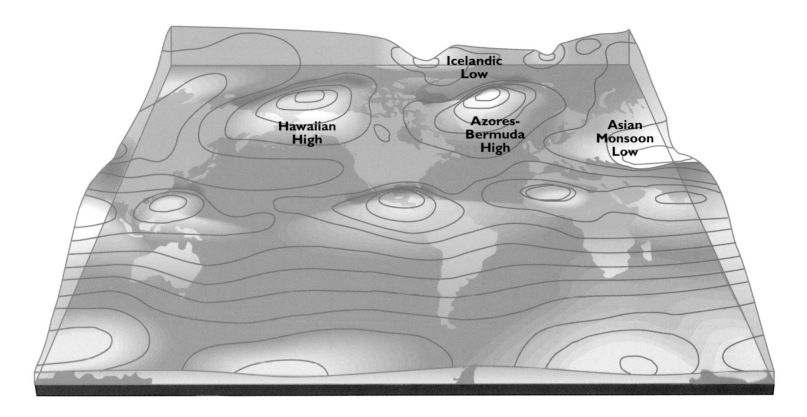

The image shows labels: Icelandic Low, Hawaiian High, Azores-Bermuda High, Asian Monsoon Low

JULY PRESSURE SURFACE MAP

Patterns of atmospheric pressure, and the contours followed by the planet's winds, change radically during the northern summer, as seen in this topographic rendering of the surface-pressure isobars averaged for July. North of the tropics, the *Siberian High* has dissipated and the *Icelandic Low* has filled, but a deep *Asian Monsoon Low* has formed over the Indian Ocean. Two dominant anti-cyclones—the *Hawaiian High* in the Pacific, the *Azores-Bermuda High* in the Atlantic—dominate midlatitude weather, feeding the trade winds. In the southern hemisphere, winter has flattened the oceanic highs, and the southern cliff of low pressure, while still steep—and stormy—is less precipitous.

movement of air along contours changes here to that of a skier going fast enough to keep from slipping off a near-vertical slope. The winds in this southern quadrant of the world, almost free of obstruction in the form of land masses, go howling eastward around and around the Earth, carrying their legendary storms with them.

The first mutiny on the *Bounty* might have come when Captain Bligh pushed into this region in March 1788, sailing upwind around the tip of South America, Tahiti-bound. The famously uncompromising skipper pushed his 215-ton merchantman against the banshee winds for a month before, his crew and ship exhausted and in grave danger, Bligh turned east and, sailing with the winds, took the easier, five-month-long road to the Pacific.

But the captain would not have fared much better had he tried the same journey in summer. The Southern Hemisphere quiets a little then—the sheer cliff of low pressure that drops off below the tip of South America becomes slightly less sheer—but the winds still howl and the waves still rise.

Between the tropics, along the atmosphere's wandering, weaving counterpart of the planet's Equator, summer breathes life back into the easterlies, which build and pulse in shallow currents across the equatorial ocean. At higher latitudes, the westerlies ease in intensity but they remain always well defined. They are the currents in which most of the world's weather is borne along in a loose plait of winds, some converging toward zones of low pressure, where they rise and spread and cool, others sinking down the slopes of high pressure, drying and heating and moving out across the land. For most of the world's people, this splendid progression of the westerlies *is* the atmosphere.

Currents of Life

Along the Potomac River at dusk in late October, a puzzling clatter that at first seems to be the sound of a broken machine becomes audible. Only when its source is overhead is it clear that the noise emanates from a vee of Canada geese, leaving behind the advancing northern winter. The winds are the roads that a goose finds and uses. But at this time of year, the flight south means tacking across the lower reaches of the prevailing westerlies.

For these and other birds and for some insects, the seasonal changes of the prevailing winds are more than merely geophysical diversions. They are tides of life that ebb and flow, provoking a restless shiver in animals noting that the Sun flies lower in the sky, that winter chills the autumn air, and that some deep instinct resonates—that it is time to embark on the exhausting annual journey of migration.

Following navigational cues from the retreating Sun and the Earth's other invisible shell—a bipolar magnetic field—the migrants may move a relatively few miles or travel from one polar circle to another. Ukraine's big, tough-looking crows fly only a few hundred miles to eastern Austria, where the hard winter is evidently less hard than the one at home. Terns cantering in summer along the gravel beaches of Point Barrow, on Alaska's northern coast, can be found during the northern winter darting along the bleak shores of Tierra del Fuego.

The flyways between seasonal homelands seem to have been set down thousands of generations ago, and no human is certain how much must be learned to use them. Experiments suggest that, even if the urge to migrate is inborn, the skills needed to do it are not: Birds, like the struggling aviators of 50 years ago, must somehow *learn* celestial navigation if they fly at night; they may also need to learn secrets of the magnetic environment. But no amount of adaptation and learning makes these journeys safe. According to some scientists, many

Canada geese rouse at dawn after a night on a frozen pond in Batavia, Illinois. After breeding in Canada and the northern United States in spring and summer, the geese migrate as far south as Mexico in the fall as their northern homes begin to ice over.

The wind blows a tumbleweed from a Russian thistle plant, scattering its seeds across a treeless steppe in Asia. Common also on the plains and prairies of North America and southeastern Europe, tumbleweeds break off from their roots at maturity and dry into a tangled ball that rolls with the wind.

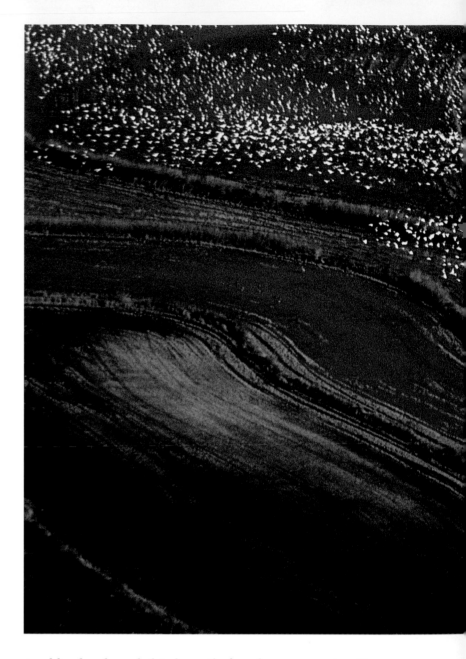

species lose half their number during a single migration to the hazards of exhaustion, predation, and simply getting lost.

The atmosphere is the medium of migration, not the cause; animals migrate less toward spas of fine weather than toward more abundant food and a reasonably secure place to reproduce—parents cannot feed themselves and their offspring in a home locked in ice and snow, patrolled by hungry carnivores. Bats, for example, migrate south following the schedule of ripening fruit; Africa's desert locusts are interested only in the food and breeding possibilities of the seasonal but infrequent rain—good rains mean a good harvest for the continent's human inhabitants, but they can also attract a whirring plague of several billion hungry insects.

Some plants, too, have evolved a kind of migration that disperses their seeds. The tumbleweeds that scoot across the world's great plains and prairies during any good wind are designed with a breakaway crown that lets them roll; as they

tumble, they leave behind a trail of seeds, guaranteeing diversity among their offspring. But most plants, however much they may turn to face the Sun, cannot migrate. To disperse their genes, many of them use elaborate strategies to persuade bees and other insects to be their pollinators, the messengers and go-betweens, the burros of the reproductive cycle. For others, especially among old species, the middleman has always been the wind.

The cottonwood and dandelion, for example, send out whiskered seeds that take maximum advantage of the passing

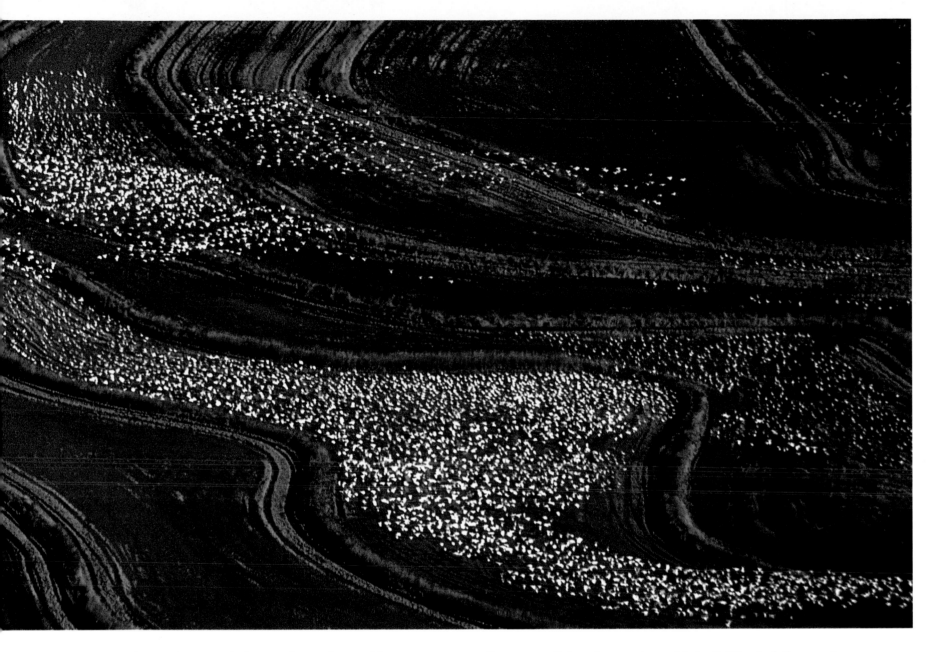

breezes, sailing miles away before settling. The seed-bearers—the fruits—of maple, ash, elm, and other such trees are winged with small airfoils that permit the seeds to spin helicopter fashion. Some species deploy small airworthy vessels that bear seeds, or plumed ones that spew out potential progeny by the tens of thousands in the hope that a few will land, take root, and grow. Seeds may travel only half a mile (800 m) or go nowhere at all. But a storm can send a dandelion's winged seeds out 20 miles (30 km), and some seeds drift for hundreds of miles before landing.

Snow geese flying above a rice paddy in California follow a migration route that allows them to bypass large stretches of open water. When birds do fly over water, they seek out the shortest possible crossing even if it is not the most direct route to their destination.

For the more active migrants there are geographic rules of thumb. Most species of birds, like pilots in single-engine airplanes, shun long flights over water—the price of exhaustion is too great. Thus flyways tend to follow the land. The routes also part around mountain chains, choosing instead

Slow and weak in flight, these leaf hoppers depend on the wind's strength during their migrations. Capricious breezes, however, may carry the insects just as easily to a spider's web or hungry bird as to a haven safe for breeding.

north-south river valleys, and narrow to conform to the tapering shape of an isthmus. European storks offer an interesting case in point. Because they are wary of flights over water, and because the Alps are a barrier, Danish storks follow the Sun to western Africa by way of the Straits of Gibraltar, while their Balkan cousins travel south through Turkey to Arabia. The many strands of flyways between North and South America are gathered at the waist in Panama, making that country one of the world's richest in bird species.

Insects also migrate, although few rival birds in their willingness to test themselves with journeys lasting thousands of miles. The North American monarch butterfly is a notable exception. In spring the monarchs of the United States—as many as five generations from the southern states—fly north to the Hudson Bay area, following a reflex set down in some distant epoch. In autumn, members of the last generation of the year leave their dying comrades and return to Florida, Texas, and California, where they hibernate in forests and other sheltered areas, waiting for summer and the long haul back to Hudson Bay. Borne like autumn leaves upon the air, the monarchs flutter as much as 80 miles (130 km) in a day.

In a way, the monarchs make the point that the planet's shifting wind currents are a silent partner in these odysseys of survival. When the butterflies go shimmering off in their Halloween colors, bound for Hudson Bay, the westerlies are strengthening, and areas of high pressure dot the continent, providing a looping route of least resistance for the monarchs. They may also benefit from the self-cancelling nature of converging and diverging winds along their route; like pilot Max Conrad, the monarch butterfly may need only to hold a course—the winds will do the rest.

River valleys are not the only paths followed by migrants; they also follow the invisible valleys and troughs between centers of high pressure, riding the winds that flow around those

Among the few insect species to migrate long distances, these monarch butterflies travel on shifting winds as far as 1,800 miles (3,200 km) from Canada and the United States. After spending the winter among fir trees in the mountains of central Mexico (*inset*), they will return in spring to their warm-weather home.

Two waved albatrosses (*above*) meet during mating season on the Galapagos Islands off Ecuador. These large birds, gliding with the prevailing westerly winds and sometimes even circling the globe, spend most of their time over the ocean, returning to land only to breed. A few months later, the young albatrosses (*right*) get their first taste of flight by stretching their long, slender wings into the strong sea breeze blowing onto the beach.

invisible features of atmospheric terrain. On its daunting autumnal sortie from North America to Hawaii and the Marquesas, the golden plover rides the southwestward-blowing winds around a mere hill of high pressure off the coast of California, down into the weakening trade winds. On its return, the plover picks up the northeastward winds around the strengthening Hawaiian High. And the wandering albatross roams the roaring westerlies of the southern ocean. Riding prevailing winds makes impossible journeys possible.

As for the geese clattering and clanking over the Potomac in October on their way south, the atmospheric way of their return will be smoothed by spring, when the reviving tropical easterlies and poleward currents on the western edge of the Azores–Bermuda High send them a fair wind for Canada.

A Vital Chemistry

Just as the winds are rivers of life, bearing organisms and pollen and seeds across the planet, they are themselves strong signs of planetary vitality. But for all its animated, protean splendor, the invisible sea of mixed gases is really just a body of fluid loosely clutched in the web of our planet's gravitation. If Earth were less massive and its gravity consequently less, this gas would go bubbling off into space, as most of it evidently has on Mars, where the thin zephyrs of a near vacuum feebly sweep the sun-blasted, rusty surface. No one expects life to endure the terrible inhospitality of worlds where there is little or no atmosphere—what could survive the vacuum-thin remnants that still cling to Earth's dead moon?

Earth has what is called a nitrogen-oxygen atmosphere. The term refers to a blend of gases that is mostly molecular nitrogen, a nitrogen molecule being nothing more than two nitrogen atoms stuck securely together. Making up about 78 percent by volume of any parcel of air, nitrogen so shuns reaction as to be almost chemically inert. And a good thing, too, for some 21 percent of air is one of the most destructive elements known: oxygen. The same properties that make oxygen the fuel for any fire, from our bodies' metabolism to a rocket engine, make it dangerously reactive. It bonds with any-thing—indeed, its combining with other elements, and the consequent release of heat, *is* fire.

Earth's original atmosphere, scientists believe, was *anoxic*—oxygen free—and such rudimentary creatures as lived here 2 billion years ago had adapted to life in an anaerobic world in which iron never rusted. Perhaps if nothing had changed, there might be life here still, but of an extraterrestrial strangeness. As it turned out, about two aeons ago things did start to change. Outgassing from the planet's interior, the creation of a sea, the arrival of plants that inhale carbon dioxide and exhale oxygen—what is cause and what is effect no one knows—all these events began pumping oxygen into the atmosphere, gradually bringing it to its present chemical composition. Almost nothing then alive survived the change—only a few anaerobic species of bacteria endure, living out of the atmosphere and its corrosive load of oxygen.

Nitrogen and oxygen are 99 percent of the present atmosphere. Of the remaining 1 percent, most is argon, with tiny fractions of neon, helium, krypton, xenon, and radon—the six *noble gases*, so called for their virtuous reluctance to react chemically with other substances in general and with oxygen in particular. Helium, the second most abundant element in the universe, contributes only a few ten-thousandths of a percent; hydrogen, the most abundant element in the universe, a few hundred-thousandths. Once major constituents of the atmosphere, those light gases bubbled off into space early in the planet's creation, before its gravity matured. And there are smidgens of such stuff as carbon dioxide and ozone, both in their way as vital to terrestrial life as oxygen, especially when augmented or destroyed by the clumsy human hand.

Their anvil tops fanned into cirrus clouds by high-level winds, mature thunderstorms boil toward the tropopause in this high-level view from the shuttle *Endeavour*. Silhouetted against the sunset, the cloud tops reach into the upper limits of the troposphere, the lowest layer of the Earth's atmosphere.

Most of this accommodating blend of gases—roughly 99 percent of it—is compressed into one layer. The nitrogen-oxygen gas mixture prevails out to about 50 miles (80 km) but grows thinner and thinner until it becomes a sparse ether of widely separated molecules, atoms, and electrically charged, or ionized, particles.

VEILS OF A GODDESS

Until the early part of this century, when scientists were able to examine the real, as distinct from the theoretical, upper atmosphere, the presumption was that the atmosphere becomes colder and thinner as the distance from the Earth's surface increases. Data gathered by probes have since revealed that this shell of air has a thermal structure rather than one based on pressure, and sharp shifts in temperature trends mark boundaries between concentric, and very different, atmospheric realms.

We live in the lowest layer, called the troposphere. The prefix tropo, from the Greek for "turn," refers to its propensity for overturning and mixing, and, indeed, this is the domain of

LAYERS OF THE ATMOSPHERE

The relatively thin skin of mixed gases we call the atmosphere, shown in the cutaway at right, is actually an immense domain of air. This ocean of transparent gases thins steadily from the surface until it blends with the near-vacuum of space. Its predominant structural features are thermally determined, for the layers of the atmosphere are defined by changes in temperature (*inset*). In the troposphere, temperatures decline steadily with altitude; where they begin to rise marks the tropopause, the boundary between the troposphere and stratosphere. Similarly, the increasing temperature trend through the stratosphere reverses at the stratopause, and temperatures once again decline across the mesosphere, reaching a minimum at yet another barrier, the mesopause. There, the atmosphere once more begins to heat, in the realm called the thermosphere. But, because at this height the atmosphere is a virtual vacuum sparsely populated by electrically charged particles, the high temperatures are less the energy of heat than kinetic energy—the energy of motion.

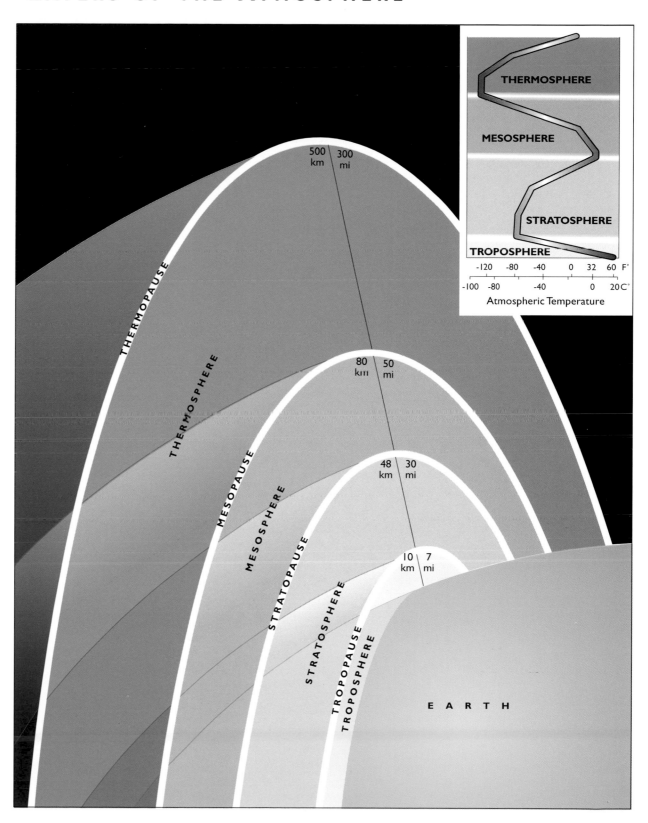

turbulence even as it is the domain of life. Only a few miles thick, the troposphere cools at a rate—called the *lapse rate*—of about 1 Fahrenheit degree for every 180 feet (1 Celsius degree per 100 m) of ascent and grows steadily thinner. The troposphere is where almost all of what we call weather occurs. It is the onion skin. To those who believe that Earth is itself an organism, a veiled goddess named Gaia, the troposphere is the veil.

The veil ends a few miles above the surface—about 5 (8 km) at the poles and 11 (18 km) at the Equator—where air temperature abruptly stops its steady decrease. This marks the *tropopause,* a thermal entity just a few hundred feet thick, which does the same thing to the global atmosphere that a temperature inversion over a city does—it inhibits the natural impulse of air to rise and so blocks vertical mixing. Just as pollutants cannot leak upward through the layer of warm air stoppering the Los Angeles basin on a smoggy day, mixing cannot easily take place across the thermal barrier of the tropopause. Then too, it is not a continuous layer, although it is often represented as one, but a cabbagelike layer of relatively warmer air covering the global troposphere with overlapping shells, the highest over the tropics, the lowest over the poles. During the year, its height varies; it is higher in summer. Sometimes a sounding shows no tropopause whatever—a gap through which air percolates out into the higher regions.

Above the few hundred feet of the tropopause, temperature becomes constant—about -60° F (-51° C) over the poles,

Frozen coiffures of large cumulonimbus clouds over Zaire are photographed during a mission of the NASA space shuttle *Challenger.* As these thunderstorms continue their development, their icy tops may poke into the stratosphere.

-100°F (-73° C) over the Equator. Then, just as suddenly, it begins to increase and does so to an altitude of about 30 miles (50 km). Here, in the *stratosphere*, the only weather is the more or less regular beat of the planetary winds, the occasional formation of thin ice clouds, the condensation trails of high-flying aircraft, and the upward poking of the frozen coiffures of powerful thunderstorms. As denoted by the prefix *strato*, this region's dynamic structure is neatly horizontal.

At about 30 miles (50 km), another sharp temperature change—this time a sudden decrease—marks the *stratopause,* and you enter the *mesosphere. Meso* means "middle," and indeed this is a kind of middle ground between the earthly atmosphere that gives and sustains terrestrial life and the increasingly hostile realm of space. As you travel through the mesosphere, air temperatures decrease until, at an altitude of about 50 miles (80 km), you find the coldest region in the atmosphere: about -130° F (-90° C). This is the *mesopause.* Beyond this point, as the old maps put it, be monsters.

In fact, from the standpoint of earthly life, the planet at this altitude has ceased to offer the slightest hospitality. Pressures are so low that, within seconds of exposure, the water in our bodies would boil, expand, and blow its frail, fleshy containers to smithereens. Temperature increases once again, but in a medium so sparse that the notion of heat is meaningless. The *thermosphere,* as this bleak region is called, stretches out for several hundred miles, the temperature of the thin medium—effectively a vacuum—varying mainly with flare activity on the Sun. When the Sun is tranquil, temperatures in the thermosphere are about 1,100° F (590° C) but rise to more than 3,600° F (2,000° C) during periods of maximum solar activity. Since heat transfer in a gas involves frequent collisions between molecules, however, temperatures here say less about heat than about particle motion—kinetic energy, the energy of motion. A molecule can go a good distance here before it finds another with which to collide.

The space shuttle, which orbits between 115 and 250 miles (185–400 km) above the Earth—technically, it is still in the atmosphere, although there is little air—was designed with the thermosphere in mind. It can operate in a temperature range from -250° to more than 3,000° F (-157° – 1,650° C); the same tiles and carbon pads that keep it from incandescing during reentry, when friction raises hull temperatures several thousand degrees, must also protect it from the conditions of the thermosphere.

At an altitude of about 350 miles (560 km), molecules—and liberated atoms seared into ions by solar radiation—have so little prospect of running into anything that they boil away, accelerating to a velocity that lets them flee gravity altogether. This is the *exosphere,* a vaguely defined region where only a scholar can tell the atmosphere from space.

A Science as Clear as Air

Until the 18th century, the atmosphere more or less took care of itself. For sailors, heavy weather was just another terrible hazard of a profession filled with them. Of course, people had not completely ignored the atmosphere. They had populated this invisible realm with all kinds of imagined creatures and phenomena—the unseen has always worked upon the human imagination. And they must have known thousands of years ago that moving air—wind—exerted force, for they quickly put it to work filling sails and turning mills. They also observed that wind brought them weather.

Despite such ageless insight into what the winds are saying, however, air was not a very interesting substance to the

In the 16th-century painting *Perspective Plan of Venice,* the Italian city's travel and trade is shown thriving on the force of the four winds. Early residents of Venice were able to use the shifting Adriatic breezes to sail among the city's 118 islands and extend their trade into the Mediterranean and Atlantic, but it was 400 years more before scientists discovered that winds were produced by gradients of pressure and heating—not clouds.

The immense force of water as it falls, swirls, and froths is captured in this drawing (circa 1507) by Leonardo da Vinci. His interest in the dynamics of fluids came from his involvement in the design of innovative aqueducts in the Po and Arno river valleys of Italy. But what he and other early scientists learned about water did much to shape our understanding of another fluid: air.

pioneer students of the behavior of fluids—fluid dynamics. The great Leonardo da Vinci was not attracted by air; he was drawn to the behavior of a denser fluid: water. So were his disciples and their descendants. Curiously, their work is memorialized less in waterworks and pump stations than on the instrument panels of modern aircraft, where many of the dials commemorate a theory or discovery made by an early scholar of hydraulics that was later applied to measuring some property of gases.

The study of these lighter, compressible fluids seems somehow to have fallen to the scholars of colder climes. Robert Boyle, a chemist and natural philosopher in 17th-century London, appears to have possessed one of those clear, innovative views of the physical world seen in many great scientists. Thus unfettered, he arrived at the first law of gases, which states that, at a constant temperature, the volume of a gas varies inversely with the pressure of the gas—in other words, increasing a given pressure twofold reduces the volume by half, and vice versa. Called *Boyle's Law* in most places, the same law was also discovered a few years later by a French investigator, Edme Mariotte, and sometimes bears his name.

The second law of gases was formulated in 1787 by the French physicist Jacques-Alexandre-Cesar Charles and named

for him and chemist Joseph-Louis Gay-Lussac, who published the idea in 1802. This law states that, at a constant pressure, the volume of a gas varies directly with its absolute temperature—that is, the hotter the gas, the greater its volume. The beauty of these two laws, besides their wonderful simplicity, is that they can be used together. Moreover—although this was almost certainly not their discoverers' intention—the gas laws can be used to explain most of what we see in the atmosphere.

And yet, having provided the means by which this invisible entity could be comprehended—equations, laws, fluid-mechanical reasons for things—these pioneers seem to have had trouble putting their new theoretical tools to work. By the end of the 19th century, the world had begun to fill with schemes for reporting and forecasting weather. Linked by the new continent-crossing telegraph wires, weather stations could report local conditions every hour, providing a vast mosaic of data in which the invisible terrain of wind and atmospheric pressure began to be discerned. But despite all this activity, there was no real vocabulary of atmospheric behavior. It fell to the Scandinavians to teach the world how to talk about the workings of the atmosphere.

Real atmospheric science began in Norway, among a small group of pioneers whose clarity of vision matched the transparency of what they studied. It may be that the pivoting centers of action in the lower atmosphere operate more vividly at the high latitudes. Certainly one feels the force of weather along the fjords of Norway, and the sky there forms a wonderfully lit background for the passage of weather. But there is also the sense that these men saw the atmosphere whole and clearly for the first time in human history.

Vilhelm Bjerknes was the first of these pioneers; it can be argued that his work makes him the father of modern atmospheric science. The son of a mathematics professor in Christiana (now Oslo), he had, like so many other mathematically inclined young men before him, become fascinated by the dynamics of fluids. His postgraduate studies took him to Leipzig to work with the famed German physicist Heinrich Hertz on the electromagnetic waves whose frequencies are now measured in cycles per second, also called *hertz*.

Back in Scandinavia in 1893, Bjerknes taught at Stockholm University. But as he built a family and a career, he was evidently thinking of the atmosphere in a way that his predecessors had not—as a vast fluid mantle covering the Earth, driven by inequalities in solar heating. No one knows today whether he experienced a leap of insight or a gradual illumination, but he saw the atmosphere as no one had before him. Applying what he knew of water dynamics to winds, he found he could explain much of what had until then merely been experienced—the valley and mountain currents, the sea breezes, and the parade of highs and lows.

In 1904, Bjerknes proposed turning his ideas into a practical weather forecasting scheme, which eight years later he tried to implement as the new director of the Leipzig Geophysical Institute. World War I brought other priorities, however, and, for a citizen of neutral Norway, deteriorating working conditions. Bjerknes returned to Norway in July 1917 and became the first director of the new Bergen Geophysical Institute, which he established as a center for atmospheric research.

By this time, Vilhelm Bjerknes had been joined by another rising star in the atmospheric sciences—his son Jakob, just 19 when his father moved to Bergen and with a year's research study in Leipzig. He became the chief forecaster at the Bergen

Vilhelm Bjerknes, the father of atmospheric research, founded Norway's Bergen Geophysical Institute in 1917. Just over a decade after the institute was founded, its researchers had discovered the basic principles driving the forces of weather and used the contemporary wartime imagery of armies and fronts to describe what they had found.

Jakob Bjerknes analyzes a weather map at the Geophysical Institute in Bergen, Norway, in this photograph taken about 1922. He and his father, Vilhelm, obtained data on air masses and their boundaries, forming the basis of modern weather forecasting.

institute. Between them, they began to beat what had been a scholarly art into a science.

Using a dense network of surface observers and instruments, the Bjerkneses constructed large-scale maps of the terrain of pressure, temperature, and wind overlying Scandinavia and northern Europe. Soon they began to see the finely drawn features of order among the whorls and barbs of a chaotic atmosphere. The work of the two Bjerkneses and their colleagues soon defined a point of view: the Bergen School. The Bergen Geophysical Institute became a magnet for like-minded researchers: Halvar Solberg, Tor Bergeron, Carl-Gustaf Rossby, Erik Palmer, and Sven Otto Patterson, among others. In a dozen years, these men utterly transformed their science and left a legacy that has become familiar to almost everyone on Earth: the swirls and tentacles of our daily weather maps.

WAR OF THE WINDS

The Bergen model has become the way we look at our atmosphere. Because one of the imperatives for establishing the Bergen institute had been neutral Norway's isolation by the war, it was natural for the scientists there to describe their model in terms borrowed from the terrible battlefields of Flanders and France. Like that ravaged gray land, the atmosphere hosted a succession of warring air masses, competing along boundaries the researchers called fronts.

In this model, the main line of battle is the polar front, separating the warm, moist air masses of the tropics from the cold, dry ones of the poles. This front, a wavy, 100-mile-wide (160-km) boundary, runs a scalloped course around the globe between about 30° and 60° of latitude north and south of the Equator. But the polar front is not a smooth boundary—like the rest of the atmosphere, it is wrinkled with disturbances. Warm air may bulge inward on the polar side of the line, cold air may bulge outward into the domain of tropical air. If the bulge extends farther into enemy territory—and it requires allies in the form of favorable conditions in the high troposphere to do so—the intrusion may create a zone of low pressure around which air converges and begins to rise.

On one side of the low, the polar front buckles inward as a warm front—an intrusion of warm air—rides up and over the denser mass of cold air. On the other side of the low, cold air cams beneath the warmer air. Moving like revolving doors, the slow-moving warm front is swiftly overtaken by the faster-moving cold front. As the disturbance reaches its maximum intensity, so does the weather it creates. Then the cold front dies out and the polar front grows quiet until another bulging intrusion causes the process to start all over again.

This never-ending parade of alternating highs and lows, of warm and cold fronts between air masses, was what weather was all about, at least from the standpoint of us surface creatures. But the Bergen scholars had begun to see not just a horizontal order to the atmosphere but a vertical one as well. The polar frontal boundary is not a vertical wall, they found, but one that slants poleward as it rises from the surface. If you follow this slanted surface to the top of the troposphere, you

A lenticular, or lens-shaped, cloud hovering over Oregon's 11,235-foot (3,404 m) Mount Hood traces the wavelike flow of wind over the snow-capped volcano. Such clouds form on the rising side of the standing, or stationary, waves associated with strong, upper-level winds, and vanish on the descending side.

find that the tropopause is interrupted and that a great, global band of wind howls along the polar front at this lofty altitude.

That is precisely what Carl-Gustaf Rossby did, using high-flying aircraft and instrument-bearing balloons. What he discovered turned out to be the very cores of the westerlies: the jet streams. Capable of blowing at speeds as high as 300 miles per hour (450 kph) or more and driven by the large thermal differences between the air on either side of the polar front, the jet streams girdle the planet, following the meandering, shifting seasonal path of the polar front, two or three jet streams to each hemisphere. In lockstep with the front whose boundaries they mark, the jet streams shift toward the equator in winter and intensify.

Rossby also found something else: a large, symmetrical undulation in the jet stream that echoes the smaller, more transient waves along the polar front. Called *Rossby waves* for their discoverer, these swells are formed when polar air moves toward the Equator as tropical air is moving toward the poles—like dancers linking arms, they spin. But in the atmosphere, they spin up cells of high or low pressure—the major seasonal features of the atmosphere's invisible terrain.

By the late 1930's, Rossby and Jakob Bjerknes had come nearly full circle in their thinking. They had found that the procession of highs and lows seen at the Earth's surface were actually the footprints of waves in the great westerly current. Where the waves bring air downward, pressing and spreading

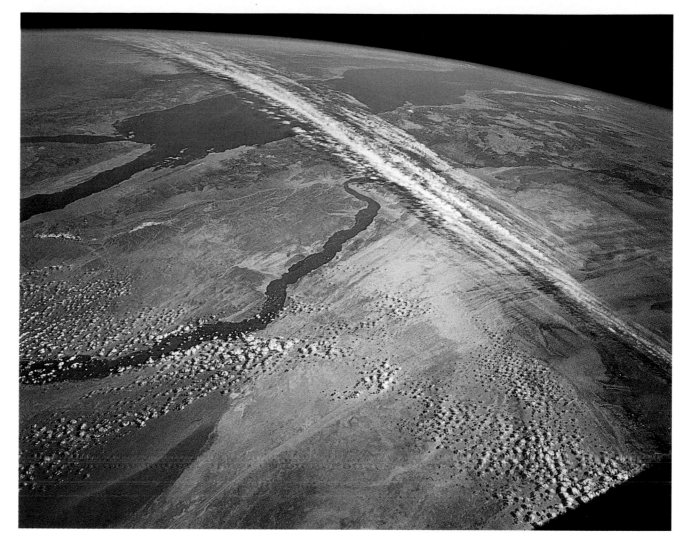

Visible evidence of a jet stream, ribbons of cirrus clouds stripe the skies above the Nile River valley and the Red Sea in this photograph taken from the *Gemini XII* spacecraft. This globe-girdling tube of westerly winds moves at up to 300 mph (500 kph).

it across the ground, atmospheric pressure increases; where the waves take air aloft, pressure decreases and air flows in to fill the relative void.

The terrain of pressure, like the daily passage of the Sun across the sky, is really a necessary illusion. The air moves from high pressure to low and is coiled by the Coriolis effect, and there is a terrain of high pressure and low that guides the way the winds blow. But that terrain exists because the wind is blowing—it is carved by wind as surely as the pinnacles of the southwest Australian deserts are.

ACTION AT THE POLAR FRONT

The Scandinavian pioneers of meteorology were the first to see in detail that low-pressure systems—cyclones—are spawned where masses of warm air and cold air meet. Cyclogenesis occurs as a sequence of events, each taking place 12 to 24 hours apart. As illustrated here, each of these events is shown as one of six numbered sections in the diagram below. The events occur along the wedge-like edge of the polar front, the line of demarcation between cold air to the north and warm air to the south.

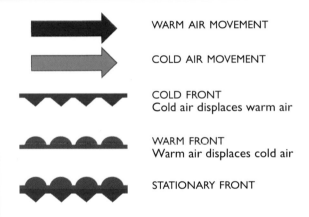

WARM AIR MOVEMENT

COLD AIR MOVEMENT

COLD FRONT
Cold air displaces warm air

WARM FRONT
Warm air displaces cold air

STATIONARY FRONT

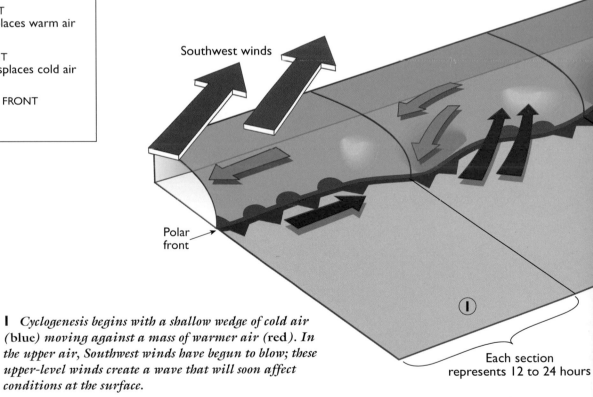

Southwest winds

Polar front

Each section represents 12 to 24 hours

1 *Cyclogenesis begins with a shallow wedge of cold air (blue) moving against a mass of warmer air (red). In the upper air, Southwest winds have begun to blow; these upper-level winds create a wave that will soon affect conditions at the surface.*

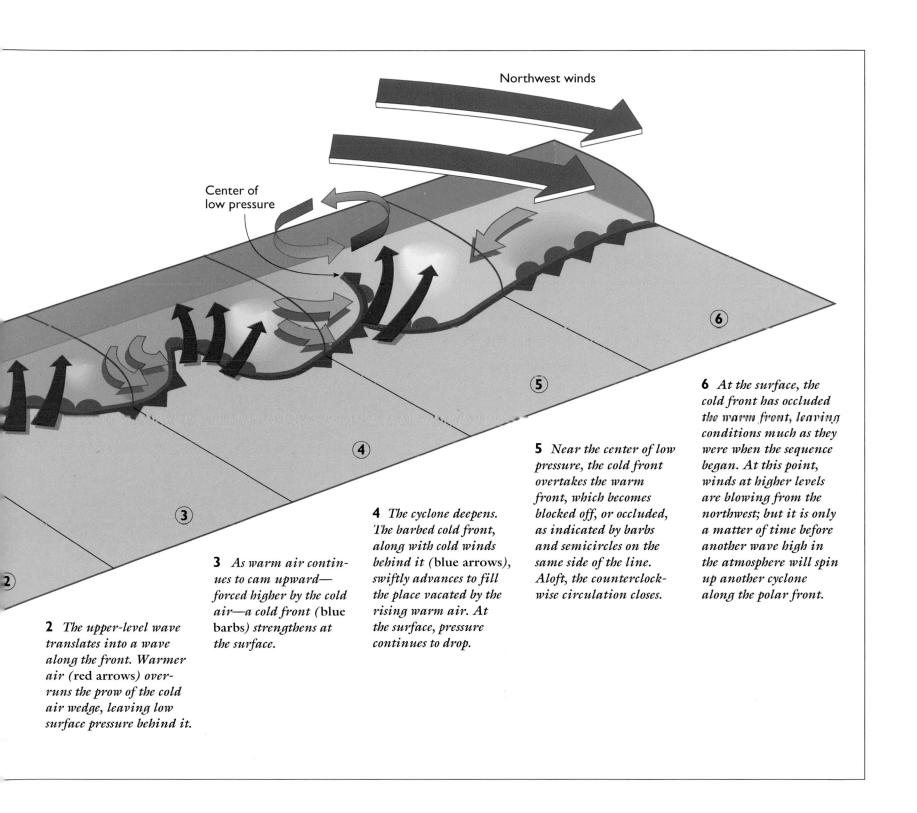

Northwest winds

Center of
low pressure

⑥

⑤

④

③

②

6 *At the surface, the
cold front has occluded
the warm front, leaving
conditions much as they
were when the sequence
began. At this point,
winds at higher levels
are blowing from the
northwest; but it is only
a matter of time before
another wave high in
the atmosphere will spin
up another cyclone
along the polar front.*

5 *Near the center of low
pressure, the cold front
overtakes the warm
front, which becomes
blocked off, or occluded,
as indicated by barbs
and semicircles on the
same side of the line.
Aloft, the counterclock-
wise circulation closes.*

4 *The cyclone deepens.
The barbed cold front,
along with cold winds
behind it (blue arrows),
swiftly advances to fill
the place vacated by the
rising warm air. At
the surface, pressure
continues to drop.*

3 *As warm air continues to cam upward—
forced higher by the cold
air—a cold front (blue
barbs) strengthens at
the surface.*

2 *The upper-level wave
translates into a wave
along the front. Warmer
air (red arrows) over-
runs the prow of the cold
air wedge, leaving low
surface pressure behind it.*

THE MISSING INGREDIENT

Something odd has happened to our basketball model: Models are toys, and toys never behave quite like the real thing, whether it is fire engines or atmospheres. The tilted basketball spinning in the light of a simulated Sun can make a point or two but it is nevertheless a laboratory creation. The Bergen Model shows us what changes to expect and where to expect them, but in many ways it has gone the way of the horse and buggy, driven out by the torrent of numbers produced by today's truly global weather-observing network.

More troubling is the metaphor of a simple heat engine to describe the impossibly complex workings of the atmosphere. Elegant the metaphor certainly is, and it is capable of making the point that the real atmosphere is a prodigious transporter of thermal energy across the globe. The problem is that it works in convection ovens and saucepans much better than it does in the chaos of the real world.

If the atmosphere were just a heat engine, moving solar energy from the Equator toward the poles on the great conveyor belts called Hadley cells, it would perform admirably for a little while—and then shut down. The reason: As a thermal engine, the atmosphere is terribly inefficient. There is enough energy in the system to do all that we observe, but only about 1 percent of all that heat is transformed into the energy that makes the atmosphere go. Thus, our poorly rigged model is out of gas before it really gets started.

But the atmosphere does keep on going. It runs not just on heat transformed into motion but on the violent stuff, too. An internal combustion engine needs thousands of explosions a minute to keep the pistons pumping and the crankshaft cranking. So it is with the atmosphere—it also needs those explosions. It finds them in the storms that spin in the prevailing winds, their huge appetites devouring colossal quantities of heat energy and feeding it back into the atmosphere in the form of motion, momentum—the stuff of work.

On Chesapeake Bay near Annapolis, Maryland, a sailboat huddles under a mass of storm clouds. Depending on countless constantly changing variables, this roiling front may unleash a vicious thunderstorm—or slide by silently with the barest hint of a cool breeze.

GIFT FROM THE SEA

Nothing seems to lie ahead of the *St. Christopher* as she
backs out of her slip in the French port of Calais and
takes up the slightly curved course to a matching slip in
Dover, across the English Channel. The gray December sky is a stam-
pede of low clouds herded toward the southeast by a stiff winter wind
off the North Sea, but in the half-light of that December dusk the sea
seems calm. The ferry glides past the old pillboxes and bunkers of
coastal France, England-bound.

Half an hour out, everything has changed. The sea beneath the
huge passenger vessel begins to heave like the flanks of some great
dreaming beast, and the rising wind can be heard above the drum-
ming engines. Rain and the mushy ice called *graupel* rattle on the
glass-paned windows and doors. Soon the *St. Christopher* rolls crazily
from side to side, so that the crew walks only by climbing along bulk-
head rails. Most of the passengers hunker down in their seats, trying
to ignore the ocean's invitation to nausea.

A good, solid storm at sea is not merely gut wrenching and exhausting—it is as exciting as anything you can do in an airplane, as exciting as war, no doubt, for mariners. On this night the vessel is caught in dirty weather descending from a high-latitude cyclone. A few hundred miles to the northwest, a deep core of low pressure has spun up between masses of warm and cold air, creating a frontal band of storms that will dominate the entire North Sea and Channel for days.

This is no time to hunker down—it is a time to go get wet, to stand in the night with the familiar atmosphere suddenly gone mad around you, the usually distinct boundary between our oceans of water and of air suddenly blurred into a single thrashing entity. The bow drops into another gorge separating the mountainous traveling undulations called *swell,* the ship vibrates with a staccato hammering of wind-driven waves. As the bow plummets, the ship's screws accelerate with a mechanical scream as they rise up out of the braking action of the water; then there is just the wailing gale as the propellers once again submerge.

After crossing the storm-tossed Channel, we see the yellow lights and the ghostly chalk cliffs that mark the port of Dover. Ours is the last ferry but one to leave Calais tonight. Now the sister ship plunges past like a rusted white charger, vanishing in the swell, her screws briefly exposed to the air; then she rises again and pounds toward the calm of the enclosed harbor.

St. Christopher turns toward the lights, passing gingerly through the breakwater, and pivots back into her berth. But here she falters, unable to hold her bow into the gale. Then, across the heaving water of the harbor, a determined little tug

The lights on a rugged North Sea oil rig blaze through a stormy night. Even in the storms that are legendary in the region, the rig remains upright, stabilized much like an iceberg by the mass of its submerged structure.

picks its way, there is the drama of lines being cast, of near collisions, as the smaller vessel darts about, trying to get hold of the crippled ferry. Finally securing lines, the tug pulls the larger vessel's bow so that it stands against the wind, and the captain backs us in against the slip.

That same night, farther north, another ferry capsizes and sinks like a tiny *Titanic.* Up there the nocturnal adventure became a nightmare of dark night and black water for scores of terrified passengers and crew. These are stormy times, and during the next fortnight almost every day will bring word of some near or actual maritime catastrophe. Incredibly, this time there is no report—as there often is—of death on one of the North Sea oil platforms, the resilient giants that squat on metal legs in waves taller than most buildings.

Despite this pervasive sense of peril from the sea, maritime travelers are no more at the mercy of water than anyone else on this planet. In fact, the energy driving the storm on our rough crossing is the same stuff that propels a typhoon across tens of thousands of square miles of ocean off Japan or that explodes in a line of thunderstorms along America's tornado alley. So close is the trafficking between water and atmosphere that you may now and then lose sight of their boundary. But it is in this traffic that most atmospheric violence is born. The currency of this energetic exchange: hydrogen oxide. Water.

British painter J. M.W. Turner lashed himself to the deck of a boat to capture this English Channel winter storm in 1842, an atmospheric tour de force which he called *Snowstorm: Steamboat off a Harbour's Mouth.*

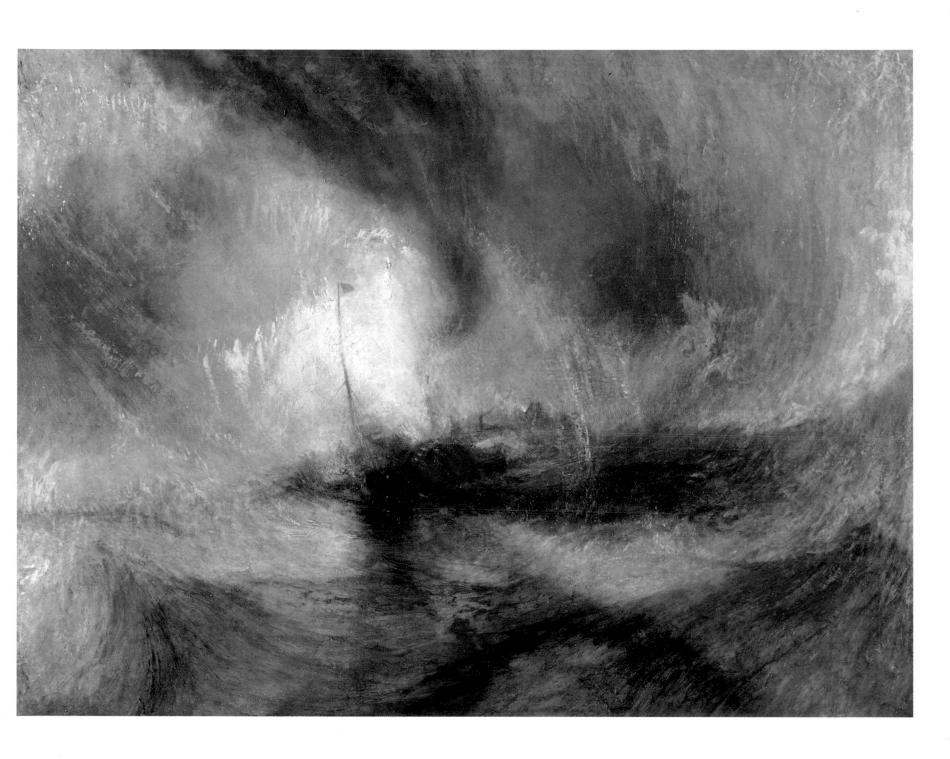

Water: The Stuff of Life

Water is literally the stuff of life for biology of the terrestrial variety—we and the other living things that we know about are mostly made of water; our bodies run on such water-based solutions as blood and bile. Even the seemingly waterless bacteria of the Antarctic find a way to extract water from their arid habitat. Despite the efforts of science and fiction-eers to imagine beings whose vital fluids are based on such substances as hydrogen sulfide or ammonia, the apparent dearth of water elsewhere in the universe is a dismaying sign of infertility. Learning that space is largely arid—the term greatly understates the irradiated vacuum that lies beyond our atmosphere—has been one of the hard lessons of extraterrestrial exploration.

Hope for life outside our atmosphere has always been water based. We have conjured rich rainforests on Venus, our Earth-sized neighbor toward the Sun, only to discover that the perpetual drizzle there is not life-giving water but sulfuric acid. Designs seen on the surface of nearby Mars were once taken to be canals, evidence of water and so of life. But Mars probes returned images of a radiation-blasted surface devoid even of the organic building blocks of life. Now and

Seen from *Apollo 17*, Earth glows with the rich vitality of a water planet, nearly three quarters of its surface covered with a global ocean, its poles buried in permanent ice caps, and its atmosphere marbled with water vapor in the form of clouds.

Although Mars appears to have neither life nor liquid water, scientists believe that ancient rivers may have cut such features as this great rift valley, a vast canyon that measures 3,000 miles (4,800 km) long, 75 miles (120 km) wide, and 4 miles (6.5 km) deep.

then, word comes that the possibility of water has been deduced for some far reach of the solar system—an ocean under the ice shell of the Jovian moon Europa or deep beneath the Martian surface. Perhaps there is, and we will find it. Perhaps we shall never know.

If we could look at Earth from the perspective of those neighboring planets, there would be no mistaking the magnitude of what we would find. We would see the disk of the planet colored sapphire blue by its mantle of water—the immense ocean that covers nearly three quarters of the globe. As with other planets, there would be a white frosting coating either pole—but of water ice, not the frozen carbon dioxide that caps the poles of less hospitable worlds.

This dazzling azure-blue cloak contains about 326 million cubic miles (1.3 billion km³) of water, 97 percent of it in the reservoir of the sea and all but a trace of the remainder locked in polar ice and glaciers. This endowment is billions of years old and has endured for all that time without measurable change—the present inhabitants drink the same water that their prehistoric relatives did.

At any particular moment, only some 3,100 cubic miles (12,400 km³) of the world supply of water may be suspended within the atmosphere, and much of this is in the form of an invisible gas—water vapor. And yet, this is enough to band the earth with clouds, link land with the ocean reservoir, moderate inequities in solar heating, and fuel the great storms that drift through the lower atmosphere. This is the stuff that

adds all that missing energy the atmosphere requires to keep going—the explosions.

Seeing that water was so plentiful here, constantly shifting its phase from one to another of its several states, we would know that this strange and beautiful blue planet is a garden of life and is kept so by the peculiar properties of an excellent molecule. But we would also know that its atmosphere would be lively as well—that, for example, the vast pinwheel dipping a line of nasty weather southward into the English Channel would be nothing but whirling dry air without its explosive cargo of water.

After splitting from coastal glaciers, or "calving," icebergs drift in Newfoundland's Labrador Sea in the region known as Iceberg Alley. Millions of cubic miles of water are sealed in the ice and glaciers that ring both poles.

THE DESIGNER MOLECULE

As there appears to be nothing comparable to our blue water planet within hailing distance, there appears to be no other compound in the universe quite like water. Anomalous, quirky but stable to a fault, power-packed, destructive, and indispensable, it is the ultimate designer molecule. With neither taste nor odor nor hue, this compound is an almost universal solvent, an elixir of just about everything. In the atmosphere it is not just a vital sign—it is also the wild card, the nitroglycerine that fills the Earth's placid rivers of air with the detonations we know as weather.

Water is the inevitable marriage of oxygen—the most abundant element on Earth—with hydrogen—the most abundant element in the universe. The two atoms could hardly fail to be drawn together. Elemental hydrogen has a simple single-proton nucleus with a single shell containing one electron and space for another. An oxygen atom has six electrons in its outer shell but space for eight. Because atoms with vacancies in their outer electron shells are unstable, they cannot exist naturally in their elemental, atomic form. (Single atoms of hydrogen and oxygen can be found in the atmosphere but mainly at great altitude, where solar radiation acts as a deterrent to stability.) Like fictional characters in search of a fulfilling author, hydrogen and oxygen atoms quest after electrons to satisfy their outer shells and so will combine with almost anything that comes

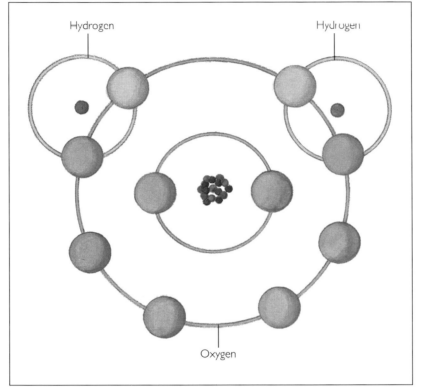

In the water molecule, vacancies in the outer electron shells of a large oxygen atom and two smaller hydrogen atoms are reciprocally filled by one another's electrons, creating a Mickey Mouse-like configuration that is one of nature's most tenacious molecular bonds.

along—with others like themselves, of course, but especially with each other. And, once assembled, water molecules are electrically charged so that they tend to congregate.

This penchant for assembling is part of the water molecule's versatile difference from nearly every other type of molecule. Strong bonding between water molecules imparts an unusual surface tension—it explains why some insects can canter over ponds and why a pan can be slightly overfilled without water spilling over the sides. The propensity to congregate favors the formation of water droplets and ice crystals, the forms in which water in the atmosphere is returned to the oceanic reservoir—and to us. Because its attraction to itself is matched by an attraction to inorganic materials, water is always ready to enfold and incorporate a passing bit of anything, which is why the sea—whose molecules have incorporated, or dissolved, all that sodium chloride—is salt.

If water were a "normal" molecule, we would expect it to freeze at -148° F (-97° C) and boil into gas at about -132° F (-91° C), not 32° and 212° F (0° and 100° C) as it does at sea level. Earth would be no more hospitable than a moon of Jupiter. As it is, the strong bond between molecules makes it harder to disperse a congregation of liquid water into the looser grouping of a gas but easier to freeze it into the rigid structure of ice.

Cooled toward its freezing point of 32° F (0° C), water behaves as most materials do, contracting and becoming

With waterproof hairs on its underside and sprawling middle legs that distribute its weight, a water strider scurries across a pond. The tendency of water molecules to associate causes the surface tension that keeps the insect from sinking.

Dewdrops on a blade of grass begin to freeze and expand as the temperature plummets. If the temperature continues to fall, the drops will metamorphose into the characteristic six-sided crystal of solid water—ice.

steadily denser. But then at about 39° F (4° C) it begins to go its own way. Held in a rigid structure by the hydrogen bond between molecules, water expands in volume by about nine percent as it turns into ice. Thus, ice has fewer water molecules per unit of volume than liquid water does—it is less dense. Again, a molecular quirk saves the day for life forms. If water followed the way of most substances, its solid form would sink in its liquid form, and the world's ocean basins would long ago have filled with the accumulated ice fields of more than a billion winters.

The bounce that this strange substance imparts to the atmosphere comes from the great stability of the water molecule itself. As it is heated or cooled, water gains or loses heat gram by gram, degree by degree, like all materials. But when it reaches one of its critical temperatures—the temperatures at which it vaporizes or freezes—water becomes either profligate or stingy about heat. This oddity was first observed systematically in 1761. Joseph Black, a Scottish physicist who studied

Slabs of ice checker the sea off the Antarctic Peninsula. Because ice is less dense than liquid water, its frozen fragments float, forming vast icy armadas called *floes*.

the phenomenon called this extra increment of stored or released energy *latent heat* (see page 51).

On regional and local scales, that latent energy is what feeds the furnace of a storm. On a global scale it is one way the atmosphere moves solar energy received in the tropics toward the poles, with each water molecule acting as a tiny mule for transporting stored energy. Where the Sun's rays strike land, they are partly reflected back into the atmosphere and space. Water absorbs this radiation and transforms it into heat, to which the atmosphere is virtually opaque. Then the excellent molecule distributes this converted energy across the planet's surface. The Sun may be the prime mover, but water is its courier. Air could not do it alone.

The Sun's rays thrust through patchy clouds, carrying light and heat to California's Sacramento Valley. Up to 45 percent of the solar energy striking land is reflected skyward; it would return to space were it not absorbed by water in the atmosphere.

A MOLECULAR MULE TRAIN

For the thermal engine of the atmosphere to crank through its cycles of warming and cooling and sustain its molecular mule train of fuel bearers, water must find a way into the air. The jump from a liquid surface into the atmosphere requires overcoming the hydrogen bond between molecules of water. Some molecules are ripped away mechanically by wind and the action of breaking waves. But most water enters the atmosphere by absorbing enough energy to change to its vapor phase—to evaporate.

Waves crash along the edge of the Pacific Ocean near the windy California coast, spraying water droplets into the air. While winds sweep some water into the atmosphere, most of it enters the gaseous envelope through the process of evaporation.

When a water molecule makes the leap from liquid to gas—and individual molecules may do so well below the boiling point, when the entire body of water is hot enough to vaporize—it takes enormous latent heat energy with it, as anyone knows who has stepped from a shower into dry air or has held a drink chilled by the melting of ice cubes. Evaporation goes on as long as the air can continue to soak up water vapor—sometimes outlasting the supply of water, as in dust-bowl droughts.

The amount of water vapor that can exist in a given volume of air varies with temperature—the warmer the air, the more active its molecules and the more water vapor it can hold. (In absolute terms, a volume of air can be as much as seven percent water vapor.) When its capacity is reached, the air is *saturated*: it can hold no more.

LATENT HEAT

Releasing huge quantities of latent, or absorbed, heat with each transformation, water changes phase from vapor to liquid to solid in this chilly winterscape along the shores of Lake Superior.

Joseph Black discovered that all materials require a boost of energy to push them from one phase to another—from solid to liquid to gas and back again. But in water, this boost is unusually large.

Going from vapor to liquid form, each gram of water must release 597 calories before it can condense. When liquid water is cooled to its freezing point, another 80 calories per gram must be released. Likewise, when ice melts to water, 80 calories are absorbed; when water turns to water vapor, 597 calories are absorbed. The energy absorbed or released in these exchanges is called *latent heat*.

It is through these exchanges—water changing constantly from one form to another—that water molecules modulate the flow of energy through the global atmosphere.

Towering trees and thick undergrowth form a lush green canyon for the Segama River on the Southeast Asian island of Borneo. With almost steady rainfall six months out of the year, this hot, humid equatorial island supports countless species of plant and animal life.

Relative humidity, the term we hear most often expressed as a percentage, is the ratio of the amount of water vapor actually present in a volume of air at any given temperature to the amount of water vapor that would cause that volume of air to become saturated. For example, a value of 50 percent relative humidity means that, in terms of water vapor at least, the air is only half full. Raising the temperature effectively increases the volume of air—the size of the atmospheric water tank—so that a measurement of 50 percent relative humidity in warm air represents a good deal more water vapor than it would in a similar mass of cool air. This is why on a hot, humid day on the Equator you might begin to wish for gills, so choked is the air with moisture. As they say, it's not the heat, it's the humidity that gets you.

The rate at which evaporation occurs is determined by the difference between *vapor pressure*—the proportion of atmospheric pressure exerted by the water vapor already present in the air—at the water surface and the air in contact with the surface. High vapor pressure retards further evaporation, while low stimulates it. The warmer the water and the lower the vapor pressure, the greater the evaporation rate. Evaporation is greater during the day than at night, during the summer than winter, in the tropics than at the poles.

Air movement also plays a crucial role in the evaporation rate. In still air or when the winds are blowing only lightly, the shallow layer of air near the surface of the water is quickly saturated, increasing vapor pressure and reducing the amount of additional evaporation that can take place. But turbulent air near the surface acts as a conveyor belt, moving saturated air away so that evaporation can fill the empties still upwind. Nothing is done for nothing, however. Every time a single gram of liquid water takes off as vapor, the ocean pays 597 calories of latent heat.

Gray storm clouds move in over Mississippi Sound at sunset. The storm's winds sweep the moist air off the surface of the bay and funnel it into the atmosphere, where it will fuel another storm somewhere downwind.

The Forms of Water

For people, what the ocean gives the air is academic. We tend to be more concerned with how and where the airborne water spends that energy when it once again becomes negotiable as sensible heat. To do that, water vapor must return to either its liquid or solid phase—it must condense or freeze.

Condensation is everywhere around us. The insides of auto windshields, having cooled the adjacent air to saturation, become covered with droplets of water. So do the relatively cool surfaces of mirrors in a bathroom filled with steam. The water vapor in our breath condenses on cooler lenses so that we can wipe our glasses.

Clouds, the heralds and harbingers of all the weather we experience, are streamers marking a place where water vapor has been cooled to this point of condensation. It is reached when the parcel of air becomes saturated, either because it has taken on a full tank of water vapor or because its temperature has dropped, causing water vapor to spill out as condensed liquid. The temperature at which condensation occurs is called the *dew point*.

But something else is always needed to make the atmosphere do what it is supposed to do. Even with a superabundance of water vapor—*supersaturation*—yet another ingredient

A dew-covered grasshopper hides in Queen Anne's lace on an early autumn morning. When air cools to the dew point—the temperature at which it can no longer hold the amount of water vapor it has absorbed—water droplets will form on anything from car windows to insects.

A close look at the feathery frost on this cold windowpane reveals the delicate hexagon forms of ice crystals. As the water vapor condenses and freezes on the glass, it releases back into the atmosphere the latent heat it has absorbed.

must be added to provide a surface for the water to land on. In theory, condensation begins as soon as relative humidity exceeds 100 percent—by definition, the atmosphere can hold no more. In nature, of course, the impossible is often the rule. Thus in pure, filtered air, relative humidity can rise to an impossible 400 percent—it is full four times over—without condensation occurring. But add a puff of smoke or fine dust, some whiff of tiny particulates, and the cup immediately runneth over with excess moisture condensing into fog.

Condensation seems to require a solid substance onto which the invisible particles of water vapor can collect into droplets. And, in fact, when looked at under the electron microscope, water droplets have been found to contain microscopic nuclei of some solid material—fine dust, exhaust products from engines and fires, and particles of sea salt are most common. The giants among them, the sea-salt crystals, may reach five microns—five millionths of a meter—in diameter and occur in concentrations of about 100 to

Hampered by fog on a wintry day, gulls make their way over the Grand Canal in Venice, Italy. Fog, which is simply a cloud that forms at ground level, occurs when moist air reaches its dew point.

Like a diamond on its velvet field, this perfect snowflake nestles in a row of hemlock needles. Actually an aggregate of many individual ice crystals, snowflakes grow as ice crystals fall through subfreezing air.

10,000 particles per cubic inch (600 to 60,000 per milliliter) of air. The air is never very crowded with them; a cubic inch can hold up to about 16 trillion cubic microns.

Even condensed into a liquid, water still carries a purse full of latent heat that can be converted only by moving to another phase—by freezing. And, as before, it is not just a matter of cooling water to 32° F (0° C) to produce an ice crystal. Left to itself, water can be supercooled tens of degrees below its freezing point. Without a tiny crystalline scaffold, such as of silica or quartz, it freezes only reluctantly. But with a *freezing nucleus*, as these particles are called, water—and water vapor, too—hardens into ice almost on schedule and shells out its 80 calories per gram in the coin of latent heat of fusion. Having collected all this energy, the atmosphere reciprocates in kind—its thermal engine keeps on turning.

SUNDOGS AND RAINBOWS

With the sun as a projector, the atmosphere's burden of water paints luminous illusions of wondrous beauty. The rainbow is purely an optical effect, spun by the combination of sunbeams, water droplets, and an observer with the Sun at his or her back. Sunlight penetrates raindrops, which bend, or *refract*, them; then, the far inner surface of the drop reflects the light back toward the observer, tilted 42 degrees off its original path from the Sun. This tilt builds the rainbow's grand arch, which may rise to the zenith. Because each of the colors in white light has its own angle of refraction, the bent light is a spray of color. Ground observers see only a portion of the rainbow. But most pilots have had the luck to look down and see the full circle that is every rainbow.

Ice crystals are less prisms than mirrors, so that their magic tends to project false images of actual things. Mock suns, or sundogs, for example, are produced when sunlight filters through a layer of ice-crystal clouds, bending the light 22 degrees en route to the observer, who sees the real Sun flanked at 22-degree intervals by false ones.

Parhelia, *or sundogs, illusions spun by ice crystals between the observer and the light, flank the setting Sun in this winterscape from Saskatchewan, Canada.*

A rainbow adds its arch to the dramatic limestone formations in Utah's Bryce Canyon National Park, a land dramatically tinted by the oxidation of iron and etched by eons of moving wind and water.

Wind beneath Their Wings

With powerful water bombs strung invisibly beneath their wings, the winds—the movements of air—become infinitely more complicated than they would be in a dry atmosphere. In the lower troposphere, a rising mass of waterless air is only that; in contrast, a rising mass of moist air is a potential explosion of latent heat. The winds may circle the planet and rule the larger motions of the atmosphere, but at the scales of size we care about—between the surface and about 18,000 feet (5,500 m)—water, not wind, spins the plot.

Air in the troposphere gains or loses heat *adiabatically*— that is, without heat being added or withdrawn by some other agent—as it rises or descends. As moist air ascends, it is gradually cooled to its dew point, and its burden of water vapor begins to form into droplets about a thousandth of an inch (0.025 mm) in diameter around microscopic nuclei. We see the aggregation of these droplets in the sky as clouds; when the air cools to its dew point along the surface, moist air condenses at ground level as fog. Pilots—and others who watch weather—know that having only a digit or two between the dew point and the temperature probably means instructions from the tower to divert to a runway they can see. Water vapor also condenses in the form of dew or, if the air is below freezing, as frost.

Sometimes the lifting is gentle, causing water vapor to condense into flat, shallow layers of cloud called *stratus clouds*.

A sheet of stratocumulus clouds follows a cold front sweeping across the tundra of northern Manitoba, Canada. Despite their vast expanse, these midlevel clouds are usually too shallow to produce precipitation.

These clouds form at all levels of the atmosphere and, as their name implies, exhibit nothing more than a desire to follow the atmosphere's strong impulse to stratify horizontally. Localized instabilities such as extreme heating or cooling create the opposite type, a turbulent species that grows vertically. The resulting inoculation of the air with large dollops of latent heat feeds a vertical development that is strong enough to overturn the natural, stratified order of things. These clouds begin as cottonball puffs of white; then, if there is enough water to condense and freeze, they boil toward the very arches of the troposphere. These are called *cumulus* clouds. A storm is not a storm without them.

Looking like a picture in a child's storybook, fluffy cumulus clouds glide by in a majestic aerial flotilla. *Cumulus*, the Latin word for "heap," is an apt name for these billowing towers of vapor and ice.

A Visible Sign

Between the extemes of flat stratus and rising cumulus clouds lives a family of hybrids—*stratus, nimbostratus, altostratus*, and *cirrostratus* on the stable side. These reach from near the surface up into the middle (*alto* means middle) troposphere and even into the lower boundaries of the stratosphere, where *cirrus* clouds occur as veils of wind-borne ice crystals. *Cumulus, cumulonimbus, altocumulus*, and *cirrocumulus* are their puffier

and more turbulent cousins. A kind of common ancestor of the two families is the familiar *stratocumulus*, in which the languor of stratus clouds is mussed by a scallop of turbulent air.

Clouds are a visible sign of what the atmosphere is up to and what weather it intends. The veils of cirrus that spread hazily across the sky above 20,000 feet (6,100 m)—indeed, they may creep along the ceiling of the troposphere—are incapable of producing the activity of weather. They are too shallow, their water too thoroughly frozen. Still, they may be harbingers of heavy weather upstream. Cirrus shields, on the other hand, are often the high-altitude exhaust from a distant storm system, and their advance is a fairly reliable prediction of what will follow: a steady parade of lower stratus and stratocumulus clouds that will gradually stretch closer to the ground and darken as they deepen vertically.

Dark clouds are that way not because they are full of rainwater—although they are—they are dark because they are thick enough to blot out the Sun. Conversely, a brightening sky means bad weather has begun to clear—folk wisdom that we have begun to forget. A glance skyward is enough to tell us the intentions of a consortium of clouds. If they are building and deepening—that is, growing darker—and their bases are not too high above the ground, some type of precipitation is certain. If they are thin and high, they are probably barren.

When cumulus clouds start forming, they signal the presence of an updraft; if they continue to build, the updraft is a strong one, fueled by air flowing into an area of low pressure. As they rise into gleaming towers, they start to boil because the surrounding atmosphere feeds them a huge dose of invisible water vapor, which they transform into liquid and ice, pumping themselves up on released latent heat. If the towers begin to shred, they have risen into a dry stratum of air that has choked off their water-fueled furnace.

As these giant clouds mature into full-sized thunderheads, they become a lonely kind of storm—their growth has starved surrounding cumuli into mere cotton puffs of cloud, scattered for

Seen from the ground, the dark, cloudy cathedral of an evolving storm glows as a shaft of sunlight penetrates its roiling center.

some distance around the main system. The awesome sight of a dark, towering thunderhead is a virtual guarantee of water in some form.

VAGARIES OF WEATHER

What goes up is not necessarily what comes down. In order for cloud droplets to fall as precipitation, they must grow tremendously—the average raindrop contains a million times more water and is hundreds of times larger than an individual cloud droplet. Some drops form when aggregations of ice crystals melt into rain as they fall, some coalesce through collisions among water droplets—larger droplets fall faster than smaller ones.

Flying through clouds where the atmospheric temperature is about 10° F (-12° C), pilots encounter mainly water droplets. Flying much higher, where the temperature is about -20° F (-29° C), the airplane beats effortlessly through ice crystals. But in the intermediate layers, where temperatures lie between 10° and -20° F, clouds are slurries of water droplets—some cooled well below freezing—and ice crystals. "You fly in one side," a flight instructor once cautioned, "and you fall out the other as a ball of ice." Without deicers, an airplane's control and lifting surfaces are quickly swaddled in a sheet of ice; an ice-covered airplane will drop from the cloud like a giant hailstone and, if the air below is too frigid to melt the deadly sheath, the plane will hit the ground like one as well.

What else hits the ground depends entirely on air temperature. Where the air is below freezing from the surface upward, the precipitation is snow; if surface temperature is well above freezing, it is rain. Between those certainties lie the infinite vagaries of weather. If raindrops evaporate on the way down, for instance, they may produce the wispy, dangling tendrils called *virga* or they may erode into the light, misty rain called *drizzle*. Partial melting en route may produce slushy snow. Sometimes a layer of warmer air separates a freezing level aloft and one at the surface. Descending flakes of snow hit the warm layer, melt, and then refreeze into small pellets of sleet near the ground. If they do not have time to refreeze in the air, they hit the ground as drops of supercooled water— freezing rain that turns to ice on impact.

Streaks of evaporating rainfall, called *virga*, veil the sky over the Sierra Nevada range in California. While falling through several layers of different air temperatures, precipitation often alternates between the liquid and the frozen forms; but under very warm, dry conditions, rainfall can evaporate even before it hits the ground.

A member of the ground crew at Colorado's Aspen Airport deices an airplane before take-off. Even a little ice on the leading edge of a wing can interrupt the flow of air that produces lift, causing an airplane on the ground to stay there—and one aloft to fall.

Hailstones pound Garmisch, Germany, during a summertime thunderstorm (*above*). Composed of concentric layers of ice, hailstones 0.5 inch (1.25 cm) or more in diameter (*right*) can fall during severe storms, injuring people and animals and damaging crops and property.

In the towering crucibles of cumulonimbus clouds strong updrafts and a gargantuan burden of moisture combine to forge water into its oddest form: the *hailstone*. Although not fully understood, hailstones are known to exhibit concentric shells of different types of ice, suggesting that they are built up a layer at a time, possibly by prolonged suspension of the hailstone near the edge of a powerful updraft where a mixture of particle sizes in liquid, solid, and slushy forms exists. When the stone gains enough size and weight, it falls out of the cloud. It is a powerful form of precipitation—a swath of hail can rip through a grain crop like an armored regiment.

Whatever form they may have at the end of their aerial odyssey, water molecules always return to the planet's surface, to the vast reservoir of the global sea. On average, water molecules will fly for about 10 days and travel thousands of miles, spending and hoarding heat as they change phase from ice to liquid water to vapor and back again. They may sink toward the black depths of the deep seas or join a surface current that will return them quickly to their atmospheric wandering.

This same hydrologic wheel has turned for billions of years, sending out the same molecules over and over again. Water that bathed dinosaurs could have become the perspiration of a galley slave or the blood of lambs and lions before it came to temporary rest in your coffee cup. This currency of the atmosphere is like money: You cannot live without it, but you may not always want to know where it has been.

A waterspout (*left*), first cousin to a tornado, descends from a cumulus cloud in the Gulf of Mexico off Key West, Florida. These funnels rotate at speeds of up to 50 miles per hour, drawing water as high as 100 feet (30 m) into the air. The more common member of the family—the landlocked tornado (*below*)—touches down with devastating consequences in a Kansas cornfield.

Weather's Footprint

Rain, snow, ice, hail—all are a kind of atmospheric arsenal. For, stocked with such weapons, warring fronts become more than air masses rubbing up against and finally constricting about one another, creating a center of low pressure between them. Now this arid coiling becomes a potent and warlike weather factory—and with clouds as tracers, visible as well.

Ahead of the low pressure center, an intruding curl of warm air—a warm front—rides up onto the sloping face of a cold air mass, cooling as it goes; as it rises its water vapor condenses, liberating heat, forming droplets, and beginning to sweep the Earth with drizzle. Behind the low pressure center a ram of advancing cold air—a cold front—wedges in beneath the warm air in its path, camming it sharply upward and cooling it rapidly. All of this activity causes a sudden release of latent heat and the heavier weather of a marching squall line of thunderstorms. When the cycle is completed, the warm air hovers aloft, isolated by a layer of colder air near the surface. Gradually the layers mix and cool, and the atmosphere stabilizes—and waits for another weather factory to come spinning through.

This maneuvering forms one of the connections that humans observed centuries ago between the weight of the atmosphere—its pressure "footprint"—and what the atmosphere is doing or is about to do. Where pressure declines, moist air converges at the surface and rises. Because expanding air is cooling, clouds begin to condense into visibility and precipitation starts to fall. Thus, falling atmospheric pressure has long been linked to deteriorating weather. By the same token, wherever air descends, compressing as it spreads out across the surface in its search for low pressure to surround and fill, it heats, lowering its relative humidity. These cloudless anticyclonic flows are linked with fair weather.

Along the shifting equator of the atmosphere, this linkage of pressure and weather operates with fair reliability. When the easterlies are deep and strong, areas of low pressure spin up in them, intensify, and dissipate in a gentle kind of chaos, bringing the afternoon and nighttime showers that mark the tropical rainy season. In the seasons when the trades weaken, as they do in the northern winter, these eddies spin up less frequently and there is a dry interval, even for the rainforests.

Dozens of advancing thunderstorms form an ominous squall line along the Florida Keys. Created when warm and cold fronts collide, squall lines strike quickly with heavy rains and violent winds before blowing themselves out or moving on.

A Solar Machine

Monsoon comes from *mausim*, the Arabic word for season, and evokes the regular, semiannual shifts in circulation that link the Arabian peninsula and the Indian subcontinent with the warm sea. But there are other, albeit less famous, monsoons across the world: in Africa, off northwestern Australia, and even, in a small way, jutting up across the Gulf of California into the southwestern desert of the United States. In every case the natives, whether of Dakar or of Tucson, look skyward for the telltale advance of clouds and the celestial explosions that bring rain to a parched land.

The world's monsoon systems also demonstrate that close relationship of pressure and precipitation. As the strengthening Sun warms the Indian Ocean and subcontinent during the northern spring, the atmosphere rigs itself for wet monsoon weather. The high-level jet stream winds weaken and shift northward, and a vast anticyclonic—clockwise—flow forms at high altitudes and spreads east winds high over India. Lower pressure forms over northern India, giving rise to southwesterly surface winds laden with moisture from the warm ocean.

By summer, the monsoon winds puffing up from the southwest are drenching India with the water that it cannot live without, the warm, water-laden air flows in to where a steadily warming land mass has caused air to rise—that is, created a zone of low pressure. The winds sweep in, drop their

A field on a south slope in India's Aravalli Hills is carpeted in green after the monsoons. While the rains often cause floods and other damage, they are a welcome relief from the long drought that all life in the region must endure each year.

In a monsoon deluge, street vendors in a southern Indian town rush to gather up their drenched goods. These seasonal rains soak Southeast Asia and India in the hot season, providing in a few weeks almost all of the rain that the region will see until next year.

cargo of moisture, and spiral out at high altitude to return to the sea. As this progression becomes more highly organized, the monsoonal flow fills with eddies and whorls lined with thunderstorms—*depressions*, as these relatively well-developed areas of low pressure are called. This machine runs on the spring and summer Sun. As fall approaches, the apparatus breaks down, and the subcontinent falls under the spell of autumnal drought. People then look forward to the return of the quenching—often drowning—rains of the monsoon.

A SPINNING PINWHEEL

As everyone who has been surprised by the atmosphere knows, however, not all low-pressure systems bring bad weather and not all highs are fair of face. Weather depends on where the incoming air has been and how much water it is carrying with it. Thus, when the big pinwheel of a zone of high pressure sits over the ocean, it may shunt enormous charges of water shoreward with its clockwise winds; there can be fronts dangling from a high as well as from a low. In the same way, some low-pressure systems carry little or no water to begin with—converging parcels of dry air meet and cool all the time without creating more than a suggestion of a cloud. Still, we are wise to look for the world's heaviest weather in the old mariner's "falling glass"—the shrinking column of mercury in an old-fashioned barometer.

In fact, it is less that the glass is falling than that it is falling sharply and rapidly: a sudden tailing off of pressure, together with rising winds and waves and a mammoth swell, was how a galleon skipper could tell he had come upon a traveling storm spinning in the easterly trades. If the glass fell below 28 inches of mercury (950 millibars), he could expect a hellish ride in a tropical cyclone.

Hurricanes, as the Atlantic and eastern North Pacific variations of tropical cyclones are called, provide an almost laboratory-sized specimen of how storms are born, live, and die and how heat energy moves between the sea and the atmosphere. They occur in similar forms in most of the planet's warm oceans, where they have acquired different names.

Hurricane is a term borrowed from the Caribe tribes encountered by Christopher Columbus on his early forays to

A computer-enhanced image shows details of Hurricane Allen's eyewall. Seen over the Gulf of Mexico on August 8, 1980, Allen raked the Caribbean with 185-mph (300-kph) winds and 20-foot (6-m) storm tides, killing more than 100 people.

explore the New World. Occurring in the waters of the western North Pacific, the larger and more powerful cousins of the hurricane are called *typhoons*. The name may come from a confluence of Chinese—*da feng* is Mandarin for "great wind"—and the classical educations of European explorers, who thought they saw Typhon, the monstrous mythic earth-child slain by Zeus and now the angry resident of Italy's Mount Etna. Along the low-lying coasts of the Bay of Bengal in India, where the storms take an enormous toll in human life each year, they are called *cyclones*. Australians use the aboriginal term *willy-willy* to describe the southern-hemisphere hurricanes that strike their Indian Ocean coast.

All of these arise from the warm sea, from some burble, some traveling instability, in the water-logged summer winds of the tropical easterlies. Something—uneven heating of the ocean surface, the introduction of freezing nuclei in the form of African dust or sea salts, some faltering in the troposphere's high-altitude winds—causes the development of cyclones, or *cyclogenesis*, to occur on the much smaller scale of a hurricane, without the clearly defined boundaries between air masses called *fronts*.

First, a low-pressure area forms over the sea, abetted by a kind of chimney provided by a strong flow of upper-level winds. Then warm, water-charged air sweeps up this atmospheric flue, as drier air moves in behind it and itself becomes charged with water—with energy—as it flows over the sea surface and in around the developing center of low pressure. Finally, if this circulation continues, and if water vapor begins to condense, releasing its latent heat into the lower atmosphere, the low-pressure center intensifies and the clouds forming in the counterclockwise spiral of air around it become more highly organized. In time, the great violence rests on the surface of the sea, its chimney a well-defined toroid, or monstrous doughnut, of clouds and raging winds rising all the way to the tropopause, attired in cloudy finery complete with spiraling trails of thunderstorms imbedded in long, ragged rainbands that stream out for a hundred miles (160 km) around.

Satellites have made this pale pinwheel familiar to us— this is the hurricane. What appears to be a dimple near the center of the spiral is the eye of the storm, the calm within the cylindrical dervish of violent wind. The amount of energy

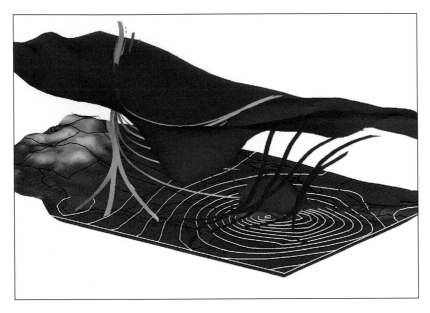

Displayed against a map of terrain and atmospheric pressure, a March 1993 extratropical cyclone that devastated the American east spins up in a University of Wisconsin computer simulation. A large cap (*magenta*) marks the sinking of stratospheric air into the storm. A conveyor belt of warm, moist air (*red*) feeds the storm's lower levels, creating a small rotary circulation near the surface (*magenta*), while strong streams of high-level air (*yellow*) add momentum.

expended by these storms, compact and short-lived as they are, is astonishing. Hurricane Andrew, for example, revved with the equivalent energy of a 10-megaton bomb continuously throughout its savage passage across southern Florida in August 1992—days, not a few seconds, of megaton-level firing.

The view from satellites and coastal radar has spun an illusion that these grand maritime storms are easily seen, finite, somehow simpler than their larger, high-latitude cousins. In fact, these violent creations of the tropical atmosphere are wonderfully complicated and inherently unpredictable—the true offspring of chaos. There is something fragile and unstable in the way the heat engine of the hurricane functions. A sudden cooling of sea-surface temperatures can cause a misfire; the storm's dynamics echo atmospheric events occurring many miles away.

The *eyewall*, the cylinder of towering cumuli and high winds that is the real heart of the hurricane, was once believed to be a kind of chimney, a conduit for energy drawn from the warm sea, a way of squeezing latent heat out of rising moist air. But it is as complex as the human heart.

Circulation into the eyewall has a shifting tilt, an asymmetry that may modulate the direction and intensity of the storm, depending on what is happening in the surrounding atmosphere. The hollow cylinder of the eyewall is punctuated with narrow columns of vertically moving air, arranged around the eye like cartridges in the rotary magazine of a submachine gun—rising currents are live rounds; descending

A lone man and his dog brave rising winds in Palm Beach, Florida, as Hurricane Andrew heads toward land. Because its most vicious winds are located at the eyewall, which surrounds the storm's eye, the hurricane's force will continue to escalate as its center approaches the city.

The remains of a Homestead, Florida, neighborhood display the violent impact of Hurricane Andrew's passage in August 1992. Andrew's eye, bounded by 175-mph (282-kph) winds, came ashore just south of downtown Miami, crossed the peninsula, and attacked the U.S. Gulf Coast two days later.

ones are blanks. As these rounds fire, or misfire, the storm intensifies and weakens, often with baffling speed, causing the eye to tighten and the winds to rise, or, alternatively, the eye to widen and its winds diminish. When we know of these dynamics, the familiar spiral of a hurricane becomes something more than bad weather—a kind of breathing beast, drifting ominously between the stratosphere and the sea.

In the northern hemisphere, tropical cyclones tend to follow a general path in which they drift slowly from east to west. Eventually they turn—hurricane forecasters say *recurve*—toward the north and northeast, and then head out into the northern ocean, where they die of the chill. South of the Equator, the only storms that are similar to hurricanes are those that

Palm saplings on a Florida tree farm are bent to the ground by Hurricane Andrew's sustained winds of 145 mph (230 kph). By the time this powerful storm had dissipated, it had destroyed homes, businesses, and vegetation and caused more than $25 billion in damage.

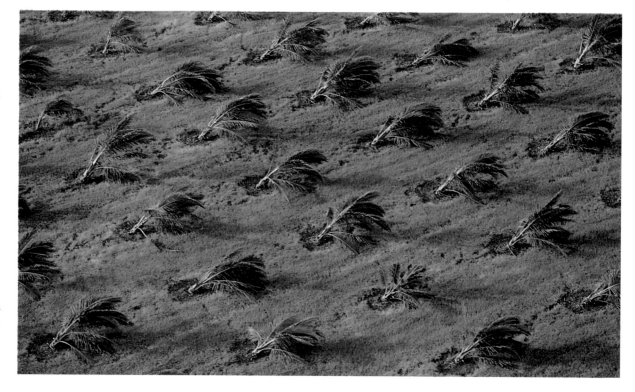

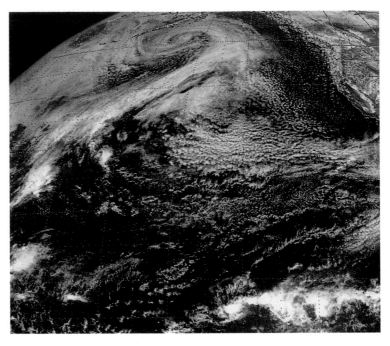

APRIL 29, 1988

APRIL 30, 1988

TRACKING AN EXTRATROPICAL CYCLONE

Under the watchful sensors of a NOAA (National Oceanic and Atmospheric Administration) geostationary satellite, a late-April depression—a region of low pressure—develops south of the Aleutian Islands in the northern Pacific Ocean. The satellite is positioned some 22,000 miles (35,800 km) above the Equator where it tracks the low pressure system, which takes just a day to spin into an extratropical cyclone with streamers of cloud bands and squall lines stretching across half the Pacific. By May 2, the system reaches the Pacific northwest (*far right*) and begins to split into disorganized patches of cloud, while a new cyclone spins up in mid-Pacific. Although the first cyclone is dying, its landfall has seeded the atmosphere over western North America with the ingredients of turbulent weather; soon the system will re-form west of the Rockies and spawn May storms all the way to the Atlantic seaboard. These four images were made in 1988 through one of several infrared channels in the satellite radiometer used to scan weather over the western hemisphere.

develop and then strike out of the Indian Ocean toward western Australia, following a path shaped by the strong westerlies of the southern hemisphere. Although hurricanes and typhoons may seem independent, they are actually steered by external forces—the prevailing bands of surface and upper-level winds, the blocking action of nearby high-pressure systems, and the temperature of the sea's surface.

All of these huge storm systems depend on water, and hot water at that—hurricanes run on sea-surface water heated to 80° F (27° C) or better. Their enormous appetite for energy leaves a wake of cold water that has welled up from several hundred feet deep. Huge appetites, however, are often signs of a corresponding frail dependency, and so it is with tropical cyclones. The heat in evaporating water has fueled their evolution from a free-form patch of imperfect weather in the easterly trades to a better-defined depression, then to the violence of the ocean gale, and finally to the hurricane. Remove the hot sea under them and they quickly reverse their evolution until nothing but a scattering of water-logged clouds remains.

MAY 1, 1988

MAY 2, 1988

At higher latitudes, a cyclone expends similar levels of energy but takes the form of a less compact, continent-sized system. Its ill-defined eye is colder than a hurricane's so that its central pressure is not as low and its winds are usually not as high as the 74 miles per hour (119 kph) that marks the lowest threshold of hurricane force. This cold center means abundant ice, supercooled water, and bone-chilling gale-force winds that now and then are the cold counterparts of the winds in hurricanes.

The 1987 cyclone that swept away whole forests of centuries-old British trees is still called *The Great Hurricane*, even though there was nothing tropical about it. Instead of a hurricane's spiral arms, hollow cylinder of cloud, and high winds around the eye, these high-latitude storms dangle conventional warm and cold fronts, soft fingers of chilly drizzle, and muscular arms of squalls and thunderstorms. This is the kind of storm that gave us our rough ride across the English Channel and enforced the point that the two oceans, one of air and one of water, often operate as one. The illusion we

experienced of having sea and sky merge violently on that night was not an illusion at all.

That the air and the sea interact closely to produce the events called weather was one of the early deductions made by modern meteorology. None of the work that scientists have done since has weakened the point but much has reinforced it. Studies taken from American and Canadian research vessels moored in the path of the great extratropical cyclones of the Gulf of Alaska—storms that create and carry winter weather from the Pacific Northwest across the North American continent and then across the Atlantic to reform into storms of the type that rattled our Channel crossing—and from the game crews of instrumented airplanes flying low through the raging winds and icy rain have revealed a degree of interaction that few researchers expected. The pressure footprint of such cyclones, for example, can be read not just on the ocean surface but on its floor as well, in storm-roiled sediments a mile and more below the tempest. That immense column of ocean is what fuels these storms.

Something for Everyone

North Sea storms that churn the English Channel are not the only disturbances that mark the winter season. An even larger and more profound interaction between the sea and the air also occurs around Christmas but in the Pacific, south of the Equator. The arid coastal lands of southern Ecuador and Peru border on some of the world's most abundant fisheries, which are fed by teeming generations of tiny anchovies. When the anchovies are plentiful, as they generally are, everything else is plentiful too, and along the desert coasts fish, birds, and fishermen enjoy good times. Such a prosperous situation requires the cooperation of both the sea and the atmosphere. The latter provides strong and steady easterly winds that, blowing offshore, push the warm surface waters away from the coast. Cold, nutrient-rich surface water wells up to take the displaced water's place, providing a banquet for the anchovies. They in their turn provide a feast for everybody else.

Some years, however, are not so good. Sometimes the trade winds weaken and the warm surface current courses closer to shore. The upwelling cold water is cut off, along with its nutrients. The anchovies vanish, and the air grows dense with the reek of death as multitudes of birds and fish starve. To make matters worse, such times bring colossal rains to the desert, greening the dry land but trying the human residents with floods and mudslides. Because this adversity begins near Christmas, the Peruvian fishermen—either in prayer or irony —call it *El Niño*, the Spanish name for the Christ child. As far as anyone knew, the El Niños that had plagued them in 1891, 1911, 1925, 1941, and 1953—and would continue to show up now and then forever—were regional events, hard luck that began and ended along the South American coast.

As early as 1924, however, a British mathematician had begun taking data demonstrating that, far from being a local wonder, El Niño had an oceanic and atmospheric root system spanning the Pacific. Gilbert Walker took over as director of Britain's Indian observatories, hoping to find a way to predict when the life-giving rains of the monsoons might falter.

Walker discovered that atmospheric pressure over the tropical Pacific and Indian oceans exhibited an odd seesawing

A fleet of fishing boats lies high and dry and out of business on the coast of Peru. The anchovies that sustain the local fishing industry die off when the normally cold, nutrient-rich currents along the coast are replaced by warm water during an El Niño event.

behavior. Whenever pressure was high over the Pacific, it fell over the Indian Ocean, the monsoon circulation intensified, and rains were heavy. When pressure was low over the Pacific, however, high pressure over the Indian Ocean caused the monsoons to falter and drought to reign. This interesting correlation was given a meteorological name that conveyed very little: the *Southern Oscillation*.

Curiously, the job of linking the distant phenomena of Walker and the Peruvian fishermen fell to a man with great experience of the atmosphere but little of the southern ocean: Jakob Bjerknes, the son and good right hand of Vilhelm and a star of the Bergen Institute. Bjerknes had come to the United States in 1940 and been trapped there by the German conquest of Norway. Unable to return, he took a position at the University of California at Los Angeles as a professor—and a prime mover—in its budding department of meteorology, one that biographers would later call the new Bergen.

Around Christmas 1957 and lasting into 1958, El Niño struck again along the Peruvian coast. By chance it occurred during the International Geophysical Year, a global cooperative study of all the Earth's natural systems, from earthquakes

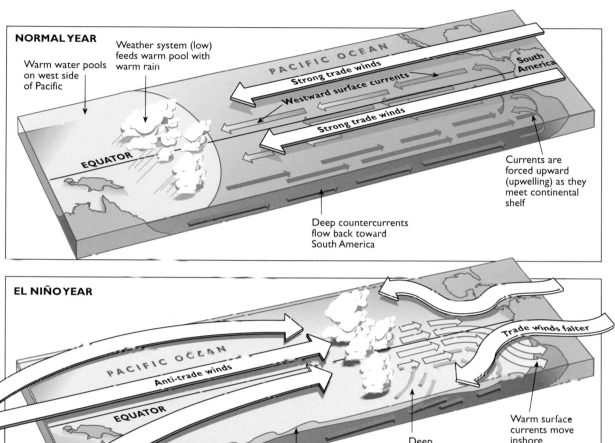

NORMAL YEAR

Warm water pools on west side of Pacific

Weather system (low) feeds warm pool with warm rain

PACIFIC OCEAN

South America

Strong trade winds

Westward surface currents

Strong trade winds

EQUATOR

Currents are forced upward (upwelling) as they meet continental shelf

Deep countercurrents flow back toward South America

EL NIÑO YEAR

PACIFIC OCEAN

Anti-trade winds

EQUATOR

Trade winds falter

Warm surface currents move inshore

Deep countercurrents weaken

Layer of warm surface water sloshes east

NORMAL YEAR Strong trade winds bolstered by high pressure over the eastern Pacific sweep along the Equator toward low pressure over the western Pacific. Here low-pressure systems produce heavy rains and a vast pool of warm surface water. In the sea, surface currents follow the trade winds. Countercurrents deep in the ocean sweep back toward South America, where the continental shelf forces them upward, causing an upwelling of cold water.

EL NIÑO YEAR Low pressure shifts eastward creating heavy precipitation and a large pool of warm surface water. The trade winds that have held the warm water to the west falter, allowing a warm pulse to spread across the surface of the eastern Pacific, driven by the eastward-blowing anti-trade winds. The deep countercurrents weaken and their upwelling is blocked by the warm surface layer along the shore.

to magnetic fields to oceans. Bjerknes turned with relish to the IGY data taken in and over the equatorial Pacific and the Indian Ocean. He had long been fascinated by the clear, intimate links between the two fluid oceans, and in the 1957–58 El Niño outbreak he may have sensed a paradigm. He showed that the "regional" El Niños of Peru correlated with Walker's Southern Oscillations—that both were part of an endless continuum of exchange between the atmosphere and the ocean.

What scientists now call ENSO—an acronym made from El Niño and Southern Oscillation—has since been studied in extensive detail, not least because of a major outbreak in 1982 and 1983 and another, extended one that began in December

1991. Ordinarily, the end of such episodes is marked by the return of less disturbing conditions, which scientists have given the name *La Niña*—the little girl.

The onset of ENSO is detectable in the temperatures of surface water. Normally, a vast pool of warm surface water covers the equatorial Pacific—except for a narrow tongue of colder water extending westward from the Peruvian coast for several thousand miles. Trade winds, bolstered by the terrain of alternating high and low pressure across the Pacific, sustain this system, keeping the warm pool piled up in the western Pacific and creating what is called the *Indonesian Low*, a massive center of tropical rainfall.

Torrential rains, flooding, and mudslides ravaged Ecuador during the 1982–83 El Niño, severing such vital links as this bridge between the cities of Guayaquil and Salinas. This El Niño's effects were felt in the form of bizarrely bad weather around the world.

Sheep in search of grazing and water roam the parched landscape of southeastern Australia. During the severe 1982–83 El Niño, which disrupted weather patterns around the world, an unusual high-pressure system over Australia diverted the expected monsoon rains and caused one of the worst droughts of this century.

When the invisible pressure terrain is smoothed, however, as it is by increasing surface-water temperatures, the trade winds weaken. The warm pool sloshes eastward, carrying the warm torrential rainfall with it. As the encroaching fingers of warm water obliterate the tongue of cooler water, the trade winds weaken further, causing the rogue weather and ocean-temperature patterns to intensify. Off Peru, the overlying warm water stifles the vital upwelling from the deep and strangles both economy and ecosystem.

El Niño has something for everyone. The 1982–83 outbreak caused the monsoons in both Africa and India to falter, raining dust instead of plenty. Forest fires swept Indonesia, drought-parched Australia, and much of Africa. And floods destroyed crops and structures in Peru, Ecuador, Argentina, Uruguay, and southern Brazil. In California record-shattering

rains and coastal storms came ashore and then swept across the United States, sowing heavy weather. Balmy Tahiti, which had seen nothing untoward in a century, was struck by six tropical cyclones that followed the atmospheric pathways laid down by ENSO.

Another El Niño–Southern Oscillation event began in 1991 and brought along its share of chaos, with unprecedented flooding that summer in the American Midwest and, some scientists believe, Europe's worst winter in many years. This record El Niño–Southern Oscillation outbreak lasted into the spring of 1994 before La Niña displaced her mischievous sibling—for how long, no one could say.

The roar of fans is only a memory in John Odonnell Stadium in Davenport, Iowa, in the summer of 1993 as it lies beneath the flood waters of the Mississippi River. Rivers swollen by the heavy rains associated with the 1992–93 El Niño crested dozens of feet above flood stage throughout the U.S. Midwest.

RIVERS IN THE SKY

But how are such storms sustained? Until only recently water vapor's journey once it left the ocean was seen as a kind of global migration, visible in weather-balloon soundings as a broad sheet of vapor drifting from the tropics up toward the poles. Then in 1993 a British-born meteorology professor at

the Massachusetts Institute of Technology discerned a new, improbable wrinkle in this global migration. According to Reginald Newell, the lower atmosphere is marked not just by great sheets of traveling water vapor but by narrow filaments as well, often flanked by banks of towering tropical clouds.

Newell called the filaments "rivers," and in a sense they are—one stream, flowing southward from Brazil toward the area east of the Andes and then out into the South Atlantic, carries a volume of water equal to half the discharge at the mouth of the Mississippi. Each river lasts for about 10 days before being replaced by a new one that materializes nearby. The rivers are typically 150 miles (240 km) wide but only a mile (1.6 km) deep and can be thousands of miles long. There appear to be about five such rivers in both the northern and southern hemispheres, flowing invisibly along the atmospheric layers below 10,000 feet (3,000 m). Newell says they are always present and coherent, although they may meander and change their form.

No one knows the precise link between these newly discovered rivers and the behavior of the atmosphere—they may be a peculiar part of the arching journey of all water vapor. But they are very likely more than simple, aimless atmospheric tributaries. These rivers have been observed to flow into the low-pressure hearts of mid-latitude cyclones and even hurricanes. Perhaps Newell's rivers in the sky are the conduits that fuel the Earth's great storms, which, like everything violent in the atmosphere, run on water, the excellent molecule—the stuff of life, and death. ☁

A dark column of torrential rain cascades through a sun-reddened sky above the Olgas, a formation of 36 rock domes in western Australia. The desert will get only a quick taste of rainwater, however—most of it is quickly swept back into the atmosphere by the arid region's high rate of evaporation.

THE ATMOSPHERE ELECTRIC

Beneath the strobing of a ferocious desert night, legions of towering saguaro cacti stand like the warriors of an alien race, their chubby silhouetted arms raised in a surreal salute to a sky gone wild. Their stunted mesquite and oak companions seem to cower in the flickering light as an exotic atmospheric artillery flashes in a thundercloud above the rocky hills; then, as if in answer, another mountain of cloud explodes with inner light. Near sheets of rain, stark, shimmering bolts shiver briefly between Earth and sky, repeating every few seconds like hammer blows. Suddenly, as if the night were a dark curtain covering a universe of blinding light, the sky seems to rip apart; a tangled, dazzling web of illumination zigzags from one horizon to another. Sometimes the sky hisses, sometimes it speaks in a rumble or a growl or a detonating *crack*!

This must have been the way the world evolved, with elemental forces unleashed in a grand, abandoned barrage. Seen from America's southwestern desert, the flickering stormscape seems extraterrestrial, the experience of it sharply aboriginal. Beneath such a sky, our strongest kinship is with the primitive men and women who, peering heavenward with curiosity and dread, decanted frightened wonder into myth. Indeed, without science, what better explanation could there be for this celestial extravaganza than an avian god—a thunderbird?

Fire from Heaven

That imaginary creature flies through all of North America's native mythology, bringing fire from heaven and a thundering cry. Among the Dakota Sioux of North America's Great Plains, legend holds that the four Wakinyan, as they call thunderbirds—one for each point of the compass—once warred with an Earth god for control of the waters. Finally, the great thunderbird of the west, Wakinyan Tanka, called his brothers

together. They agreed that the sky, not Earth, should be their realm, so they went to live there and continued fighting the Earth god from the heavens. The Wakinyan won and took dominion over water as they had over fire, thunder, and wind—dominion, really, over life and death.

In the Pacific Northwest, the thunderbird is represented on the carved totems of such tribes as the Kwakiutls by an eagle. The beating of its wings is said to cause thunder to roll across the sky. Lightning flashes from its eyes, and it is enormously powerful—often it is depicted with a whale in its dreadful talons.

The idea of a celestial bird as the agent of lightning and thunder is not just a North American notion. It appears in the artifacts of ancient Mesopotamia as the lightning bird, Zu, and on Bronze Age pots from such widely separated spots as Siberia and Peru. In the southern part of Africa the Zulu and Baziba peoples have a crimson counterpart to the Sioux's Wakinyan that is called the Lightning Bird. They say that lightning *is* a

A stocky bronze Zeus flourishes his superweapon, the thunderbolt, in this 5th century B.C. Greek statuette. Thunderclouds were regarded by the Greeks as the forge where Hephaestus, the lame husband of Aphrodite, fashioned Zeus's deadly bolts. The supreme deity hurled them as punishment for trespasses, but also out of pique, and objects struck by lightning were considered sacred.

Wings outspread, the mythic creature known as the thunderbird joins other animal deities on this colored panel painted by Nootka artists around 1850. The Nootka people were early inhabitants of Vancouver Island in the Pacific Northwest.

bird, something like the ferocious fish-eating eagle, that it may be found dead where lightning has struck, and that its body is the source of powerful medicine. To be struck by lightning, in this canon, is to be ripped by the claws of the Lightning Bird.

More often, however, lightning is portrayed not as a creature so much as a weapon—a superweapon, appropriate to the hand of a powerful, anthropomorphic deity. Many African mythologies refer to lightning as God's Ax, and some explain the phenomenon precisely the way the ancient Greeks did, as the work of a sky-dwelling blacksmith. The dreaded thunderbolt was shaped to great Zeus's hand by the crippled smithy Hephaestus and was the most powerful weapon in human experience—it sometimes killed, it could shatter trees and boulders, and it often set fires. Only Zeus, the god of gods, could wield such an instrument—and yet, improbably, it also wound up in human hands. In the myth of Prometheus, whom Zeus punished horribly for sharing fire with puny men, we discern reality: early humans receiving their first fire from a lightning-streaked sky.

The idea of the thunderbolt as a celestial weapon pervades mythology. Thor, or Donar of the Germans, also armed

In this dazzling miniature from the 17th century, Indra, the Hindu god of thunder, sits astride his white elephant while sending a fierce storm, represented by roiling black clouds, down on a royal gathering below. To match wits with Indra, another deity uses a local mountain as an umbrella to shield lords, ladies, and their cattle from the storm.

himself with thunderbolts, as did his Finnish, Slavic, and Celtic counterparts. From atop his white elephant, the Hindu storm god Indra flung lightning at the people of the Indian subcontinent. The Inca's Categuil roamed the heavens with a sling and a mace, wreaking such havoc with lightning that children were sacrificed to curb his wrath.

In the richly textured mythologies of Nigeria's Yoruba people, the great warrior-god Shango rules from heaven with his thunder and lightning. Some native priests in the Yorubaland of western Nigeria wear a stylized version of Shango's thunder ax, and believers place stone axes—stand-ins for the deity's—in forked sticks with offerings. Curiously, Shango casts a longer shadow than most gods, for he has crossed the waters to the Caribbean—in southern Haiti, he

controls the stormy heavens. In northern Haiti, however, his place is taken by an unlikely substitute: St. John the Baptist, a man, in this myth at least, so violent that God tries to make him too drunk to exert his full powers on his saint's day, which comes in the thundery Caribbean summer.

With the idea of lightning as a weapon, however, there is almost everywhere the softer contrapuntal notion that the same forces that create lightning also bring the gift of seasonal rains. The native American thunderbird, though supernatural, is no malevolent spirit. Its domain may comprise the violence of severe storms and lightning but it also brings the water that keeps the continent's rain forests, plains, and deserts alive.

In central and southern Africa, as in the southwestern United States, these rains make the difference between life and death and blend those twin strands into myth. The Songhay people of the upper Niger region, for example, tell the story of a celestial spirit named Dongo. Trying out a new ax over a village, Dongo threw the weapon—a lightning bolt—and killed men on the ground. Puzzled, Dongo went in search of a way to undo what he had done. His wise grandfather gave the penitent spirit an earthenware pot full of water, with which Dongo filled his cheeks. He then returned to the scene of his error and spewed the water over the dead, reviving them. Around the world, fear of lightning is soluble in rainwater.

A CYCLE OF ENERGY

Not surprisingly, lightning mythology has its sharpest edge where people are sometimes cut down by a bolt from heaven. This means that in the world's centers of thunderstorm activity—in the lower latitudes, where there is plenty of heat and moisture to drive the storms—people see the lightning stroke as something awesome. At higher latitudes, lightning is interesting—it is Nordic Thor's weapon of choice, after all—but not nearly the terrifying weapon it is closer to the Equator.

Two aborginal myths from north-central Australia offer a case in point. The Aborigines of the northeast coast of the Arnhem Land, which juts northward between the Timor Sea and the Gulf of Carpenteria, tell the story of the giant Djambuwal, who stalked the world to the east, guarding the beaches against newcomers. Djambuwal wielded a great spear named Larrapan. Once, however, a canoe-load of invading Makasans from near Borneo landed on his beach and, after a long fight, vanquished Djambuwal. As he died, he promised they would hear his voice in every storm. Afterwards, his spear, Larrapan, could sometimes be seen streaking across the southern heavens as a shooting star. But now and then Larrapan would miss its mark and richochet off rocks, striking sparks: lightning. For Djambuwal, lightning is not so much a weapon as a glittering accident.

Farther west in that same region, the Gunwinggu people tell a far more ominous tale. There, Namarragon, the Lightning Man, once roamed the sky, carrying in each hand a spear of lightning and wearing axes tethered to his arms and knees. For the majority of the year he stayed away from people, but during the rainy season he rode in on the clouds streaming in from the sea. Namarragon was not merely a meteorological entity. In his thunder-voice, he admonished people to do no evil. When they transgressed, however, his voice would hiss and sizzle with angry disappointment, and he would hurl his lightning-spear across the sky in a bright arc. It could split a great tree and crack the ground asunder; sometimes Namarragon even killed the sinners. In one version of the myth, he incinerates a wife and her adulterous lover in an inferno of heavenly fire.

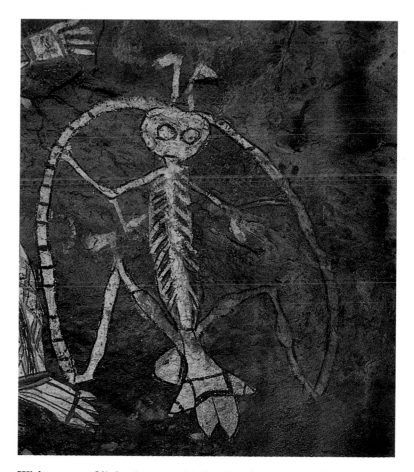

With an arc of lightning over his head and stone axes fastened to elbows and knees, Namarragon, the Australian Lightning Man, promises to punish human sinners. This rock painting is in Kakadu National Park, about 160 miles (256 km) southeast of Darwin in the Northern Territory of Australia.

The difference between the two myths may be the difference in how lightning is experienced in those separated corners of tropical Australia. One suspects that the Gunwinggu have seen terrible storms and people struck by thunderbolts and fires set. They have been awed by the atmospheric arsenal as, perhaps, their neighbors to the east have not.

Possibly nowhere else does lightning seem tamer than in China's Taoist mythology. The deity in charge is My Lord of Thunder, Leikung, a hideous, winged blue man with nasty talons who punishes humans for their secret crimes. But the actual atmospheric activity is a mild, rather familial affair. Leikung can only make thunder. Rain comes from Yu-tzu, Master of Rain, clouds are piled up by Yun-t'ung, Little Boy of the Clouds, and wind is the creation of Feng-po, Earl of Wind. Lightning is the work of Mother Lightning, Tien Mu, and is simply the flashing of mirrors she holds in her hands.

This view echoes through many mythologies, with lightning and the sound it makes seen as two discrete things—lightning something thrown or seen, thunder the thrower's or someone else's voice. In southern Zaire, thunder is called Nzasi, a storm god who roams the sky hunting with two dozen dogs, who are his strokes of lightning. Sometimes mere mortals try to adopt one of Nzasi's dogs, only to have the creature explode and send the foolish man to oblivion—while not as great as the thunder god, lightning is still dangerous.

THE SOUND OF LIGHTNING

In general, however, where intense thunderstorms are a pervasive seasonal presence, rising along the atmospheric borders between winter and summer, cold air and warm, there is no separating the thunderbolt from the thunder. When lightning is uncoiling overhead and the sight and sound come close together—as they often do over the North American plains—it makes sense to have them both embodied in the thunderbird's flashing eye, its cry, the rolling beat of its wings.

Near or distant, however, thunder is the voice of lightning. It is produced as air, intensely heated and accelerated by the passing lightning stroke, vibrates like the baffles in a speaker, quickly expanding as it heats, then contracting as it cools. The vibrations ripple away from the stroke in the form of sound waves, and we hear them as thunder. When the stroke is very close, the sound it makes is one of detonation. At a greater distance, the sharp crack blurs with other lightning-caused vibrations and becomes a muttering rumble.

Because light from the flash moves at the speed of light—which is about 186,000 miles, or nearly 300,000 kilometers, per second—and thunder travels at the much slower speed of sound, the eye and ear rarely sense them together, explaining why each phenomenon is often given a source of its own. But the two can easily be linked. Light covers one mile in 5.3 millionths of a second; sound travels a mile in about five seconds. Thus, the time in seconds between the stroke and its thunder, divided by five, is its distance in miles. (For approximate kilometers, divide by three.)

What the tellers of all these myths could not have known was that these luminous darts are the visible manifestations of what may be seen as an alternative atmosphere—one not of wind and water but of magnetic fields, high-voltage currents, and electrified molecules: the world as a current-generating dynamo. But who could have inferred the atmosphere electric? Although timelessly familiar, its signature—lightning—is inscrutably faster than the eye and seems as separate from the rest of nature as an angry god's ax or spear.

Still, there are myths that take a larger view. For example, the Desana, who live in the steaming rain forests of Colombia's deep interior, associate the crash of thunder with the voice of the owl, the silent-winged nocturnal predator who in their mythology bears the bad news of death. Sometimes thunder is a celestial jaguar's dreadful roar. Lightning is not a weapon hurled by gods, however, but a form of semen from the sun—semen that, like its human counterpart, carries the seeds of life. To the Desana—the Sons of the Wind as they call themselves—lightning is more than the human mind can grasp: part of a grand, global cycle of energy, the stuff of life and magic and fertility expressed as palpable light.

Lightning flickers between centers of electrical charge in storm clouds gathering over Las Vegas, Nevada, during the southwestern desert's monsoon thunderstorm season, when the region experiences its famously spectacular electrical displays.

Anvils of the Atmosphere

Today we know that electricity lies at the heart of our existence. Our brains crackle with electrochemically generated signals and our muscles and nerves are literally galvanized into action. Biology runs partly on electrical energy. Atoms contain positively charged nuclei in a swarm of negatively charged electrons—the attraction of opposite charges holds our universe together. But that awareness is relatively recent.

To the enlightened scholarly mind of the 18th and early 19th centuries, electricity was one of the new wonders of a world that was revealing one astonishing new phenomenon after another. To some imaginations, the phenomenon of electricity evoked godlike possibilities—Mary Shelley's young German medical student named Frankenstein was punished for appropriating the Creator's prerogative of giving life. The full title of Shelley's novel is *Frankenstein, or The New Prometheus*, and here, as we sense in the Greek myth of humans obtaining fire, lightning is the energizing agent.

Upon those of a more scientific bent, this odd kind of energy—electricity and its counterpart, magnetism—exerted an irresistible gravitational attraction. One of the people drawn early to the study of what looked like a puzzling variant of fire was the versatile American founding father Benjamin Franklin, who—almost a mythological figure himself—at a time when he was poised between careers of printer and diplomat, chose to explore electricity systematically as a self-made scientist. Today when we think of Franklin's electrical studies, we envision a plump, middle-aged gentleman in colonial American garb flying a kite linked to a metal key into a Philadelphia thunderstorm.

In fact, that very dangerous experiment in 1752 came at the end of his studies, not at the beginning of them, and was intended, like most well-constructed science, to confirm a hypothesis. Franklin had begun tinkering with electricity in 1746 after receiving an "electricity machine"—a rudimentary generator—from a friend in England. Following the lead of earlier researchers but hampered by a sketchy understanding of how to use such scientific tools as mathematics, Franklin doggedly pursued an understanding of electricity. His work

endures mainly as a vocabulary—such terms as "conductor" and "battery," and the notion of positive and negative charge are all his—and because it verified what his studies had led him to suspect: lightning was an outsized electrical spark.

Probing the nature of lightning, Frenchman Thomas François Dalibard and a fascinated crowd shrink from current flowing down the kite line from thunderclouds during a 1753 experiment. Unlike his contemporary Benjamin Franklin, who also probed lightning with kites, M. Dalibard takes care not to touch the electrified string.

Franklin was only one of several individuals to try the experiment in a thunderstorm. Researchers in France had already verified that lightning and electricity were one, although somewhat less dramatically: they were careful not to remain connected to the kite during the experiment. Following a line of thinking that most scientists used in those days, Franklin applied a hydraulic analogy to explain how lightning worked. It was electrical fire, he said, an "element diffused among and attracted by other matter." When a body containing a surplus of electrical fire neared a body with an electrical deficit, a discharge—a lightning bolt—shot across the gap, equalizing the two supplies. He was right about the equalizing but unable to perceive the real nature of the equalizing spark—a spark, it turns out, of godly proportions.

TOWERS OF POWER

The atmosphere has a number of generators capable of producing respectable lightning bolts: blizzards, dust storms, and the fount of ash and smoke from an erupting volcano may all dance with visible electricity. But most lightning is linked to thunderstorms, the electrical side of meteorological processes that transform moist air into violent cloud towers eight miles (13 km) high. Thunderstorms are spawned by thermal instability in the atmosphere induced by a number of factors: radiative cooling of cloud tops, heating of the cloud base by the sun-warmed ground, or the camming aloft of warm, moist air by an advancing wedge of cold air.

The resulting vertical motion—*convection*, as it is called— can be seen in any unevenly heated fluid. A pot of water heated from below begins to circulate vertically, the hotter water rising toward the surface and allowing the colder, denser water to sink toward the bottom, where it in turn is heated and rises. But in the atmosphere this neat, circular movement from hot to cold wears the livery of chaos, not order.

Vertical movement goes against the atmosphere's strong reflex to be horizontally stratified—it is a lazy place of gentle winds and little weather much of the time. When a cumulus cloud makes a dynamic bid to become one of the violent creatures of that world, it must push convective currents up through those stratified layers, taking advantage of thermal

A million volts of artificial lightning electrify both air and audience at General Electric's exhibit at the 1939 New York World's Fair. Like natural lightning, these giant sparks are discharges of current powerful enough to overcome the insulating effect of air between opposite charges—but they are pale imitations of the real thing.

instability—a rapid cooling of the air with altitude. Turrets of rising air laden with supercooled droplets drive the developing thunderhead along—turrets of descending, dried-out air throttle it. Shafts of rain fall desultorily earthward. It is slow

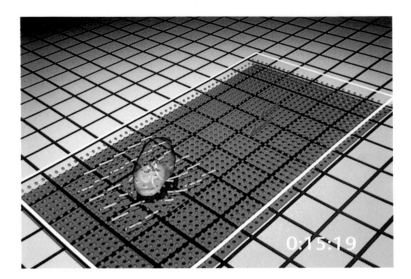

0:15:19

In this simulation by the National Center for Supercomputing Applications at the University of Illinois at Urbana-Champaign, a cumulus cloud forms, fed by an inflow of moist air (*red arrows*) from the east, and creates a central updraft. Rising (*orange*) and sinking (*blue*) imaginary particles are added to the model to trace air motion (*yellow streamers*) in and around the storm.

0:30:42

Its turbulent heart (*gold*) glowing with small droplets of water and the larger raindrops that would be visible to radar, the cumulus explodes upward around a strengthening updraft, intensifying the inflow near the surface. An anvil forms high in the troposphere and spreads eastward as cirrus clouds.

going, and it may not go at all—many cumuli puff up, secrete a squirt of rain, and fragment into wispy shreds of water.

When it works, however, it works wonderfully well. The winds that once gently converged at the surface, seeking lower atmospheric pressure, strengthen, feeding the growing tower's central updraft. Moist air flows in through the cloud's sides, mixing with and feeding the intensifying updraft. The storm's vertical momentum is fed by water's change of phase, which releases millions of calories into the updraft as vapor condenses into liquid, and liquid freezes into ice. As long as this keeps the updraft warmer than the surrounding air, the current will rise. At the top end of this chimney, high-level winds sweep away the sputtering "exhaust" blowing out the top of the rising thunderhead, producing the draft to keep the cauldron of air, ice, and water roaring within.

Inside the exploding cumulonimbus cloud, the air grows saturated and, at altitudes of 20,000 feet (6,000 m) or so, begins to freeze and coalesce into projectiles heavy enough to

fall down through the updraft. Now, as falling precipitation sets up a current of its own, the strong updraft is joined by a corresponding downdraft, which is fed and strengthened, as the updraft was, by entrained air. When fully developed, the mature thunderstorm dominates the atmospheric circulation for quite a few miles around. It may stretch out to be several miles across at its base and tower to altitudes of 40,000 feet (12,000 m) or more.

On the ground, we feel these processes keenly, although most of us have ceased to notice them. First there is the rain and a strong, cold, reversing breeze as the converging winds are replaced by the outpouring downdraft, which spreads out over the surface. This is nature's way of telling us that the storm exploding over our heads is at its most violent phase—it is here that it releases its arsenal of destructive hail, torrential rain, and raging gales and whirlwinds. It is in this phase that humans discerned great Zeus hurling the gleaming thunderbolt or saw the flash of a thunderbird's eye.

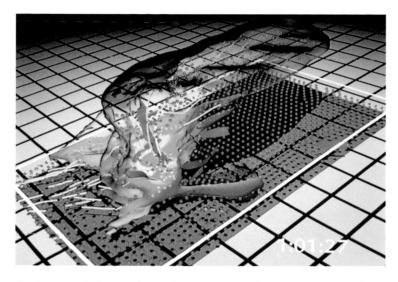

As the storm's internal circulation becomes better organized, the central core of water droplets expands and deepens, releasing further doses of latent heat to fuel the growing tempest. A gust front forms along the storm's rear flank, over which air rises up and into the heart of the cloud, where a coiling ribbon indicates the start of a rotary circulation—the storm within a storm, or *mesocyclone*.

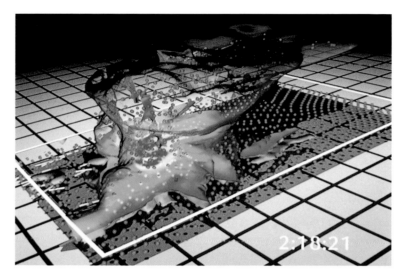

Fully developed, the thunderstorm rages across its computer landscape, fed by the mesocyclone updraft and powerful downdrafts, which fuel the surging gust fronts. Descending midlevel winds add their energy to the system. For poorly organized thunderstorms, maturity is the beginning of the end. But well-organized storms like this one are so efficient that they last for hours.

Cloudbound Circuitry

No one is quite sure how these isolated towers of water and convective air currents generate the powerful electrical currents that eventually become dramatic darts of lightning. Some researchers believe that rising water vapor and ice crystals act to separate positive and negative electrical charges. The positively charged lighter particles are swept into the higher reaches of the thundercloud while the heavier particles—water droplets and clumps of slush called graupel, for example—tend to fall, carrying their negative charge toward the cloud base. Another view holds that growing cumulonimbus clouds may acquire electrical fields from electrically polarized droplets drawn from the surrounding environment.

In either case, turning a cloud into an electrical storm is a complicated business, occurring as it does on a microscopic scale. Tiny ice crystals bump together—the warmer ones acquire a negative electrical charge, as do the saltier ones.

(The atmosphere is full of sea salt, which acts as condensation or freezing nuclei for water vapor.) Supercooled water—water that has been cooled below freezing but is still in liquid form—turns into graupel; as it drops, it acquires a negative charge. Like balky engines, cumulus clouds often misfire before their electrification can properly get under way. But when a vertical turret bursts from the lower clouds, ascending quickly with its cargo of water, it generates an electrical disturbance that doubles in strength every minute or so. Lightning marks the end of that doubling—the release of energy pent up to the point of bursting.

Normally negatively charged with respect to the atmosphere, the ground beneath the growing storm begins to be electrically transformed. As charges separate inside the cloud so that most of the positive charge is in the tower and most of the negative charge is in the base, the moving storm induces a positive charge in the earth below and for several miles around the cloud—as the storm dominates the atmospheric circulation around it, so it also dominates the electrical field. The ground charge follows the storm like an electrical shadow, intensifying as the negative charge in the cloud base increases.

The attraction of positive for negative charges makes the ground current reach toward the storm cloud—positive charge flows up buildings and up through towers, the branches of trees, raised golf clubs, anything that puts it a little closer to the link it seeks. Animals become jittery, sensing the electricity flowing from the earth through their bodies; in a spot where the electrical potential is high, the charge is enough to make human hair stand on end. (That is nature's way of telling you to flee, for lightning is about to strike.) But like a layer of insulation, air—like most gases, a poor conductor of electricity—holds the opposite charges apart. To join, they must become strong enough to overpower the insulating air—to force a conducting path.

Lightning is the flow of current across that nonconducting gap, pushed by a difference between positive and negative charges—the electrical *potential*—that may attain 100 million volts. Usually the flow is from the negative charge to the positive one and can dash from cloud to cloud or from cloud to ground. Sometimes, when positive charge has flowed up into

Lightning pierces the night sky over a wheat farm in New South Wales, Australia, reminding farmers of a thunderstorm's mixed blessings: rain to ease a chronic drought, but also crop-smashing hail and lightning-set wildfires.

Silhouetted against a churning sky over Wyoming's Red Desert, two pronghorn antelope nervously await the coming storm. They feel the increasing electrical charge in the ground as it flows up into their bodies through their hooves, making them, in effect, living lightning rods—and imparting to them a high sensitivity to changes in atmospheric electricity.

Lightning strokes appear to skid across the American Southwest landscape as wind from a storm shifts their ionized path between the cloud and ground. The camera sees each successive stroke displaced to the left, creating this illusion of ribbons of lightning.

such elevated, pointed structures as the tower of the Empire State Building in New York City—on average it is struck 23 times a year—the rule finds an exception with sparks hurled skyward from the ground.

An eerie glow sometimes seen emanating from high, pointed objects—from church belfries and ships' masts, for example—is a kind of leakage of electricity skyward in what scientists call *corona discharge* and what everyone else calls St. Elmo's fire, named, it is said, for the patron saint of those who sailed the ancient Mediterranean.

ELECTRIFYING RIDES

Electrical discharges can be triggered when conductive objects intrude between two opposite charges and inadvertently shorten the distance between positive and negative centers. Flying in a cumulus tower above the freezing level of 12,000 to 16,000 feet (3,600–4,800 m) is a rough ride of updrafts and downdrafts but also an electrifying one—the highly conductive aircraft narrows the gap between the positive charge high in the cloud and the negative charge below and often gets zapped. Usually the only sign of this is a quarter-sized

hole burned into the metal skin of the plane and some singed electronics—but not always. In 1963 the explosive blend of fuel and air in a Boeing 707's wing tanks was disastrously ignited by a lightning strike.

Perhaps the most famous triggering was seen when *Apollo 12*'s 360-foot-long (109-m) Saturn rocket lifted off into light cumuli over Cape Canaveral on November 14, 1969. The first lightning stroke hit the craft at about 6,000 feet (1,800 m), the second at about 13,000 feet (3,900 m); luckily, only a few circuit breakers popped and the mission proceeded. In March 1987 triggered lightning caused an Atlas-Centaur booster rocket to tumble to destruction, and in June of that year lightning ignited three sounding rockets on their NASA pads at Wallops Island, Virginia.

On the other hand, lightning's propensity for being triggered has been a boon to those who wish to study it. At the Langmuir Laboratory in Socorro, New Mexico, for example, scientists launch rockets trailing wire tails into thunderstorms to trigger lightning bolts—to, as one researcher puts it, "bring down lightning where we want it." By bringing it down into a grid of instruments, thunderstorm researchers can study the quick electrical life and death of thunderbolts. The laboratory could hardly be better situated. It is just south of one of North America's centers of lightning activity, in the lee of the Rocky Mountains in northern New Mexico. The other center of action—and another lightning lab, this one at the University of Florida—is close to Cape Canaveral, where *Apollo 12* received its famous jolt.

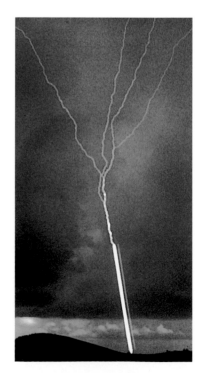

Lightning leaps down a wire spun from a rocket-borne reel. Scientists at the Langmuir Laboratory in New Mexico's Magdalena range use devices such as this to create strokes almost at will for extensive—and convenient—study.

ANOTHER KIND OF THUNDER

Even when budding thunderstorms hide in the turbulent folds of other ugly weather, they give themselves away. Undetectable by satellites, obscured from observers on the ground, the growing cloud begins to generate electricity early in its development and cannot muffle its electromagnetic growls—the rasp of static on AM radio is a sign that a thunderstorm is somewhere nearby. The familiar voice of lightning is a rumbling thunder, a burst of acoustic vibrations. But lightning's more audible voice is a broad radio signal ranging from extremely transient, localized 300-megahertz squeals to mutterings in the low-frequency range around 10 kilohertz. (One hertz is equal to one cycle per second.)

These signals pinpoint the location of the powerhouse at the heart of the parent storm; their radio frequencies reveal the storm's stage of development. When a thunderstorm is building, most of its lightning occurs within the towering cloud, and its electromagnetic signal is in the high-frequency range. But as the storm reaches maturity and begins its decline, its high-pitched signal settles into the baritone of the low-frequency range. The amounts of energy behind these radio transmissions are staggering, ranging from about 3,000 to 200,000 amperes with currents in the millions of volts. Each of the bright bolts is really a composite of several strokes—as many as 18 have been recorded for a single one-second flash.

It has always been theoretically possible to position lightning strokes by measuring the arrival times of the signal at various locations. The trouble has been that the signal moves so swiftly that even continental distances are traversed in a few ten-thousands of a second. Such short intervals of time require a brand-new technology. Only in the last decade has this technology become a reality, largely through the advent of powerful microprocessors and such synchronized sources as the Global Positioning System, which uses a constellation of earth-orbiting satellites to provide exact positioning information for navigation. During the early 1990s, what is called the Lightning Positioning and Tracking System, or LPATS, developed by Atmospheric Research Systems of Palm Bay, Florida, has come into operational service around the world.

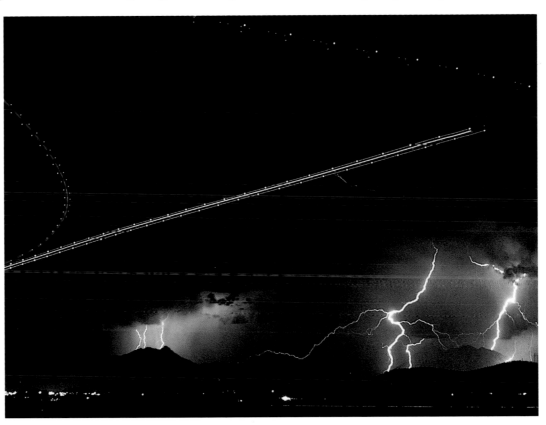

Lightning flickers in the Arizona sky over Tucson in this time exposure crisscrossed by the airplane's anticollision lights. Lightning-detection gear pinpoints each stroke and lets aviation managers keep their clients flying until the storms are close enough to pose a real aviation hazard.

When a lightning stroke occurs, its radio-frequency signal flies out in all directions at the speed of light, about 186,000 miles (298,000 km) per second. It arrives at each receiver in the widely spaced LPATS network at different—but not very different—times. This arrival time is recorded to within less than a millionth of a second by instruments synchronized to within 50 billionths of a second of one another. Arrival times are relayed to a central analyzer, which calculates the location of the lightning stroke using differences in arrival time at three receivers. The LPATS then refines that solution further and records the position, time, frequency, and other parameters of each flash. Six receivers can cover an area of nearly 400,000 square miles (1 million square kilometers), pinpointing lightning strokes—about 25 million a year in the United States—to within about half a mile (1 km).

LPATS networks are operating across the United States and eastern Canada, in Brazil, in several European countries including Germany, Spain, and Sweden, in Israel and South Africa, in Japan, and in southeastern Australia. Small-scale networks are also springing up where lightning information is critical to operations—explosives storage areas, petrochemical facilities, theme parks, mines, power utilities, and airports.

Forging the Thunderbolt

Most of the lightning we see is caused by current flowing from cloud to ground. The typical stroke usually begins as a tentative thrust called a *pilot leader*—like a pilot fish or pilot parachute, it guides the larger entity—pushing down through the nonconducting air toward the opposite charge. It creates the first rung or two of a conductive ladder made of *ionized*—electrified—air molecules. With this initial path laid down, a larger surge of current, called a *step leader*, drives the stroke another 100 feet (30 m) toward the ground. There is a pause, then another surge as the cloud's potential rebuilds itself, then another pause, another surge, and so on, step by step. The sequence continues until the ionized path is near the ground, where the step leader tangles with flickering discharge streamers rising from the ground to meet the cloud charge. When they connect, the bridge between cloud and ground is completed, and a bright bolt leaps from the ground toward the cloud in a powerful return stroke up the ionized trail.

With the ionized channel established, the return stroke is followed by another sequence of thrusts from the cloud, called *dart leaders*, and secondary returns from the ground, until the opposing charges are equalized or until the wind disperses the ionized path. The whole dance lasts less than one second.

THE BOLT IS QUICKER THAN THE EYE

The lightning stroke that seems to dart suddenly from a thundercloud toward the ground is all we see of what is actually a sequence of events—each step takes only a fraction of a second. The powerful spark that forces its way across the gap of insulating air between centers of opposite—positive or negative—electrical charge may leap from cloud to cloud, between centers inside the cloud, and even upward into the stratosphere. But the most frequently observed form of lightning is the the cloud-to-ground sequence illustrated at right, where gathering centers of opposite charge in a cloud and the earth beneath it build a conductive bridge—in effect, an invisible wire of ionized air—along which lightning's massive electrical current can flow.

As the electrical potential between cloud and ground increases, a short spark called a *pilot leader* starts a conductive channel (1), followed by *step leaders* (2) that stab downward toward streamers (3) rising from ground. The return stroke from ground (4) illuminates branches and seems to come from the cloud. The main stroke is followed by a sequence of flashes called *dart leaders* and returns (5), until the electrical potential is reduced or the ionized path is dispersed (6).

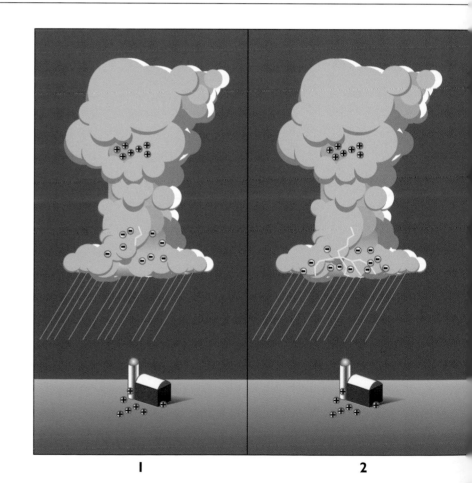

1   2

Our eyes find an illusion in the return stroke—because it energizes and illuminates air molecules along the ionized leaders, it seems to strike downward. But the eye is a poor instrument for observing a phenomenon that comes and goes in tiny fractions of a second. Because the retina retains a short memory of what it sees, we think lightning lasts longer than it does—when we photograph lightning, we often snap at what remains on our retinas but is really nowhere to be seen.

Another illusion we experience is the strike as a glowing column of light, making the bolt seem some tens of feet across—in fact, the conductive path is only inches wide. Sometimes the current flows within clouds, reflecting and

illuminating the churning currents producing it so that we see shapeless flashes or ragged streaks of light. Sometimes lightning seems to occur in parallel ribbons, an illusion produced when wind moves the conductive channel between a rapid succession of strokes. There have been reports of beaded lightning, in which the stroke is a kind of dazzling dotted line. Ball lightning is probably the most remarkable of this family of forms, reported as a luminous globe or toroid that hisses as it speeds from heaven to Earth, maneuvers at high speeds, rolls along structures, and hovers in midair. It has been seen so rarely and imaged so ambiguously that some experts even doubt that it exists.

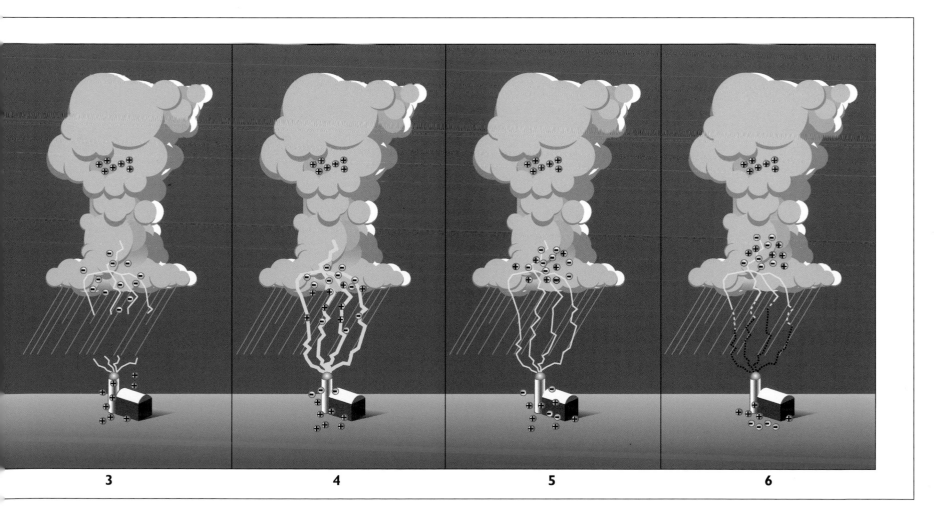

3   4   5   6

Because they are sparks, lightning bolts are sometimes likened to other, more tractable forms of electric current. Many people believe, for example, that lightning cannot cross the insulating boundary of a car's four rubber tires or that it otherwise behaves like normal household electricity. In fact, cars are safe because they offer the protection of a steel shell connected to the ground—a *Faraday cage*. That the wheels have rubber tires, or that someone is wearing shoes with rubber soles, is the kind of detail that lightning tends not to notice. Current peaks in a lightning stroke may reach 200,000 amperes or more and can literally crush the conducting structure or cause such non-conducting materials as wood and brick to explode.

Lightning is like the proverbial giant gorilla—it goes where it likes and has none of the etiquette of lesser shocks. Although this gorilla has a sobering history of death and destruction—in the United States alone it kills about 200 people a year—it may also do a zany kind of mischief. The abrupt, intense heating—air within the stroke may reach 54,000° F (30,000° C)—by a lightning

strike can make the air in fabric expand so swiftly that clothing explodes off the hapless victim's back, leaving the poor soul scorched and naked. Lightning reportedly welded shut the zipper on a soldier's sleeping bag, trapping him where he slept. There are reports of lightning roaming through houses, selectively cracking china or carving small, perfect circles in window panes. One bolt reportedly struck a house, setting it afire; a second bolt at the same house set off the alarm, summoning firefighters. Old wive's tales suggest that lightning prefers oaks to all other trees, and people once believed that

Artificial lightning darts downward from hollow aluminum spheres to strike an enclosed metal cage in a display at the Boston Museum of Science. Because the cage is grounded, it diverts the electrical charge, leaving the researcher seated inside unharmed.

A shattered oak tree shows the explosive force of a lightning strike. Finding the wooden trunk a poor conductor, the high-voltage current instantaneously heated its target by hundreds of degrees, causing water in the tree to explode as steam, sending out a dangerous shrapnel of bark.

ringing church bells would deflect an approaching thunderstorm—in fact, it often caused the unfortunate bellringers to be zapped in their belfries.

GLOBAL HOT SPOTS

These sudden, brilliant bolts from heaven and the storms that produce them are pervasive. At any given moment, an estimated 2,000 thunderstorms are raging somewhere in the world, with each storm strobing with a stroke of lightning on average every 20 seconds. Most of the world's thunderstorms occur between 3 and 8 P.M. Universal (Greenwich) Time, which corresponds to midafternoon over central Africa and the Amazon basin, when conditions favor thunderstorm formation. The thunderstorm minimum comes at about 4 A.M. Universal Time, when it is late evening in those centers of ionic action. A global map of thunderstorm days—days on which one or more thunderstorms are observed—shows where these tempests rage: the American Midwest and Southeast, the waist of Central America, the equatorial regions of South America and Africa, and the Malaysian archipelago all show regions of very high activity with more than 60 thunderstorm days a year—in some smaller hot spots in Africa and South America, there are more than 180 such days.

Because they represent atmospheric instability, these storms are associated with unstable seasons. This means that they roil the tropical sky for much of the year, dissipating only in the relatively brief dry seasons. At higher

latitudes they form mainly in the springtime, when very different air masses begin to collide, and during the summer, when solar heating overturns the atmosphere and sets the machinery that produces thunderstorms in motion. The storms keep mostly to the large landmasses. There is surprisingly little lightning over the open sea—even allowing for the fact that the ocean covers more than 70 percent of the globe, the ratio favors land by five or ten to one. In addition, there is little thunderstorm activity at very high latitudes, because there is little atmospheric instability over the perpetual ice around the poles.

A striking portrait of global lightning was constructed by Richard E. Orville and Ronald W. Henderson. Using visual data from the Defense Meteorological Satellite Program (DMSP), the researchers mapped the locations of some 32,000 lightning flashes detected by the satellite's sensors near local midnight between September 1977 and August 1978. Their 1986 journal paper shows lightning as red dots scattered over a world map—a scarlet rash of electrical activity.

When their series begins in September, the rash is concentrated in the tropics, with a few scattered flashes at higher latitudes on both sides of the Equator. October shows the rash moving south with the austral spring, flaring across Central

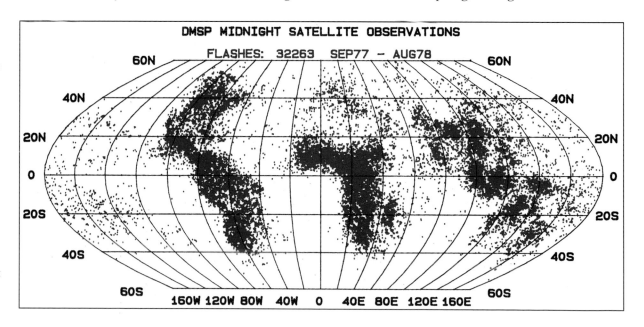

Thirty-two thousand separate lightning flashes plotted in red between September 1977 and August 1978 create a virtual map of the continents, pointing up the fact that most lightning occurs over land.

and South America, equatorial and southern Africa, the southern tip of India, the archipelago of the Indies, and west-central Australia. This pattern intensifies—the rash inflames—in November and December, then begins to ease as the southern summer gives way to autumn in March. By then, however, the lightning pattern has shifted northward and, as the northern spring returns, becomes once again inflamed over the central and eastern United States, the southern mainland of Asia, and, as before, across equatorial Africa. As the summer evolves, the rash of lightning intensifies across America and Europe before winter brings relief. Plotted seasonally, the red swaths of lightning flashes move back and forth across the Equator. But when they are plotted for the year, the total flashes take the shapes of continents—you can tell where the land is by looking at the lightning.

Seeing the seasonal advance and retreat of lightning across the continents, you sense that these are not just the massive, isolated discharges of huge electrical fields but that they are something larger. And so they are. The bursts of lightning do more than equalize differences between centers of charge—they do important chemistry as well. The atmosphere is about 80 percent nitrogen, a gas that, in its molecular form, is so stable as to be almost inert. Yet plants, which sustain all other terrestrial life, require nitrogen compounds to survive. Most of these compounds are produced by microorganisms that transform nitrogen gas into other, more usable substances. But lightning also plays a crucial role: As it cleaves the atmosphere, it breaks up and ionizes the tightly clinched pair of nitrogen atoms in a molecule, freeing them to recombine with oxygen and hydrogen as nitric acid. This vital nutrient falls to the Earth in rain. As in the Desana myth, lightning is not just an ax—it is an agent of fertility.

Flashing like a steel-mill furnace, lightning flares in a cumulonimbus towering over Tucson, Arizona. Linked to a separation of opposite charges within the clouds, such airborne activity is often a prelude to massive electrical exchanges between cloud and ground. Spectacular displays such as this one are common in Tucson during its monsoon season.

Highly Charged

Dramatic as they are, however, lightning bolts are merely the sparks from the atmosphere's vast, gingerly balanced electrical machine. Some liken the electric atmosphere to a *capacitor*, a sandwich of good conductors separated by a layer of some poorly conducting material such as air. One of these conductive plates is the solid earth. The other is the thin air of the high stratosphere and beyond, where atoms and molecules are ripped apart and electrified by incoming cosmic and solar radiation—the ionosphere.

That the atmosphere must have an electrically conducting region was an early inference of 19th-century scientists exploring the Earth's magnetic field—only a conducting layer could explain the magnetic-field changes observed on the ground. Guglielmo Marconi's turn-of-the-century radio broadcasts across the Atlantic—over the horizon—proved that such

a region existed. Once called the Kennelly-Heaviside layer after two scientists exploring its existence, this layer is now known as the *ionosphere*.

It is a region of inhospitality, a vacuum-thin realm of high-energy radiation and celestial debris. From our standpoint, its most important function may be as a shield against a barrage of deadly radiation from space. Thermonuclear processes in the Sun and other stars shower Earth's neighborhood with energetic particles—protons, alpha particles, and electrons—all carrying immense levels of various types of energy and traveling at speeds approaching that of light.

Haloed by a dim greenish airglow along the Earth's curved horizon, the *aurora australis*—the so-called Southern Lights—flickers above the southern geomagnetic pole. Interactions between oxygen and radiation from the Sun at altitudes of 50 to 75 miles (80 to 120 km) cause both phenomena.

Nearing the vicinity of Earth, galactic radiation combines with a radioactive plasma emitted by the Sun and by energetic solar particles raining earthward. In a sense, the sparse molecules of the high atmosphere are sacrificed to prevent this barrage from getting through to the surface.

This energetic shower has created a world of bizarre chemistry, of wrenching dissociation and recombination; the atmosphere becomes a thin veil of atoms and molecules that have been *ionized*—that have acquired electrical charge by losing one or more electrons—and the resulting free electrons. From an altitude of about 25 miles (40 km) out to a distance of several thousand miles, weather becomes increasingly a matter of electron densities and electrical charges. In almost imperceptible increments, the atmosphere shades into a Sun-dominated, electrical world.

In the capacitor analogy, the ionosphere is the upper conductor plate. As an atmosphere, however, it is little more than an electrified vacuum, stratified into three main layers, which are defined by the kind of radiation they absorb. The lowest layer, the so-called D region, begins at an altitude of about 37 miles (60 km) and is the zone where shortwave ultraviolet *dissociates,* or disconnects, oxygen molecules and is absorbed in the process. The ionization at these heights produces one of the atmosphere's most beautiful phenomena—*airglow,* a faint, blurred luminosity observed at altitudes of about 50 miles (80 km). Faint as distant candles, airglow appears to result from chemical changes in ionospheric atoms and molecules, which, raised to a higher energy state by solar radiation, emit excess energy as light when they relax. But the D region is a transient phenomenon, depending entirely on the ionizing blast of radiation from the Sun for its existence. It dwells only on the illuminated side of the planet.

Starting at about 55 miles (88 km) above sea level, the E region extends upward for another 20 miles (30 km) or so, creating a layer in which X rays ionize molecules of hydrogen and nitrogen. Tides of electrons ebb and flow in the tropical belt of the E region, riding the crests of gale-speed currents that sweep the electrified particles across the face of the planet and also across the force lines of the Earth's magnetic field, creating a dynamo effect. It produces electricity by moving conductors across a magnetic field, exactly the way a mechanical generator does.

Above the E region, from about 75 miles (120 km), the F region extends out beyond 200 miles (320 km), absorbing high-energy ultraviolet radiation in its lower layers; in its higher reaches it has a dense layer of electrons but little else. These electrified shells of the atmosphere wax and wane with the Sun. An active, flaring Sun can send an ionizing blast of

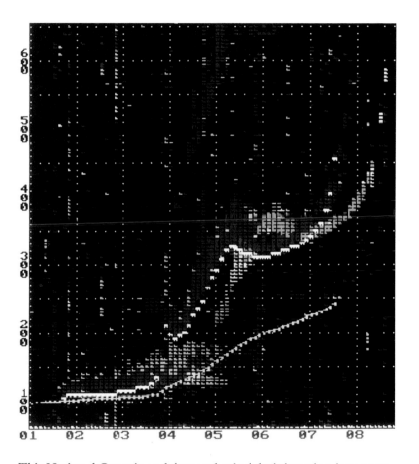

This **National Oceanic and Atmospheric Administration ionogram shows the dense electron layers of the ionosphere. Mapped with reflected radio signals, the E layer appears in red and green near the bottom of the image at an altitude of about 60 miles (100 km), the F1 layer appears as red and yellow at altitudes from 120 to 240 miles (200–400 km), and the F2 layer shimmers faintly above 300 miles (500 km). White lines indicate the true altitude of the layers, corrected for variations in the speed of the radio waves.**

radiation deep into the atmosphere, causing electrical storms and charged jets of energy to snap around the ionosphere and searing the low-lying D region.

VOICES FROM THE VOID

As they absorb incoming radiation at the short end of the spectrum, the E and F regions of the ionosphere are selectively opaque to shortwave and broadcast-band radio wavelengths at the long end. Those waves, beamed upward from the ground, carom back to Earth—a bounce that makes international shortwave radio possible. Interestingly, the ionosphere is even-handed in its opacity. The same radio frequencies that it relays back toward Earth, it also reflects back to space. Thus, humans searching for the radio signals of other populated worlds or quasars must listen through a narrow breach in the ionospheric wall. Everything else ricochets back into the void.

When most radio communications were in the same high-frequency domain, the condition of the ionosphere was

Immense radio telescopes peer skyward to gather radio-frequency signals emitted by stars and other galaxies. These faint signals are audible to radio telescopes like these 85-foot-diameter (26-meter) giants in the Very Large Array, a 27-telescope system in the New Mexican desert.

LIGHTNING AS SEEN FROM SPACE

From the superb vantage point of a space shuttle orbiting the Earth, lightning can be seen as part of the global atmosphere's enormous electrical circuitry as it can nowhere else. While groundlings see mostly grumbling flashes within clouds and powerful strokes between cloud and ground, spacefarers see the flashing of cloud-to-cloud strokes from above—they peer down into the labyrinth of clouds where the bolts themselves are forged. From orbit, bolts can be seen springing from cloud tops deep into the stratosphere, presumably completing the electrical connection betweeen the Earth and the ionosphere.

The view from space has also turned up what may be another species of lightning—mysterious high-altitude flashes that leap across the upper atmosphere as much as 60 miles (100 km) above the ground in broad corridors. Also reported by the flight crews of high-flying aircraft, the flashes are much longer than a lightning stroke, lasting 10 to 20 thousandths of a second, and much fainter, presenting more of an auroralike glow than the sharp bright line of an electrical spark. They are as much as 50 miles (80 km) across and appear to occur with less frequency than lightning in the storms below: hundreds of cloud-to-ground discharges occur for every high-altitude flash. Puzzled scientists can only speculate as to the cause of this strange phenomenon: a new variant of atmospheric electricity, perhaps, or luminescence from molecules excited by X-ray and ultraviolet emissions from electrified clouds.

Seen from the moonlit cargo bay of the space shuttle Columbia *in April 1993, thunderstorms building over Mexico flicker with blue-white cloud-to-cloud and intracloud lightning* (**left and far right**), *contrasting with the golden free-form light patterns that mark cities. The large patch of light beyond* Columbia's *vertical stabilizer is Mexico City.*

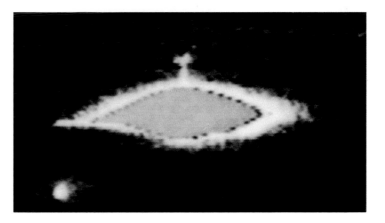

A plasmalike vertical flash of lightning lances the high upper atmosphere in this image made by a low-light-level video camera that is mounted in a space shuttle cargo bay. Very different from the sharply defined lightning bolts between clouds and the ground, such flashes may reach altitudes of more than 30 miles (50 km).

vital. For radio operators on ships and aircraft, a D region disturbed by an active Sun tended to soak up everything they had to say, and storms in the higher E and F regions could send their signals off into electronic oblivion. But at night, when the D region is quiet, even AM radio has a grand reach—driving under a starry Kansas sky, one can listen to stations a continent away.

Predicting the state of the ionosphere is still big business, not just for radio but for the corresponding disturbances produced in the Earth's magnetic field, which allows the detection of submarines, among other things. While most of today's communications use higher frequency line-of-sight transmissions that find the ionosphere transparent, if you want your over-the-horizon radar or shortwave radio to function, you need to know which radio frequencies the ionosphere is reflecting and which it will absorb.

ACCENTUATE THE NEGATIVE

Although it is not ionized by a barrage of space radiation, the lower atmosphere is itself perpetually electrified, even when no thunderstorms are present. This fair-weather electrical field sends a current down toward the planet's surface. In dry climates, the rubbing together of particles in dust storms, like the rubbing together of brushes in an electrical generator, produces electricity. The collisions among blowing snowflakes and ice crystals produce current, as does a turbulent flow of air or the charged effluent of volcanoes and industrial smokestacks. Thus, even in fair weather, the atmosphere is charged.

Human nature being what it is, the constant presence of positive and negative ions in the air we inhabit and breathe cannot be ignored. Surely something so pervasive must affect our well-being and behavior. Some scholars probing this presumed link have cited behavioral and mood changes when seasonal winds increase the local concentrations of positive ions and note that some cognitive tasks are handled more efficiently in an environment charged with high levels of negative ions, which seem also to have some beneficial effects on houseplants. The reason that air following a thunderstorm smells fresh and cool, they say, is that a flood of negative ions rids the air of dust and pollen.

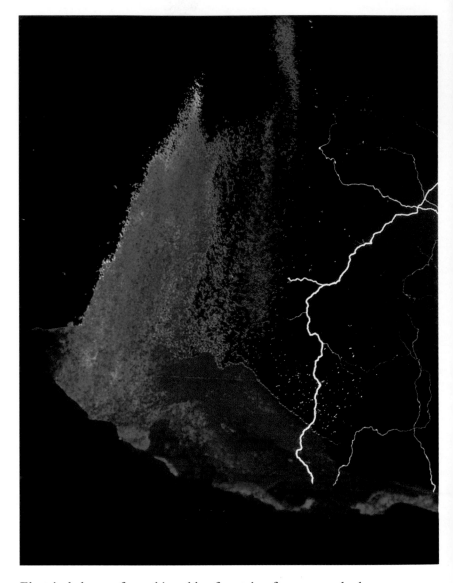

Electrical charges from this golden fountain of magma and ash generate powerful bolts of lightning on Mount Kilauea, one of Hawaii's active volcanoes. With the largest crater in the world, Mount Kilauea is 2 miles (3 km) wide and towers 4,090 feet (1,246 m) above sea level.

More than one canny entrepreneur has found a market in such speculation for devices they call *ion generators*, which purport to allow individuals to alter their ionic environment to suit what they believe to be their personal needs. Some employers even use these ion generators in the workplace in an effort to obtain greater productivity, alertness, and contentment from their employees.

But such laboratory work as there has been suggests that the relationship of humans to ions is neither simple nor straightforward—workers' performance sometimes slips in a negative ion environment, for example, and men respond to electrical fields differently from women. Moreover, there is some uncertainty as to whether the observed effects are electrical or thermal. Does cool air refresh because it is cool or because it carries negative ions? No one knows for sure. Nevertheless, people buy ion generators and seek out communities whose electric atmospheres are reputed to be rich in energizing negative ions.

THE OTHER SIDE OF LIGHTNING

Electricity in the air has far more important effects than just calming people and plants: it preserves the very structure and stability of the atmosphere. Between the Earth and ionosphere as between a thundercloud and the ground below it—a huge electrical potential exists, one reckoned in hundreds of thousands of volts. This potential is sustained by an electrical current of about 2,000 amperes distributed over the planet's surface—a current generated by the legions of local thunderstorms always in progress somewhere in the world. The electrical activity in a thunderstorm produces an upward current that spreads out horizontally near the base of the ionosphere and then descends to the surface in storm-free areas, a perpetual circulation in an electric atmosphere that is as vital to the planet as the atmosphere of air is to people.

If you happen to live above the Arctic Circle, you will not see much of this stormy apparatus in action, but the electric atmosphere will nevertheless pervade your life, especially when there is an active Sun. The energetic gale of a gusting solar wind filters through the Earth's *magnetic field*, a large, irregular doughnut of magnetic force enclosing the Earth—the doughnut's "holes" are above the North and South magnetic poles—and extends well into space. Although the field is generated by the internal dynamo action of the spinning planet, it is part of a vast web of magnetism that spreads across the

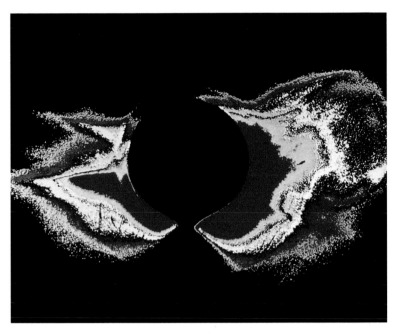

With the Sun masked to create a mock eclipse, the halo of light called the corona shows the dramatic explosive effect of a solar flare reaching millions of miles into space. This image was made by *Skylab* astronauts in August 1973.

solar system—a web that, like the planet's surface, is plagued by its own type of storm.

Until recently, some researchers believed that geomagnetic storms were related to material sent earthward from the flares exploding upward from the surface of an active Sun. Now it appears that each storm starts as a ripple when the solar magnetic field tears apart, ejecting massive quantities of material from the Sun's atmosphere, or *corona*. This potentially deadly shower of energetic particles and radiation speeds across space, where it meets the Earth's magnetic field. This barrier bounces low-energy particles back into space. But high-energy particles burrow through, becoming trapped in the radioactive clouds called *Van Allen belts* that surround the planet or dancing down lines of force through the holes of the geomagnetic doughnut toward the Earth's magnetic poles— the northern one near the northwest corner of Greenland, the southern one over Vostok Station in the Antarctic.

As incoming particles collide with molecular nitrogen and oxygen, the liberated atoms emit distinctive colors of light: nitrogen a bluish glow, oxygen a greenish-yellow incandescence, and other substances a dark red shimmer. Seen from above the atmosphere, these diaphanous curtains and sheets of light congregate along an oval belt that stretches some 1,200 miles (2,000 km) across—much broader when the solar magnetic field is perturbed—and is centered eccentrically on the magnetic pole. As the planet turns beneath the glowing belt, the lights form arcs, bands, and patches that move toward the pole, then away from it, as the illuminated oval seems almost to breathe. They are named for the Greek goddess of the dawn: *aurora borealis* in the north, *aurora australis* in the south.

The auroras are, in a sense, the other side of lightning. As the thunderbolt visibly expresses the electrical life of atmospheric storms, the auroras mark the passing of the great, unseeable storms of the ionosphere and geomagnetic field. They are the other dazzling face of the atmosphere's electrical coin, a soft ethereal lightning for the polar bears and penguins watching from the eternal ice.

Mountains of the Alaska Range frame ghostly curtains of the aurora borealis, or Northern Lights. This phenomenon is caused when showers of charged cosmic particles slide down geomagnetic lines of force toward the Earth's magnetic pole and interact with atmospheric atoms. Because they are linked to disturbances in the Sun's magnetic field, the largest, brightest auroras occur during periods of high solar activity.

GOING TO EXTREMES

If the Earth's surface were covered with water, the winds would arc across the planet unimpeded, rising and falling as the air became hotter or colder, wetter or drier; here and there it would explode into a thunderstorm; the great oceanic tempests would spin into extratropical cyclones and hurricanes, brush such tiny islands as they encountered, then wander off across the world; lightning would flicker harmlessly, like airy sparks. Compared to the real thing, this ocean-moderated atmosphere would be relatively tranquil, its best punches reduced to mere jabs of wind and water.

To attain the extremes of atmospheric behavior, the sea of air must flow across vast slabs of land, wrinkled with mountains, called continents. These are the roomy spaces in which a trajectory of a thousand miles or so produces some highly focused, often destructive effect. It is where the killer thunderstorms and terrifying tornadoes are assembled; it is where torrential rains swell riverbeds to bursting, where enormous whorls of moving air steep the land in Siberian cold or poach it in killing humidity and heat.

Blowing Hot and Cold

The factory where California's desiccating downslope winds are manufactured is not along the Pacific coast at all but far inland in the intermountain regions of Utah, Idaho, and Nevada. There, winds boom down a steep slope of high pressure, accelerating as they descend, and spread out in a clockwise fan to head west and southwest. As the air drops seaward, it is heated by compression and wrung dry of its last particle of moisture.

Without the coastal ranges the winds would blow down across southern California and out to sea, bringing a breaking wave of moderate discomfort. The mountains make the difference, often a terrible one. As Giovanni Battista Venturi, an Italian physicist of the late 18th and early 19th centuries, learned from his studies of hydraulics, fluid passing through a narrowing, cone-shaped throat—what he called a *reducing section*—is accelerated. In a carburetor, this acceleration squirts a fuel-air vapor mix toward the spark. In a rocket engine, the nozzle, which tapers to a narrow throat before spreading into an expansion cone, speeds up the expanding gases that push the projectile along.

Venturi's theory is well expressed by the canyons separating coastal California from the hot, dry air sweeping down from the intermountain plains. The winds rip through the gorges and arroyos, heating up still more, to burst howling out of the Sierra Nevada and into the Santa Ana valley that gives them their name. Author Raymond Chandler called them the Red Winds, "those hot dry Santa Anas that come down through the mountain passes and curl your hair and make your nerves jump and your skin itch."

As arid as the breath of a hair dryer, the Red Wind pushes temperatures above 100° F (more than 38° C) and imparts a gritty, scorched feel to the normally sea-sweetened coastal air, turning southern California's brushland into incendiary tinder. It also, some say, deflects the denizens of Los Angeles and San Diego toward crimes of passion or despair; although there is little quantitative proof of this, everyone senses that a link exists between heat and hatred. No one doubts, as each year brings an ever more destructive outbreak of fire to the tinderbox beneath the Santa Anas, that the Red Wind speaks to the very soul of arson.

Housing developments sprawl across the floor of southern California's Santa Ana Canyon, namesake of the scorching winds that funnel seaward through narrow gaps in the Sierra Madre.

In a November 1993 outbreak near Malibu, California, Santa Ana winds blowing up to 100 miles per hour (160 kph) fan brush fires into gales of superheated flame—at 1,700° F (927° C), hot enough to melt a firefighter's water hose.

DESTRUCTIVE DOWNSLOPES

On the eastern slope of the Rocky Mountains, the same wind is called a *chinook*—an Arapaho Indian term for "snow eater"—and comes in winter. Where the Santa Ana brings discomfort, grass fires, and bad cases of the jitters, the chinook itself can be violent and destructive. In Colorado the breaking wave of air crosses mountains at altitudes of more than 14,000 feet (4,200 m), then spills toward the plains in a roar of invisible surf, a westerly wind gone mad.

After miles of downhill running, the descending winds accelerate to more than 100 miles per hour (160 kph). When the chinook blows, more than snow disappears: roofs yield their shingles and the sides of frame houses flutter like the walls of a beating heart—and often fail. It is a frightening, screaming wind and, like its California cousin, it is not of strictly local manufacture: the weather systems pushing those winds up one side of the mountain are spawned in the Pacific, then refined and modulated as they cross the coastal ranges and the high plateaus, gathering strength during the long, landlocked fetch from Seattle to the Rockies.

In Europe the famous downslope wind is the *foehn,* a warm current out of the Alps that may drum upon the eastern plains of Austria for days at a time. It offers little physical threat but is said to spawn an atmospheric malaise, confirming the suspicion that all these hot, dry continental winds somehow connect with and possibly influence human behavior. Chandler suggested that when the Red Wind begins to blow, Angelinos begin to kill one another. The foehn, an Austrian will tell you, makes the Viennese kill themselves. One of the grand ironies of the human condition is that we are soothed by the breaking of ocean waves but driven to murderous despair by breaking atmospheric ones.

But the most formidable of all European winds is probably the *mistral,* the cold torrent of winter air that spools off a center of high pressure hovering over central France and hurries toward a low-pressure area over the northwestern

The eastern slopes of the Colorado Rockies become a flume for the chinook winds that pour down into the plains in winter, testing the deep anchors of these venerable pines.

Mediterranean. A fast-moving, transparent river perhaps two miles (3 km) deep, the mistral floods the Rhone River valley, whose narrow throat, like the mountain passes east of Los Angeles, acts like the nozzle of a rocket engine, speeding up the fluid passing through it. Gusting to more than 100 miles per hour (160 kph), the mistral brings a bone-chilling kiss of Siberian air to the otherwise balmy winters of Provence.

This quintessential wind of winter gained further fame from British author Peter Mayle, whose first months in Provence acquainted him with the phenomenon. "We had heard stories about the Mistral," he wrote in his book, *A Year in Provence*. "It drove people, and animals, mad. It was an extenuating circumstance in crimes of violence. It blew for fifteen days on end, uprooting trees, overturning cars, smashing windows, tossing old ladies into the gutter, splintering telegraph poles, moaning through houses like a cold and baleful ghost, causing *la grippe*, domestic squabbles, absenteeism from work, toothache, migraine—every problem in Provence that couldn't be blamed on the politicians was the fault of the *sacre vent* which the Provençaux spoke about with a kind of masochistic pride."

No doubt the mistral spins off to chill the North African desert, as well. But Africa now and then strikes back. A northward-setting wind called the *khamsin*, a hot, gritty gale that reduces visibility to a few paces and sprays the countryside with an ochre coating, blows out of Libya for 50 days at a time—indeed, it takes its name from the Arabic word for "fifty." A warm, windy explosion from a pinwheeling low-pressure system over the desert to the south, the khamsin drives across the waist of the Mediterranean to pall the skies of Italy, Malta, and Sicily with desert sand. In Algeria, the same wind bears the legendary name *sirocco*; it is *shahali* in the central Sahara, and *haboub* in the northern Sudan.

Perhaps such regionally familiar winds as the *alm, bora, halmiac,* and *jauk* of former Yugoslavia, or Croatia's *jasna bura* and *mracna bura*, also speak to violent hearts. The *Schneefresser* and *Traubenkocher*—respectively, "snow eater" and "grape cooker"—of Switzerland sound merely practical, but mayhem could lurk in the *bornan* and *vaudaire* that sweep down upon Lake Geneva, or in the Wind of Valais. Argentines

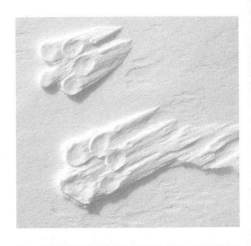

The sculpting winds of northern Canada preserve this wolf pawprint in raised relief. Compacted by the wolf's weight, the snow under the print resists the wind, which erodes the looser snow around it until a small paw-shaped dune emerges.

Stiff, steady gales have permanently deformed this *lenga* tree in Torres del Paine National Park near the southern tip of Chile. A sunny day like this is rare in the normally bleak wilderness.

may grow more than usually edgy when the *zonda* roars down the eastern slopes of the Andes, and Chileans may find neurasthenia in the suffocating air of the *puelche* flowing off the Pacific side of the Andean cordillera. Weather in the Gobi Desert of north-central China and southern Mongolia resembles that of the North American high plains, a dry, windy place that constantly presents some new extreme—year in and year out, the Chinese say of Gobi weather that it is "most unusual this year." The atmosphere over every continent rattles and reverberates with such winds, and every language has its share of names for them.

But why do these winds have names at all? The chinook is just a westerly wind, after all, the Santa Ana, an easterly, and the khamsin a southerly. They could all be labeled generically by direction. It is not that they are more violent than other winds—few equal the destructive power of a hurricane, for example, although chinooks sometimes seem to try. These winds have names because they are so reliably what they are, and so much a part of living on the continents that spin them up and send them howling down mountain slopes into the affairs of humans. They are not just perennial companions, but companions of an extreme kind, like gunslingers riding into town, or cossacks, or pillaging barbarians. It is this quality of being dependable and of visiting us from the violent fringes of atmospheric possibility that leads us to name these odd currents of the air.

Tunisian villagers cover up against the ochre gale of the khamsin, which screams out of North Africa's southern desert with an unseasonable winter blast of heat and dust for Mediterranean Europe.

Chilling Out

These fringes are truly the work of continents, which, acting as hot plates, nozzles, baffles, and refrigerators, do much to determine what new and outrageous guise the air will adopt. Although the planet is not entirely covered with water, 71 percent of it is, and the overlying atmosphere benefits from the moderating effects of water's peculiar thermal properties and its tendency to react sluggishly, rather than explosively, to change. Thus, concerning weather in the southern hemisphere, where less than a quarter of the surface lies above water, the ocean is king. The southern continents of Africa,

Elephant seals haul themselves out of the sea during a winter storm in the rough ocean off Tierra del Fuego, in Chile's extreme south. Thick, subcutaneous layers of fat insulate them from the cold ocean as they shuttle between the barren shores of southern Chile and Antarctica.

Australia, and South America extend only a modest portion of their land mass into the realm of temperate weather and so experience little of the extreme atmospheric chaos that makes northern continental life so challenging. And the Antarctic…is virtually another planet, where the atmosphere is concerned.

Land areas come into their own in the northern hemisphere, where more than a third of the planetary surface pushes above the sea. With water and heat from the ocean to drive the regional atmosphere, the continents are places where major meteorological events occur.

During the northern winter, for example, one of the most prominent atmospheric features is the great dome of high pressure—and of frigid air—over much of Eurasia: the Siberian High. Latitude has much to do with the legendary badness of Siberia's winter, but not everything. London lies about as far from the Equator as Moscow but does not endure a subzero winter—it is not on a continent and its weather is steered by the surrounding sea. On the European continent, however, air spreads over the enormous, frozen land in winter, gradually acquiring the character of the continent itself. Because there is little instability—nothing thermal that would produce convection, or vertical motion—it becomes steadily colder the longer it remains over that vast domain, following the atmosphere's strong impulse to stratify, with the colder, denser air always at the bottom. By the time the air reaches the Russian frontier, the oceanic influence has mostly disappeared and there is just the deepening cold, a type of weather composed of wind and such frozen water as it transports down from the polar seas. The combination is a winter of awesome depth, a season of unrelenting cold and a biting gale that whips south along the flanks of this high pressure with its winter residence over Siberia.

RUSSIA'S SIBERIAN STRATEGY

Perhaps no one has tasted that Russian winter more bitterly than those who have invaded that country from the west. The cruel winter, coupled with Russian willingness to scorch the earth before the advancing legions of France, made Russia the world Napoleon could not conquer and caused his imperial juggernaut to founder in ice, snow, and famine in 1812.

Adolph Hitler's vaunted Eastern Front did no better against the Soviet armies of Joseph Stalin and the winters of the early 1940s. The frozen plains of Ukraine and western Russia stretch across world literature as a symbol of overreaching human ambition. But that terrible winter on the westernmost frontier of the Asian continent is just the beginning, for it keeps getting worse.

As the cold air travels east, across the Urals, out across the steppes and northern taiga forests, deeper and deeper into the frozen continent, it crosses no moderating body of water; only land, chilled to Arctic temperatures by the low winter Sun and the flow of air off the northern ice fields. The little oil town of Baykit, for example, about 2,000 miles (3,200 km) east and a bit north of Moscow, endures the heart of Siberian cold: temperatures that plummet to -75° F (-60° C), a world in which soup freezes before one can put a spoon into it and spilled milk is ice by the time it hits the ground. East of Baykit there is nothing but the cold, all the way to the Pacific.

Flowing out of Siberia's frigid, land-locked heart, an outbreak of polar air—the Siberian Express—roars across Eurasia and northern Canada, deep-freezing the planet's northlands.

Constant low temperatures turn the Neva River in St. Petersburg into a pedestrian thoroughfare. The river, which bisects Russia's historic city, remains frozen each year from November to April.

Impervious to cold, a solitary polar bear (*left*) shakes snow off its thick, coarse, cream-colored fur. Unlike their southern counterparts, these huge animals do not hibernate, but roam the Arctic in a constant hunt for scarce food.

Siberia is generous with this frigidity. The immense land injects masses of frozen air into the tributaries of the mistral to the south and west and into the rivers of air pouring down over southern Asia. A bad winter across Europe and the United Kingdom is usually a gift from Russia, and the torrent of frozen air that sometimes spills out into eastern Canada and the United States is familiarly called the Siberian Express. Buried beneath this seasonal blanket of cold air, however, Siberia is not an especially stormy place—the skirts of Siberian air become the cold side of the polar front, which keeps to lower latitudes.

In winter that front is dominated by cold air over the poles, which pushes toward the Equator, shoving warmer air ahead of it. With the front driven to perhaps 40° north latitude, Europe and central Asia see little in the way of sudden, violent weather beyond the winds whipped south by pressure systems in the north—there is little of the vertical instability needed to produce severe storms. Where the continents touch the oceans, there are opportunities for terrible winter

storms; but the farther inland one goes, the more tenacious becomes winter's hold and the less variety the atmosphere offers.

As the Sun returns in spring and summer, the polar front shifts northward, weakening before the advancing tropical air. Over western Europe this passage brings unstable weather, fueled by moist air off the sea. But there is little opportunity for great mischief over the warming steppes of central Asia—there is scant water to fuel it. Eurasia has its thunderstorms, and sometimes they are grand; but the vast, dry continent tends to damp out the extremes of summer weather. That may explain why a good wheat harvest in Russia has always been dicey—every warm season contains the seed of drought.

Size and latitude count for a lot in the weather game. Europe, for example, is a smallish continent: Paris is only about 500 miles (800 km) from Vienna, and it is only another 500 miles from Vienna to Kiev. In the northern spring, when the jet stream—and so the polar front—follows its scalloped

Wheatfields surround a monastery in Pereslavi-Zalesski, a Russian town north of Moscow. While wheat, rye, and other grains constitute a major portion of the country's annual crop, yields tend to be low because of antiquated equipment and an unpredictable climate.

Their distinctive dorsal fins creasing the surface of Norway's Tysfjord, a pod of killer whales forages in the calm coastal waters of a Scandinavian spring. The largest member of the dolphin family, the often-friendly *Orcinus orca* earned its name from canny, wolflike hunting during seasonal forays across the world's oceans.

global path at about 40° north latitude, almost all of Europe and most of Asia are still to the north. By summer the line has moved up toward Scandinavia, taking most of its weather with it. Above the Arctic Circle thunderstorms are rare or nonexistent, and even in summer there is little instability. Good weather along the polar sea is a clear sky with a good chance of fog blowing in off the water.

In the southern third of Asia the Himalayas, rising more than 20,000 feet (6,000 km) above sea level, act as a barrier between polar and tropical air masses. South of that 2,000-mile-long (3,200-km) wall of granite, the atmosphere is once more dominated by the sea and by the kind of weather that wanders the tropics—isolated thunderstorms, the odd maritime storm, and the seasonal reversals of the monsoon winds. Below the Equator, tropical Africa has its share of thunderstorms but, as over the Indian subcontinent, much of the seasonal change is ruled by the ocean and the cycles of the rain-bearing monsoons. Coastal areas enjoy the balm of a relatively warm ocean in winter—relatively cool in summer—which eases the bite of those seasons. Thus, in coastal Australia and southern Africa the seasons are not very different in the weather they bring. Nor are they in those parts of South

America that lie outside the tropics, except in the far south, where the continent shades toward Antarctica.

The monsoon storms of Africa and India, the dust clouds of Mongolia and central Australia, the deep chill of a Siberian winter, the legion of pet winds blowing very hot or very cold—these constitute a brand of weather that should be bad enough for anyone. But they are not the worst the atmosphere can do. For that, one goes to the United States, where, for reasons having nothing to do with politics or economics, the really violent stuff of the continental atmosphere is hammered out, season after season.

A brilliant rainbow bridges the top of the world above the 26,470-foot (8,021-m) Hidden Peak in Pakistan's end of the Himalayas. The mountain range serves as a granite barrier between polar air to the north and tropical air to the south.

The Weather Factory

Indeed, if you wanted to build a factory for the production of weather with an evil, destructive diversity, you would turn immediately to the American model. The factory's foundation would be a continent located just north of the Tropic of Cancer (roughly equivalent to northern Mexico) and extending to about 50° north latitude (not quite as far as the southernmost edges of the Canadian provinces)—the approximate range of the polar front's north-south movement during the year. Atmospherically, this placement guarantees that the continent will be a battlefield of air masses and explosive weather. Having Arctic air to the north and the warm trade winds to the south would add frequent winter storms and occasional hurricanes to the mix. To fuel all this, there would have to be water everywhere—oceans on the upwind and downwind sides and a shallow, warm gulf in between. North-south chains of mountains would wrinkle the continent at intervals of some hundreds of miles. Great rivers would drain the land, but imperfectly, so that there would be seasonal flooding, sometimes on a colossal scale.

Take the way the continent handles ugly winter weather. The North American winter has its steady, Siberian side—Canada and the northern tier of states endure a killer chill that would make a Scandinavian feel very much at home. When the Sun is low in the southern sky and the mercury rests at -40° F (-40° C) and the wind is a whip of blowing snow, there is little to choose from between a wheat farm in Montana and the steppes of Central Asia. As far as your skin is concerned, stepping into a forty-below day in Fargo, North Dakota, is like stepping into one in Minsk.

Unlike Central Asia, however, North America has five sizable bodies of water—the Great Lakes—that add their moisture to the passing masses of freezing air. Cities along the shores of these lakes all get something extra in winter—

Winds sweep across frozen Lake Michigan with a massive charge of ice and snow for the Wisconsin city of Sheboygan, one of many cities on the Great Lakes' shores where huge amounts of lake-effect snowfall pile up each winter.

Chicago's famous wind is the bone-chilling flow off adjacent Lake Michigan. But the extreme is reserved for communities at the downwind side of the lakes. Air blowing over the cold water becomes saturated by the time it reaches shore, where, lifted by terrain, it dumps snow by the ton. Meteorologists call this *lake-effect* snowfall. In Buffalo, New York, which lies at the eastern end of Lake Ontario, residents call it winter.

THE NORTH AMERICAN GAUNTLET

Much the same thing happens as air flows east above the near-frozen Baltic Sea, threading its way between Scandinavia and Germany en route to the iced-in palaces of St. Petersburg. The difference is that American winter storms derive their peculiar intensity and identity from the fact that they run a continental

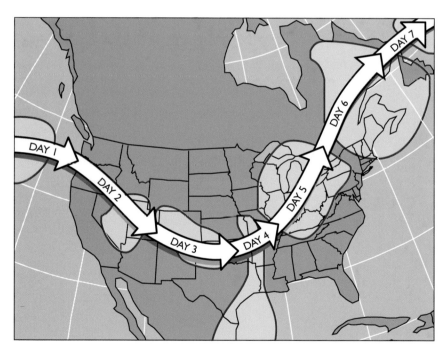

In this seven-day itinerary, the low-pressure area (outlined in red) of a typical winter storm waxes and wanes during its passage. After making landfall in the Pacific Northwest, the storm weakens, then reforms over the Rockies and heads for Oklahoma. As it dips southward, the cyclone taps the relatively warm waters of the Gulf of Mexico for added energy, intensifying the stormy low before spinning northeastward into Canada.

gauntlet flanked by large bodies of water—the Pacific to the west, the Atlantic to the east, the Great Lakes and Hudson Bay to the north, and, along the southern edges of real winter, the relatively warm, energy-rich waters of the Gulf of Mexico. Low-pressure systems that spin up in the Gulf of Alaska and the eastern North Pacific blow into North America, along with their garlands of storms, between Alaska and southern California and go reeling across the coastal mountain ranges with their huge burdens of water, leaving a deep trail of snow.

Once across this barrier, the disturbances eddy, seemingly exhausted by the passage, then reform over the Great Basin—Utah, Idaho, Nevada, and northern Arizona—until the prevailing westerlies blow them into the western slopes of the Rocky Mountains. The climb across the peaks and high passes drains the storms of even more water in the form of snow before they push out over the plains east of the mountains. Sometimes air moving around the lows is thrust back against the foothills, causing an *upslope*, a lifting flow of air that is still moist. It is the opposite of a chinook wind and one of the few sure things in meteorology: upslope currents of moist air from the east mean low clouds and usually precipitation along the foothills of the Rockies.

By now, the storms have begun to lose the punch imparted to them during their Pacific passage. Many go wheeling north and east, heading for the ocean; some boom through the Great Lakes and some dip toward the central midwestern states, then curve back northeastward. If they still have a strong low-pressure center when they reach the Atlantic, they may revive, drawing energy from the warm Gulf Stream off New England and pounding the coast with counterclockwise gale winds from the northeast—the famous nor'easters.

DOUBLE TROUBLE

As they cross the continent, these winter storms are constrained by the atmosphere's dynamics to spin more or less along the polar front, erratically following the ground track of the high-altitude jet stream, which in winter drops well to the south over the United States. For many disturbances this southerly trend means a second chance at mayhem—a chance to be reconstituted by heat energy flowing northeastward out

Plunged in Arctic air, a snow-bound Minnesota farmhouse (*left*) endures one of America's infamous winters, with months of subzero temperatures and deep snow.

A winter storm whips wind and waves through the stilted legs of empty vacation homes (*below*) on the Long Island shore. Deep pilings are often not enough to keep the structures anchored in a bad nor'easter; the ruins of those unable to withstand the gales litter the eastern seaboard.

of Mexico and the tropical Pacific, as well as out of the Gulf of Mexico. Watched from space, these systems converge with a nice inevitability, one spinning down from the northwest until it entrains what seems to be a great river of cloud streaming southwest to northeast across the Gulf.

Once those northern and southern forces have been joined, the reinforced storms whirl back toward the northeast and, depending on the jet stream and surrounding wind currents, head for the Atlantic. Many follow a curve from Louisiana up through the Carolinas and then toward New England, often rooted in the energy-giving ocean. The hard 1993–94 eastern winter was just such a meeting of energies, with storms born in the Pacific doing their worst in the West, then linking up with the untapped power waiting in the Gulf to hammer the land from the Appalachians to the East Coast.

The Heat Wave—Weather to Die For

The fact that the American weather factory lies closer to the Equator than that of other temperate continents does more than put it up against the endless summer of the Gulf—it also sets the stage for an incomparable continental summer. Statistics do not do it justice. The steppes of Kazakhstan see temperatures of 130° F (54° C) in a hot summer, despite that land's distance from the Equator. But this comes from the blazing Sun of any desert, available in southern Arizona and the southern rim of Asia and across much of Africa—to natives of a temperate zone the stab of light and heat in Africa comes like a blow to the head. There is a type of summer heat in the American heartland, however, that is as dangerous and oppressive as anything in the world: the heat wave.

Given its terrain and geographic situation, North America is bound to have hot summers. The advancing Sun reinforces warm, moist tropical air, which pushes the weakened polar front back toward its northern sources. Its parade of cyclones and anticyclones still snakes along the midlatitude westerlies, but their file shifts northward, marked by the scalloped course of the jet stream, which stays to the cool side of these systems as they form and spin and die below it. The Gulf states' April rains become June thundershowers on the Great Plains; the humid Georgia spring turns into the muggy summer of Illinois. While the atmospheric machinery sustains the alternations of instability and equilibrium, hot and cool, moist and dry, North America moves through its normal summer—hot and humid, to be sure, but normal.

In some years, however, the wavy path of the jet stream alters, possibly responding to a meteorological burble half a globe away. Instead of tracking along the Canadian border, as it normally does, the jet stream bends northward over the Great Lakes, and its alternating patterns of weather go with it. Hot, humid air from the south and southwest pours into the

A summer heat wave broils a stretch of Interstate 90 south of Tomah, Wisconsin, creating a shimmering mirage of wet pavement in the distance. Heat-wave weather kills more people each year in the United States than hurricanes and tornadoes combined.

In a stark Depression Era image, a farmer in the Oklahoma panhandle bucks the Dust Bowl winds that blotted out the Sun and turned fertile fields to dust during the late 1930s.

vacated region, spreading over the surface. Above it a high-level center of high pressure creates an impermeable cap of descending, compression-heated air currents. A wicked cycle begins. The land heats up, heating the atmosphere, which heats the land. What had been merely fair weather turns to earth-cracking drought.

As every winter is a hard one for some corner of the land, every summer brings some sort of hot spell to a region. But the real scorchers, like the worst winters, indelibly etch a place in human memory because heat, like cold, is not just uncomfortable—it kills. Records show that the summer of

1830 scorched the north-central interior, and the 1860 heat wave dried up the Great Plains. In 1901 heat-wave weather killed 9,508 people in the United States. During the incomparable Dust Bowl droughts of the 1930s, each summer was hotter than the one before, with temperatures edging well above the 100° F (38° C) mark from the Dakotas to the sea. Heat killed nearly 15,000 people from 1930 through 1936.

Even today, a temperature record is also a record of heat-related deaths: both peak in July, the hottest month, and in years with high average summer temperatures.

THE BREAKDOWN OF HUMAN DEFENSES

The reason heat and human mortality are so closely linked is that we are *homoiotherms*—warm-blooded creatures who maintain a constant body temperature regardless of the thermal environment outside our bodies. Because the human body also functions as a metabolic furnace—a creator of heat—it often must labor mightily to remain on the cool side of its upper thermal limits. The body does this work reflexively, under the control of a small peanut-shaped entity at the top of the brain stem: the hypothalamus.

TENDING THE INNER FIRES

Whether we do it with layers of flannel, fur, fat, or feathers, we warm-blooded creatures must keep our internal temperatures within careful bounds. In very cold temperatures, most homoiotherms are less interested in keeping the chill out than in keeping the heat in, using insulation to do it. Layered clothing creates gaps of air that slow the outward flow of body heat; so do ruffled feathers and the raised hairs of fur. When things get too warm, our internal thermostat makes us unbutton those coats, smooth those feathers, lay down that fur. And most creatures have some means of carrying the heat-bearing blood closer to the skin surface, where it can be used as a natural thermostat to adjust the delicate thermal balance between the body and the surrounding air.

The downy albatross (right) keeps warm by louvering its feathers to provide more or less ventilation. This albatross keeps cool by balancing on its heels, exposing its orange feet and intricate webs of blood vessels to the cooler air. A northern elephant seal (below) imitates its big African namesake by using its flippers to shower itself with cool, wet sand.

Like the hot-engine warning light in a car, the hypothalamus responds to the temperature of our blood. A surge of blood heated above 98.6° F (37° C) sends the hypothalamus into action. It signals the heart to pump more blood, dilates the blood vessels for the increased flow, and activates bundles of tiny capillaries just beneath the skin, causing the skin to flush. At the same time, water diffuses through the skin in the form of *insensible perspiration*, so-called because it evaporates before it becomes visible—the skin still feels dry to the touch.

But these are fine-tuning adjustments. If the hypothalamus continues to sense overheating, it goes further, calling upon the millions of sweat glands perforating the outer layer of the skin. These tiny glands can shed huge quantities of water—and heat—in the form of *sensible perspiration*, or

California sea lions (left) swim in natural drysuits of thick blubber, using their lean, vein-streaked flippers as efficient heat exchangers to regulate their inner temperature.

Masked to prevent frostbitten faces, tourists huddle in heavy winter gear on Canada's Ellesmere Island, their vital internal warmth retained by the insulation of thick coats.

sweating. Perspiration, both seen and unseen, handles about 90 percent of the body's heat-dissipating function.

The closer environmental temperatures are to the nominal body temperature, the chancier this process becomes. The body cannot rid itself of heat through the blood because there is no heat-drawing drop in temperature between skin and air. At this point the skin's elimination of heat by sweating is the body's only hope of maintaining a constant temperature.

Sweating by itself does nothing to cool the body. The water has to be removed by evaporation to do any good, and high humidity retards evaporation. Thus, when the air temperature is in the 90's F (30's C) and relative humidity is above about 75 percent, the body's cooling apparatus must labor flat-out to keep internal temperatures within limits. The heart is pumping a torrent of blood through a network of dilated blood vessels. The sweat glands are spewing liquids and such essential dissolved chemicals as sodium and chloride onto the surface of the skin. And finally, like other mammals and birds, we pant, blowing hot air back into the atmosphere. Sometimes nothing is enough, and the thermal limits are exceeded. When this happens, the homoiotherm does not doze, reptile-fashion—it dies.

Among the vital statistics kept in the United States are those labeled "death by excessive heat and insolation"—these are the people, usually several hundred in a year, who succumb to the direct effects of heat-wave weather. *Heat syndrome*, as this health hazard is called, refers to disorders ranging from the vague malaise of heat asthenia to lethal heat stroke, which marks the collapse of the thermoregulatory system. But heat does much of its killing, not by heat syndrome, but by indirection, stressing the body until something breaks. Like a predator, it kills most easily when its victim is very young or very old or infirm. The mild heat cramps of a 17-year-old boy may become heat exhaustion for a man of 40 and heat stroke for a man in his 60s. Men seem to be more at risk than women—females appear to exhaust fewer vital chemicals in their perspiration. No one knows how many deaths are "encouraged" in this way, how many diseased or aging hearts surrender that would not have done so under better conditions—how many bodies could not run another summer race.

Here Be Monsters

Superposed on the weather factory's line of bad winters and hot summers is a string of products that, while not uniquely American—nothing happens in the North American atmosphere that doesn't happen somewhere else as well—are clearly different. They are built on scales of intensity and size and destructive power unknown to other continents. If violent weather were automobiles, American skies would build Indy racers and Lamborghinis.

Thunderstorms offer a notable case in point. They occur the world over and are both ubiquitous and perpetual in most of the areas bounded by the tropics, vanishing for a brief dry season every year. But at those latitudes the thunderstorm is generally seen as a towering white cumulonimbus cloud, splendidly capped with a dark anvil of cirrus, that has sucked up so much of the surrounding water and energy that it has come to dominate the area; its stunted relatives wither into patchy little cumulus puffs. The successful thunderheads, reaching toward the tropopause in isolation, are seen everywhere; they spring up along any mountain range, over any desert, over any warm sea if there is instability and water—that is, latent heat—enough to fuel them.

Meteorologists are loath to differentiate among phenomena, preferring lightning to be lightning and wind to be wind. But tropical thunderstorms, especially those forming over the sea, seem softer than their continental cousins, more inclined to yield rain than a destructive swath of hail. And, although scientists say their lightning is the same as other lightning, there is something muted in the way these thunderbolts perform. Perhaps the most telling measure of severity, however, is that pilots routinely fly into towering tropical cumuli—cumulus clouds on their way to becoming thunderstorms—even in small aircraft and, while the ride is rough, it is not regarded as one that will shake the plane apart.

A cumulus cloud towers above eastern California's Mono Lake, fed by surface air moistened by lake waters. As the cloud climbs higher into the troposphere, high-level winds will shred its gauzy crown into streamers of cirrus ice clouds.

Silhouetting a Wisconsin wheat farm's buildings, nocturnal lightning darts between the earth and sky, where warm and cool air masses battle along turbulent, unstable fronts.

This is not to say that the big storms that lurch across Africa and India in the monsoon-moistened trades are trivial, or that such meteorologically even-tempered places as England have little interesting weather. Even in England, the sky now and then darkens with a rising cumulonimbus, and pounding hailstones lay waste to a field of corn. Indeed, what is the eye of a hurricane if not a ring of powerful thunderstorms?

Still, the thunderstorms produced in the U.S. weather factory are special. The electrified giants that crash across the American Midwest in spring and summer are often part of an atmospheric mob. On satellite imagery, you can see a broad column of such storms marching along a frontal boundary hundreds of miles long. As one bright white tower dims, another swiftly takes its place. It is disquieting to view their seemingly determined advance from a vantage point in space; seeing the green-black congregation of towering thunderclouds from the rain- and hail-swept ground, their innards flaring like steel mills with near-constant lightning, is awe inspiring. The only pilots who fly into these storms are those in armored, all-weather warplanes or those who have wandered into harm's way. The cloudy ramparts of these storms look granite-solid, and their rainshaft is a black wall of wind and water. Ancient mappers of atmospheric possibility would have observed such a rowdy crowd of storms devouring the sky over central Oklahoma and noted: Here be monsters.

Most monstrous of all these raging thunderclouds is the *supercell thunderstorm*—a storm of much greater endurance, violence, and destructive potential than its less-daunting cousins. Supercells, as their name suggests, are powerfully organized vertical machines of heavy weather. They can pump and recycle precipitation-driven energy for hours at a time. As with all thunderstorms—and, indeed, with such larger storms as hurricanes—surface air converges around a core of relatively low pressure and rises through the troposphere to blow out at high altitude, creating a kind of heat engine that runs on new moisture swept in at the base and on the release of latent heat in the rising central column. But in ordinary storms this machinery dithers and backfires after a half hour or so, and the storm dissipates.

In the supercell, the rising column of air evolves into a spiralling mile-wide updraft called the *mesocyclone*—*meso* meaning "middle," suggesting a middle-sized cyclone. Meteorologists believe that this spinning column of rising air begins when fast-moving winds aloft brush over friction-slowed currents near the surface, imparting a spin—invisible surf. The central updraft that marks the formation of any thunderstorm then transforms this spin into the vertical spiral of the mesocyclone, creating what will become the heart of the supercell. But only the heart.

Powerful as they are, supercell thunderstorms, again like hurricanes, require a good deal of cooperation from the larger atmosphere around them to get up and running. While the rotary circulation of the mesocyclone begins to organize and deepen the growing storm's inner circulation, cool, dry air from the middle levels of the troposphere at 10,000 to 20,000 feet (3,000–6,000 m) flows in, evaporating some of the precipitation in the cloud. Then, laden with water, this cooled midlevel air sinks toward the ground, producing a strong downdraft in the rear flank of the storm, but also a wedge of descending air that takes up its station on one side of the advancing cell. Called a *gust front*, this wedge is actually a dwarf cold front moving in the direction of the storm and, like a cold front, it cams warm, wet surface air up and into the storm, stoking the central mesocyclone with fresh heat energy. There is also help from above. Strong winds at 30,000 feet (9,000 m) and higher help exhaust the effluents from the updraft at the top of the storm. These stiff winds sweep the effluents out into the anvil form, sometimes 60 miles (100 km) long, that heralds the storm's approach.

With that elaborate machinery in place, the mesocyclone becomes an efficient heat engine, sucking energy from incoming moisture and momentum near the surface, but also producing conditions aloft that help sustain the powerful storm. This inner spiral of rising air pumps surface air into the cloud's anvil top between 40,000 and 60,000 feet (12,000 and 18,000 m), where the air is finally exhausted into the surrounding atmosphere.

Behind the gust front, the powerful downdrafts become draped with dark curtains of torrential rain, hammering hail, and near-continuous streaks and flashes of lightning—the supercell is also an efficient electrical generator. But something much worse than any of these may also lurk inside the vortex of the mesocyclone, in the instability and spin of air currents in the thunderstorm. It is the tornado, the most violent creation of the atmosphere.

Cumulus clouds explode upward in this developing thunderstorm over Iowa, as a strengthening updraft at the core of the storm drives the cloud tops toward the tropopause.

SHEAR TROUBLE

Wind shear is the meteorological term for any sudden change in wind speed or direction. Although it has acquired ominous overtones, wind shear does not always mean trouble, and pilots push their machines through zones of shearing wind currents without thinking much about it. But when an airplane is in that unstable realm of transition between being a multiton surface vehicle and a huge machine that flies, wind shear can be a deadly surprise. In its most lethal form, the shifting wind is part of a *microburst*. Less than two and a half miles (4 km) in diameter, the microburst is a fast-moving cataract of air expelled downward by a thundercloud—or by a turbulent surf of winds in clear air.

Stalking wind shear in thunderstorms near Orlando International Airport, a NASA pilot (left) flies a heavily-instrumented Boeing 737 from a specially equipped second cockpit in the plane's midsection, guided by a color video display from a forward-looking camera. A scientist assigned to the mission (right) watches for signs of dangerous wind shear in a fan-shaped area ahead of the plane, displayed on the screen at upper right.

column, and the spreading surface wind now comes from behind—a tailwind. In the cockpit, it registers as a sudden burst in airspeed. The pilot quickly reduces power—often too late.

But the Federal Aviation Administration and National Aeronautics and Space Administration are developing ways to neutralize the dangers of wind shear. In the early 1990s, government scientists used an instrumented Boeing 737 from NASA's Langley Research Center in Hampton, Virginia, to test airborne devices capable of making the atmosphere's invisible hammer visible. The result: a family of remote-sensing instruments that can "see" the telltale circulation that

The shift in wind speed and direction always comes suddenly and invisibly, and its touch upon the airplane itself can create a fatal illusion. Flying into one side of the spreading microburst, an airplane preparing to land encounters a headwind, decreasing the craft's speed relative to the surrounding air; on the instrument panel inside, it appears as a sudden drop in airspeed. With no visual clue, and not wanting to lag on the approach, the pilot follows his reflexes, increasing power to bring airspeed back into line. But by that time the plane has flown across the microburst

marks microburst activity and that can provide flight crews up to 40 seconds' warning. One of these, a microwave radar that detects the movement of water droplets in a thunderstorm, is already under development by private industry and is earmarked for installation in commercial airliner cockpits. Another, a *lidar*—the laser equivalent of radar—can monitor the motions of microscopic particles in cloudless air. It has entered an advanced development stage and may eventually join the microwave system aboard passenger aircraft. Soon the atmosphere will offer pilots one less surprise.

The Whirlwind Reaps

For most people, tornadoes are merely strange and dangerous, perilous abstractions to be avoided if one can, to be endured if one cannot. Strictly speaking, tornado country is just about everywhere, but the American weather factory leads the world. About 900 tornadoes a year are seen in the United States, with Australia's sparsely settled interior running a distant second with a few hundred reported; but the funnel-shaped storms have been seen almost everywhere, if rarely.

Like thunderstorms, they depend on the atmospheric instability that comes with renewed warfare between warm and cold, moist and dry air masses. In the United States, they are most frequent from April to June, but their center of action drifts across the land with the seasons. In winter, they are most common along the Gulf Coast and in the southeastern states. By April and May, they spread northward, concentrating in the southern plains. May is the cruelest month nationwide for tornadoes. In June and July they stalk the northern tiers of midwestern states from the Dakotas to New York. They have a kind of punctuality, occurring mostly between 3 and 8 P.M. local time, and they have a land of their own: the swatch from Texas up across the plains to Illinois and Indiana is called Tornado Alley.

Curiously, even in the Alley, most people have never seen one. Still, the sight of a funnel cloud dipping earthward from a thunderstorm has become a familiar sight, a fixture of the nightly news, along with the repeated signatures of damage— a windy vandalism that smashes structures to matchwood and scatters their contents with wild abandon. Tornadoes may have been rendered less frightening by all this exposure, at least to those who do not live among them. Indeed, the violent little storms have entered our literature mainly as Dorothy's conveyance from Kansas to Oz.

Small compared to the thunderclouds that produce them, tornadoes also lose some of their ability to awe us because they so closely resemble other, relatively harmless atmospheric relatives. There are always vortices—spinning currents—in any moving or unstable fluid. Pull the plug in a bathtub and, as the water runs out, little submarine tornadoes will swirl

In its last few seconds of existence, a ropelike tornado whips through Washita County, Oklahoma, on a late spring afternoon. This twister found relatively few targets besides a metal hay barn, which it shredded.

around the drain. The difference is that the air in whirlwinds is moving up, attracted by a center of very low pressure and whipped to high speeds as it converges around it. On any windy day in any desert, heating will produce a whirling devil of sand or dust. Thunderstorms and even fair-weather winds

The rotary circulation of what may become a tornado spins the lower layers of a cumulonimbus over Lake Superior into a dark, hook-shaped vortex. Not until a funnel cloud touches down does it officially become a tornado.

can whip up a waterspout. Sometimes a tornado will poke its funnel cloud down from the outflow area of a middling thunderstorm, writhe interestingly for a few minutes, and dissipate, much like the eddies near a bath drain.

Even among the extreme cases of the continental atmosphere, the tornado seems to be an anomaly, one of nature's outlaws, as unpredictable in its assaults as Billy the Kid. Usually only about 200 feet (60.6 m) across, these skinny, transient tentacles that flick down from thunderclouds can be deadly and destructive—you often see their hand in a mobile home community kicked apart by winds or in a metal roof twisted like a candy wrapper. But they are, relatively speaking, alley cats and ocelots compared to the twisters spawned in supercells. There, at the storm's 10,000-foot-high (3,000-m) waist, the spin of the mesocyclone communicates itself to air flowing into the storm's updraft area, initiating a rotary motion as much as a mile (1.6 km) in diameter. Helped by the Coriolis effect that is applied to rising and descending air, but also by the rotational forces already active in the cell, the growing vortex builds upward on the updraft—and downward as well—protruding into the clear air below the rear quadrant of the storm.

EXPLODING HOUSES

From the ground people often see the larger twisting of the storm's dark collar of cloud, an echo of the mesocyclone revving up within. Then, as the vortex comes into view, moisture condenses around it into a funnel cloud that reaches earthward, groping like an elephant's trunk. As it nears the surface, its winds sweep dust and debris into the funnel, causing it to darken ominously. Sometimes lightning plays along the whirling cloud as it strides across the land, lifting off for a moment, then settling again to earth to mark its terrifying signature. Witnesses describe the sound as similar to that of bombers overhead, or many locomotives; but there is a general sense that these comparisons do not do justice to the banshee voice of the whirlwind.

The forces at work in a large tornado are incomprehensible. The winds rage at speeds of up to 300 miles per hour (480 kph), and there is extreme low pressure at the core—the

ACTUAL TORNADO CLOUD, OMAHA, NEB., MARCH 23rd, 1913.

"Having a great time; wish you were here!" Two lucky photographers, in the right place at the right time to shoot tornadoes on March 23, 1913, in Omaha, Nebraska (*left*), and June 2, 1929, in Hardtner, Kansas (*bottom*), sold their pictures to eager publishers, who printed them as postcards.

TORNADO, JUNE 2, 1929, HARDTNER, KANSAS

greater pressure inside houses can cause roofs to explode off a structure into the passing vortex. Dorothy's being swept away in an intact house was not entirely a fiction— tales abound of people being hurled, house and all, into the Kansas sky and surviving the ordeal.

Anything swept into their fierce winds, from autos to structures, becomes a projectile, part of the tornado's destructive apparatus. But there seems almost a kind of whimsy in the power of these twisters. Tornado winds have plucked chickens and pounded straws into telephone poles and wooden poles into steel. Chicken houses have been swept away without cracking a single egg. Houses have had all their furniture sucked out but have survived intact. Perhaps because they are so destructive they have left histories of odd coincidence: for example, tornadoes hit Codell, Kansas, in 1916, 1917, and 1918—all on May 20. Sometimes they move across the land with a kind of stately slowness, but sometimes they approach at 70 miles an hour (110 kph), fast and destructive as a giant runaway train.

The interior of that frightening vortex remains one of nature's mysteries—few have looked inside a tornado and lived to tell about it. Retired Army Captain Roy S. Hall was one who did. On May 3, 1943, a tornado swept down on the Hall family's home in McKinney, Texas, about 30 miles (50 km) north of Dallas. Hall managed to get his wife and children into one of the bedrooms just as the roaring twister began clawing at their house. The winds ripped away the walls protecting them—then, abruptly, the dreadful roar passed into silence and they were bathed in an eerie bluish glow. "Something had billowed down from above," Hall wrote afterward, "and stood fairly motionless, save for a slow up-and-down pulsation. It presented a curved face, with the concave part toward me, with a bottom rim that was almost level." It was the base of the funnel; Hall and his family were inside it.

Above them, Hall recounted, a smooth, opaque wall of cloud, like "the interior of a glazed standpipe," stretched up to perhaps a thousand feet (300 m), swaying and bending in the thunderstorm's surrounding winds. At the bottom, Hall estimated the funnel was about 450 feet (135 m) across. "Higher up," he recounted, "it was larger, and seemed to be partly filled with a bright cloud, which shimmered like a fluorescent light." He thought the column looked like a stack of huge rings, each moving independently of the other, but linked by a wave that rippled down the length of the sides. As each ripple reached the bottom, Hall said, the funnel flicked like a whip. Minutes later, moving away from his ruined house, the tip of the tornado flicked at a neighbor's house and blew it away "like sparks from an emery wheel."

RECORD-BREAKING HAVOC

Every spring someone takes a terrible hammering from tornadoes in the United States. But a few outbreaks linger in human memory for their duration, their severity, and the hundreds of victims they claimed. The Great Tri-state Twister of March 18, 1925, is in this tornadic pantheon of superstorms. At times a mile (1.6 km) in diameter, the funnel touched down that afternoon in Annapolis, Missouri, razing Main Street's buildings in about 20 seconds. Spinning crazily toward the northeast, the lethal twister swept through Murphysboro, Illinois, tossing trees, buildings, and underground pipes about as if they were toys; at least 234 people died in Murphysboro. Still

gaining intensity, the tornado headed for the nearby farming town of DeSoto, population about 600. The twister killed 69 of them and flattened every structure more than one story high. It marked its trail with shredded clothing and human flesh, taking a total of 689 lives before vanishing in southern Indiana at the end of its 219-mile-long (350-km) rampage.

More often, the memorable tornado is not one but a squadron of them, advancing like cossacks along a broad front of heavy weather in Tornado Alley. One of the worst came on April 11—Palm Sunday—1965, when nearly 40 destructive tornadoes galloped through towns in Wisconsin, Iowa, Illinois, Indiana, Michigan, and Ohio, killing 256, injuring 3,000 more, and destroying some $300 million in property. One of that outbreak's unforgettable images: twin tornadoes, descending like dark stumpy legs from their thundercloud, march along a highway near Elkhart, Indiana.

But never in human memory has there been an outbreak to equal the one of April 3 and 4, 1974. A textbook meteorological situation—warm humid air pressing against cool humid air from about Chicago eastward, with dry air to the west pinched by cold air moving down from the northwest—triggered a line of severe thunderstorms 1,000 miles (1,600 km) long. As it marched through Tornado Alley, it spawned 148 tornadoes, which touched down and left tracks across the Midwest from Illinois to West Virginia and from Chicago to the Gulf of Mexico. In Xenia, Ohio, some 3,000 structures were demolished. Across the southeast-to-northwest paths of the marauding storms, entire towns were wiped out, 307 people were killed, more than 6,000 injured, and an estimated $600 million in property devastated.

GROUND ZERO

The so-called Super Outbreak of 1974 revealed yet another dangerous side to thunderstorms. Among the unmistakable signatures of tornadoes scrawled across midwestern America was something written in a violent hand—something more ordered than the chaotic vandalism of most tornadoes. T. Theodore Fujita, a professor of meteorology at the University of Chicago and a renowned tornado researcher, looked at the damage from the air and noticed a pattern he thought he

had seen before. Before coming to America in 1953, Fujita had taught physics at the Meiji College of Technology in Japan. In 1945, the 24-year-old scholar had been one of a team asked to examine the damage wrought by two atomic bombs, one dropped over Hiroshima, the other over Nagasaki. There, he discovered, the nuclear detonations above the cities had produced a strangely symmetrical pattern of destruction—a kind of starburst of structures blown away from ground zero, the point directly below the explosion.

Shaken townspeople in tiny—population 250—Campbellsburg, Kentucky, wander among the ruins of their block-long business district that was flattened by a twister, part of a major outbreak along the Midwest's Tornado Alley in April 1974.

Flying over West Virginia, Fujita saw a similar pattern of damage, as though a powerful explosion had occurred at the center of a rough starburst of destruction. No one had seen this effect before or had thought much about the destructive

potential of the downdrafts known to spread out from the bases of thunderclouds. Fujita proposed that this was no ordinary downdraft and coined a new term for atmospheric weaponry: *downburst*. The term is now used to signify a powerful downward cough that hits the ground and spreads out, leaving a distinctive damage signature behind it.

Whatever the patterns of destruction, aerial views of towns like Xenia, Ohio, shattered into splinters by the winds of one tornado or a mob of them, can still move us; but nothing outside the actual experience of a tornado can quite communicate the horror of that howling, sudden storm. "If I live forever," said one survivor of a Kentucky twister, "I will never see anything so horrible as this again."

Watching the tiny, blanket-draped figures standing shocked and stunned amid the wreckage of their lives, the neighborhoods transformed into a trash of shattered homes and scattered belongings, the dazed survivors saying bravely to a camera that they have lost everything, *everything*—watching all those now-familiar scenes, sharing in a distant way the horror written there, we also acknowledge a sad home truth. These terrible sights are as normal to this heart of the American weather factory as the drenching monsoon rains are to the heart of India, terrible cold to Siberia, or the shrieking sirocco to the sandy shoulders of Africa. Deadly weather is part of continental living. ☁

Photographed from a scant mile (1.6 km) away, a half-mile-wide (1-km), 1,000-foot-high (300-m) tornado funnel churns up the earth near Hesston, Kansas, on March 13, 1991. As friction with the ground tilts the dust-darkened twister, it begins to shower the area with a deluge of swept-up dirt and debris.

PROPHETS AND MAGICIANS

There is something about our ocean of air that tantalizes and seduces the intellect. Perhaps because we are ourselves creatures of this larger chaos, we are compelled to find order in it—in the random dance of excited atoms at one end of the atmospheric spectrum, the global march of fronts and giant storms and Earth-girdling stratospheric winds at the other. Perhaps because the atmosphere seems beyond understanding, we must try to peer into its hidden future—even make it do our bidding.

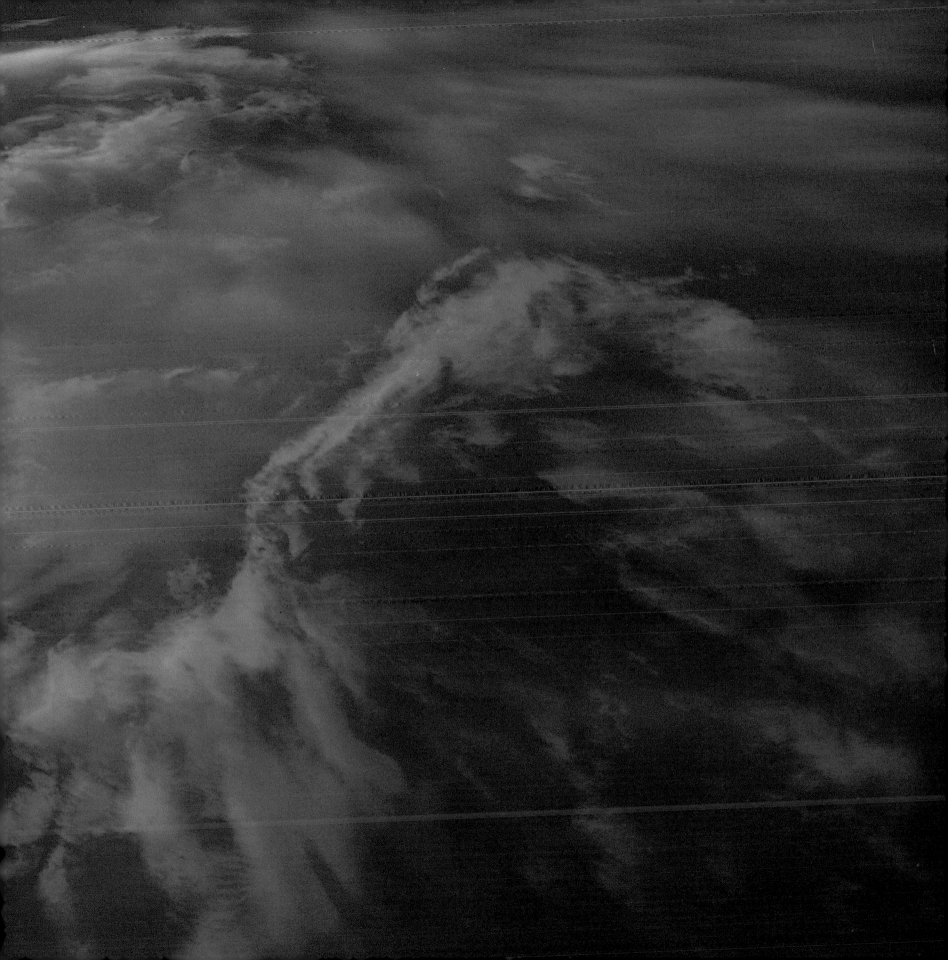

A Dangerous Intruder

Raw weather, left more or less to itself, rampages through the world, exhibiting a chilling indifference to life. In the developing countries a tropical cyclone can destroy tens of thousands of lives even after a timely warning has been broadcast. In the weather-conscious industrialized nations, weather kills with something like abandon, a few hundred here, a few hundred there. The atmosphere is not just a mystery, then, but a dangerous intruder that must be watched and, if a way to do it can be found, disarmed.

That our dealings with this intruder from the atmosphere contain an element of futility is heard in Mark Twain's description of New England weather. "In the spring," he told the New England Society in 1876, "I have counted one hundred and thirty-six different kinds of weather inside of twenty-four hours," adding his own prediction: "Probable nor'east to sou'west winds, varying to the southard and westard and eastard and points between; high and low barometer, sweeping round from place to place; probably areas of rain, snow, hail, and drought, succeeded or preceded by earthquakes with thunder and lightning." He is not merely being funny—he is throwing up his hands, acknowledging a variety and complexity that is beyond human comprehension. "One of the brightest gems in the New England weather," he concluded, "is the dazzling uncertainty of it."

"Everybody talks about the weather, but nobody does anything about it," goes another aphorism often attributed to Mark Twain. In fact, it is more likely the creation of Twain's sometime collaborator Charles Dudley Warner, editor of the *Hartford Courant*, where it appeared in August 1897. Regardless of its provenance, the axiom has become part of the dogma of meteorological futility—of the impossibility of doing business with that great confuser called chaos.

Certainly, like all axioms, Warner's contains a kernel of truth; but that kernel, as is often the case, is soluble in

After a night's torrential rain in 1991, a truck in Britannia Beach, British Columbia, is nearly interred in a field of boulders bulldozed into town on a flash-flooding stream.

Heavy rains turned paved roads into waterways for farmers in China's Anhui Province—a region of low-lying land and numerous rivers—during the 1983 season.

serious reflection. A moment's thought makes one realize that, in fact, a great deal *is* done about the weather, and was then. By the time the *Courant* ran the clever line, the United States had operated a national meteorological service for about 27 years, Great Britain for 43. Today most of the nations of the world collaborate in watching the global atmosphere minute by minute, around the clock and calendar, fielding a vast array of breakthrough technology to make what once must have seemed an impossible task part of a daily operational routine. They are in the weather business not so much to let the citizenry know when it is time for umbrellas, galoshes, or parkas—although that is one of the many things they do—as to protect aircraft from fatal ice, ships from dangerously rough seas, farmers from ruinous wind and water, travelers from

meteorological traps; the harm must be detected if people are to be warned out of its way.

Nor is this work merely watching and waiting. Enormous progress has been made since the 1950s in *predicting* what the global atmosphere will do on various scales of time and space and, perhaps more difficult, what the atmosphere will do over regional scales reckoned in hundreds of square kilometers or miles—the scale of river valleys and communities, where serious weather happens quickly and kills with the suddenness of a bomber raid or an earthquake.

Adding a Third Dimension

Despite the truisms about the unpredictability of the atmosphere, most of the history of meteorology has dealt with discovering order in the movement of wind, water, and energy over the planet's surface. Meteorological pioneers seemed to find predictable events in the blossoming and withering of fronts around a center of low pressure, in the enormous circulations of Hadley cells and globe-girdling winds. The Sun's yearly contribution—the rough equivalent of fuel added to the atmospheric tank—was pretty well understood. But the magnitude of the entity being studied boggled the mind.

Nevertheless, technology has seemed to bring that entity more and more within human grasp. The advent of the telegraph in 1845 meant that weather observers could consolidate *simultaneous* observations over great distances. Meteorological

Turn-of-the-century telegraph clerks provide the first communication links between widely separated communities—and weather stations—which used telegraphs to report simultaneous measurements to a central meteorological office in Washington, D.C.

networks began to spring up. A small meteorological department that was established in 1854 in Britain's Board of Trade began issuing information on weather and currents at sea for mariners; by 1860 it was telegraphing regular weather reports to points throughout Great Britain, aided by data from other national systems beginning to operate on the European continent. The idea of weather reporting and forecasting spread across the British Empire.

In the United States, President Ulysses S. Grant signed a joint resolution of Congress establishing a national weather service in February 1870. That same year, observer-sergeants in the Army Signal Service took surface observations at 24 stations around the Great Lakes and telegraphed them to Washington. Like the sister agencies just beginning in Europe and its empires, this official brand of meteorology rested on centuries of active interest in the weather—on diaries, municipal records, and experimental preoccupations with lightning and fluid mechanics, in all the places where earlier scholars had set down what they thought was predictable order in the atmosphere. At first, the government reports comprised pressure, relative humidity, and temperature at the surface, plus what the station observer could see—how much of the sky was covered with what kind of cloud moving how rapidly in which direction. By 1888 about 75 of these reports flowed into the U.S. Signal Office in Washington, D.C., three times each day, to be laboriously transferred by hand from coded telegraph messages to notations on continental maps.

EXAMINING THE ELEPHANT

Sometimes the reports were predictive in a rudimentary way. For weather that moved in an orderly fashion, and at a good clip, a telegraphed report of conditions upstream—usually to the west—meant that those conditions would be a few hundred miles farther east by morning. Cold waves, for example, could be forecast for points downwind some 30 hours ahead with reasonable success—it was like predicting where a train would be 24 hours down the track. But most weather was more complicated than that, and meteorologists were like the proverbial blind men examining an elephant. The great beast of the atmosphere could not be seen in its entirety. A cyclone reforming west of the Rockies, then coiling out across the plains, dipping into the energy reservoir of the Gulf, and spinning up the Atlantic seaboard—the size and shape of such behemoths could only be inferred from the meager data coming in from surface stations.

Indeed, not much more than the ground track—the footprint—of the atmosphere could be read in these reports. Practitioners of the new science of meteorology realized early in the game that the planet's thin film of atmosphere was, from the perspective of tiny humans, a very deep ocean of air and that to understand it they would have to send their instruments aloft. At first they used the time-honored means of sounding the atmosphere, one pioneered in 1749 by two Scottish students when they measured air temperature with a thermometer attached to a kite.

The kite was the only flying machine available to researchers through the 19th century—and not just any kite would do. From 1898 to 1906 American meteorologists used box kites 8 feet (2.5 m) or so on a side, capable of lifting a

Forecasters at the Marquette, Michigan, weather station pose with the different box-kite designs used to hoist meteorological instruments into the atmosphere. During the 1920s the kites were replaced by airplanes carrying meteorological instruments.

small adult. They were launched from spools wound with thousands of feet of piano wire and reeled in with electric motors. The kites, often launched in a series so that each successive kite added its lift to the system, carried an ingenious device called a *meteorograph*, capable of recording atmospheric pressure, temperature, relative humidity, and wind velocity. These frail platforms added a third dimension to weather observation, but not much of one. Kites reached the end of their longest tethers at about 4.5 miles (7 km) altitude— Virginia weathermen sent a record-making train of five kites to 23,835 feet (7,222 m) in 1910. But this was hardly two-thirds of the way to the tropopause, and most kite soundings went only to 10,000 feet (3,000 m).

After World War I, airplanes gradually replaced kites as instrument platforms, and, from 1925 until the late 1930s, meteorographic soundings were made by having a score of instrumented biplanes take off from a number of widely separated fields

and simultaneously spiral upward to 17,000 feet (5,100 m), then spiral back to the field again. Launching all the members of a scattered squadron at the same time was an expensive means of obtaining upper-air information, and the airplanes of the day could carry instruments only to about 20,000 feet (6,000 m) at the most; they also had to hurry back to the field while their data were still relatively fresh. Another flaw: in bad weather, when meteorological information was needed most, the planes were grounded.

A meteorologist attaches a meteorograph to the wing struts of a weather plane before a 1926 takeoff. The airplane would spiral up, then back to land, bearing measurements of atmospheric pressure, temperature, relative humidity, and wind velocity from the surface to 17,000 feet (5,100 m).

BALLOON BLOWERS

Balloons offered a possible alternative. Filled with one of the light gases—volatile hydrogen or inert (but rarer and more expensive) helium—they would rise through the atmosphere just like an air bubble rising through the water; as the bubble rises, surrounding pressure decreases, the bubble expands until its internal pressure exceeds the strength of its walls—and it pops. Small, 30-inch-diameter (75 cm) *pilot balloons*, so-called because their movement traced the motions of the wind, were used from 1918 onwards, launched from the ground and tracked with a surveyor's calibrated telescope—a *theodolite*—to determine wind patterns aloft. Alas, the little balloons were fair-weather friends—once they entered a cloud, they vanished forever.

During the 1930s, a new balloon-borne instrument package called a *radiosonde* began providing a third dimension to atmospheric data collection. The instrument package recorded temperature, relative humidity, and barometric pressure and radioed these back to its ground station. The receiver automatically plotted the data as the sonde rose through the troposphere. When the balloon expanded to its elastic limit in the thin air of the stratosphere, it burst and the radiosonde dropped free to parachute back to Earth. Such soundings often probed the atmosphere to about 75,000 feet (22,700 m), and heavier balloons could routinely carry instruments to better than 100,000 feet (30,000 m).

By the time World War II began, the radiosonde had become more than a tool of modern meteorology—it had become its symbol as well. Across the world, meteorologists became known familiarly as "balloon blowers," a sobriquet they have cheerfully applied to themselves. After all, there was nothing pejorative in being nicknamed for using state-of-the-art technology that told the world about the upper atmosphere, present and future.

Forecasters at the Washington, D.C., Weather Bureau office launch a balloon carrying a device called a radiosonde, capable of transmitting its data to a ground station, during a test in the 1920s. By the next decade, balloons had largely replaced aircraft as instrument platforms for routine soundings to the top of the troposphere.

Seeing It Whole

Besides providing instrument platforms, aviation gave meteorology an urgent respectability. Farmers and mariners and all kinds of commerce and industry had always been weather-dependent to a degree—a forecast of good weather meant sheaves could be brought in, barns raised, an English Channel or Great Lakes transit made without the perilous agony of violent storms. But airplanes actually went into the atmosphere itself and flew there at the mercy of wind and water. An airplane moves *through* its medium, so that its speed is partly determined by which way the air is moving and how fast. A wing feels the enfeebled touch of heat-thinned air and is an

Before modern meteorology, pilots were on their own, weatherwise. Here, a Cessna 130 and a 135 fly over Alaska's Arrigtech Peaks at the Gates of the Arctic National Park, keeping their distance from the mountains and their unpredictable wind currents.

excellent nucleus around which ice can aggregate. Weather in an airplane is experienced first hand—one feels the atmosphere's embrace around the machine, one time helping, another time hindering, flight.

At first, pilots handled their own meteorology: they muddled through, or did not, depending on how well they read the prospects for killer downdrafts, ice-filled clouds, wind shear, thunderstorms, and headwinds that gripped the ship as its fuel was steadily consumed. Flying a small plane in the Arctic and along the Andes is still a bit like that, despite a sprinkling of weather stations along the line of flight. The weather seems always to be not quite what one was led to expect—the weather, as pilots put it, is what you find. Sometimes there is not space or visibility or fuel enough to endure what is found, and plane and passengers are lost to the atmosphere. Even so, for a time, it was enough that pilots were able to muddle through alone.

MAPPING A NEW WORLD

It was not until aviation came of age in the years before World War II that the new industry's meteorological needs became clear. Aviation, it turned out, was not just about flying—it was about taking off in one weather regime and landing hours later in another thousands of miles away; it was about flying fast in airplanes whose weight was reckoned in tons, not pounds or kilograms, carrying a load of cargo, people, or bombs. As these new generations of aircraft probed higher and higher, the atmosphere yielded a few close secrets. World War II bombers flying in the high troposphere over Europe discovered that the prevailing westerly winds had a central fast lane—the *jet stream*—that could add up to 200 miles per hour (320 kph) to a plane's airspeed. Almost inadvertently, the heavy traffic in the upper reaches of the troposphere and lower stratosphere mapped a new world of thin, fast winds—westerlies and counterflows, winds that reversed biannually, the mixing of air across the inversion of the tropopause.

Airplanes also offered scientists an unprecedented opportunity to enter into the atmosphere as they would a laboratory, to study weather where it happened. Much of this work derived from military programs, both during the war and afterward.

The ENEMY is listening

...ts to know ...ou know

...P IT TO YOURSELF

Filling in for male meteorologists gone to serve in World War II, this trio of women forecasters plots the day's weather. After the war ended, such jobs in meteorology—as in most other industries—went back to the returning veterans.

A meteorologist aboard a Navy WV-2 Hurricane Hunter uses a 1940s-vintage radar to probe a tropical cyclone from within. Flights into hurricanes became routine in the 1950s, with airplanes taking instruments into the hearts of the storms to measure them.

Hurricane hunters, for example, began their work in the Pacific war, when meteorologists needed flights into tropical cyclones to find and plot their low-pressure centers—and where, incidentally, the earlier practice of giving female names to hurricanes and typhoons began. The foundations of atmospheric physics and chemistry now applied to studying microscopic changes in atmospheric composition were laid by instrumented bombers sampling the stratosphere downwind of Soviet and Chinese nuclear tests. The peculiarities of the tropical atmosphere were mapped by postwar researchers in military amphibious aircraft, tracing equatorial wind and water in long, slow flights that evoke the odysseys of albatrosses. It was a university meteorologist in the back seat of a Navy jet who discovered supercooled water blowing out of the chimneys of hurricanes.

WINGED LABORATORY

Most of the world's leading meteorological services employ specially equipped aircraft to probe events in the atmosphere as they occur. Britain's National Meteorological Library at Bracknell flies this modified Lockheed C-130 Hercules, XV208, which has been transformed into an odd-looking bird bristling with sensors. The normal snub nose of the Hercules has been drawn out into a long, candy-striped probe that enters undisturbed air a split second before the giant craft roils it. At the tip of the stinger, a pitot static head senses air speed and direction, a gust probe—a set of vanes—measures winds relative to the plane, and other sensors record the amount of liquid water and ice and take the temperature of air just ahead of the airplane. The right wing is hung with a maxipod containing a holographic laser and a minipod with a holographic camera for three-dimensional cloud imagery; a maxipod on the left wing holds a multichannel radiometer, one of a number of temperature- and radiation-sensing devices located around the aircraft. A spectro-photometer probe next to the left-hand maxipod uses scattered light to infer the sizes and densities of solid particles suspended in the air. Perforations in the pressurized hull permit direct sampling of outside air and water. The Hercules carries a weather radar in a teardrop-shaped radome above the cockpit and a Doppler antenna in the belly. Researchers work at computer stations inside the almost windowless, cavernous fuselage of their flying laboratory.

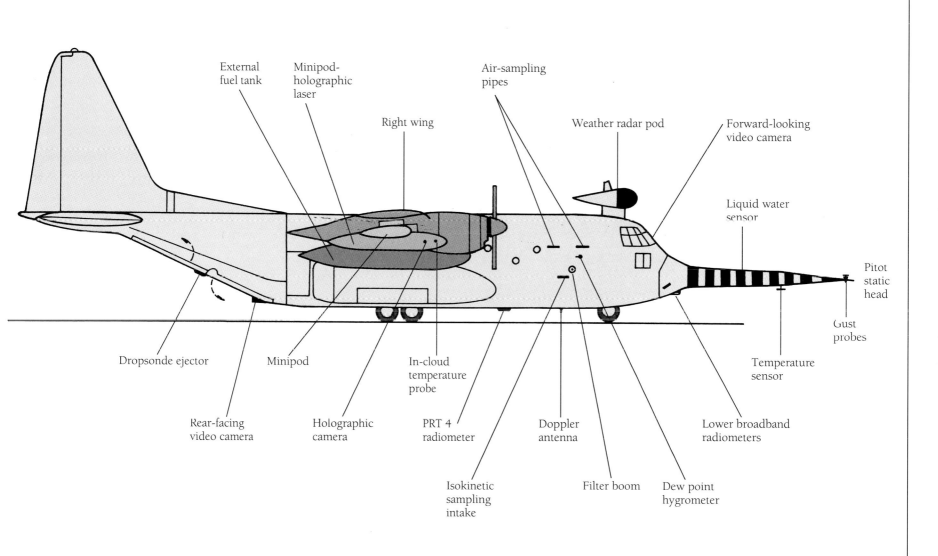

External
fuel tank

Minipod-
holographic
laser

Right wing

Air-sampling
pipes

Weather radar pod

Forward-looking
video camera

Liquid water
sensor

Pitot
static
head

Gust
probes

Dropsonde ejector

Minipod

In-cloud
temperature
probe

Temperature
sensor

Lower broadband
radiometers

Rear-facing
video camera

Holographic
camera

PRT 4
radiometer

Doppler
antenna

Dew point
hygrometer

Isokinetic
sampling
intake

Filter boom

On left wing (*not shown*):
•Forward-scattering spectrophotometer probe
•Maxipod-multichannel radiometer
•Two-dimensional cloud probe

Eyes on the Sky

But it was not just a new breed of aircraft. A new generation of research meteorologists had opened an era of exploration that would be to the air what the great navigations of the 15th and 16th centuries had been to the seas. As that earlier exploration had grown around the advent of ocean-worthy ships and talented navigators, this meteorological one developed around observation platforms and new instrumentation—or rather, new uses of existing ones. *Radar*—the acronym taken from "radio detection and ranging"—is a perfect case in point. Developed during World War II as an antiaircraft detection system, it soon found its way aboard naval ships and military aircraft, where it was used not just to find the enemy, but to keep track of one's allies as well. It worked by sending out a radio-frequency pulse, which objects in its path reflected back to the radar antenna; this information gave observers a distance and bearing to the object.

Meteorologists were quick to note that this object need not be an enemy airplane. At some frequencies the beam was also reflected by water droplets in the atmosphere; the bigger the target was, the stronger the reflected signal. Thus, radar could see the liquid-filled heart beating *inside* a thunderstorm. Sometimes it discerned a hook-shaped formation in an area

A five-man Signal Corps crew (*left*) works a primitive SCR-268 during the 1944 campaign in Italy. The radio-ranging device required three operators to watch for echoes, one to monitor the target's track, and one to monitor its height. Meteorologists later adapted radar to "see" water droplets in clouds, using such platforms as the Navy's modified R5D2-2 flying radar laboratory (*above*) to test antennas and techniques. Four radar sets are mounted on the outboard wings and a 15-foot (4.5-m) mast housing meteorological instruments raises and lowers in flight.

where tornadoes occurred. It revealed the full structure of the hurricane, which appeared on the scope as a pale spiral of violent clouds ringing an empty eye. In the early postwar years, radar joined the operational weather services, usually in the form of a surplused military set installed at a ground station. Now, with a radiosonde balloon to probe the atmosphere overhead to 100,000 feet (30,000 m), and a radar beam to sweep the sky for several hundred miles around, a weather station had its best view yet of the surrounding atmosphere. Stations with overlapping coverage could provide something like a continuous three-dimensional view of the weather across a continent.

And yet, something was still missing. A 1952 U.S. Weather Bureau pamphlet plaintively began, "If it were possible for a person to rise by plane or rocket to a height where he could see the entire country from the Atlantic to the Pacific...." and displayed an artist's rendering of what meteorologists thought North America would look like from that vantage point: a continent banded by well-defined fronts and tidy formations of clouds. At about the same

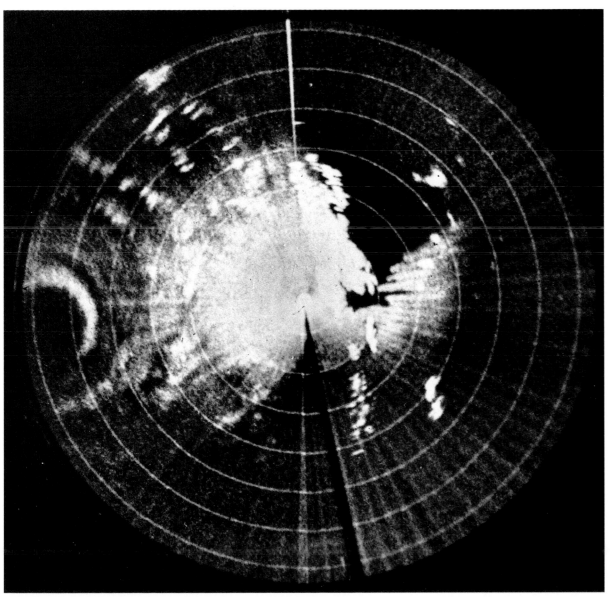

Hurricane Connie, one of the Atlantic storms of 1955, reveals herself to a Hurricane Hunter's airborne radar from the plane's position at the center of the storm. More modern radar views of the big storms show structure, precipitation, and wind fields in finely drawn detail.

time, captured German V-2 rockets pressed into research were carrying cameras to altitudes of about 100 miles (160 km) and showing us—this may have been among the first visual proofs—that the planet's horizon was indeed a curve, the Earth really round. Moreover, the V-2 cameras revealed that, while major frontal systems looked something like theory, there was nothing neat about the way clouds were scattered across the landscape.

A Vantage Point in Space

The V-2s were heralds of a new age, one in which the meteorologist's vantage point would shift to an Earth-circling orbit. Soon the planet and its atmosphere would be seen as must have been intended, from a distance rather than from within. Post-Sputnik meteorologists fantasized about the possibilities weather-watching satellites would bring: better warnings

Carrying a camera instead of an explosive warhead, a March 7, 1947, flight of a German V-2 rocket shows the planet's curvature, providing one of the first views of the atmosphere from very high altitude—the V-2 flew to about 100 miles (161 km).

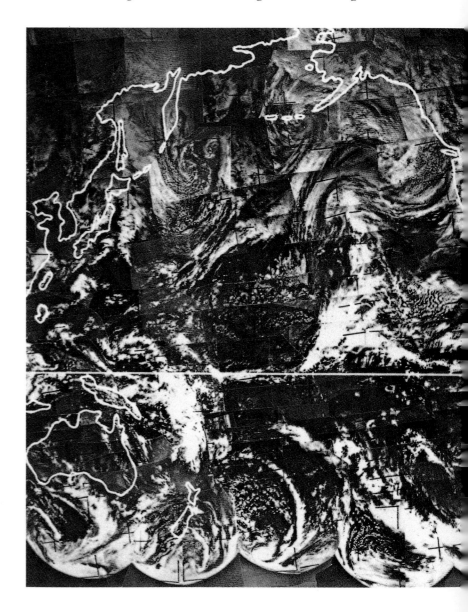

of dangerous storms, a continuous view of the entire atmosphere as it unfolded, a quantum jump in the quality of the human condition.

The responsibility for turning this fantasy into reality lay at first with the Advanced Research Projects Agency, a threshold research activity within the U.S. Defense Department. In 1959 the year-old project moved to the newly formed National Aeronautics and Space Administration and became Project TIROS—the acronym for "television infrared observational satellite." TIROS I, the first meteorological satellite to carry a television camera, was launched at 6:40 A.M. on

American meteorologists assembled this first complete view of a cloud-mottled atmosphere, a mosaic of 450 individual images transmitted by the TIROS weather satellite, during a single 14-hour period in February 1965. Land masses, outlined in white, are slightly lighter than the ocean areas.

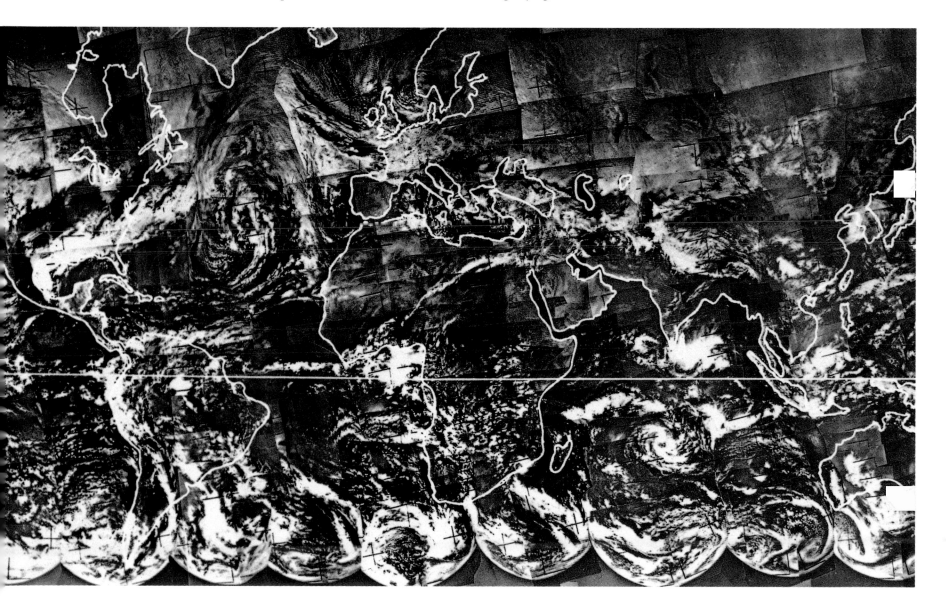

April 1, 1960, from Cape Canaveral. It spent its 78-day operating life taking and transmitting some 23,000 images of Earth—images that confirmed the atmosphere's befuddling complexity. Even today, looking at the planet through the blurred lens of TIROS I is daunting: there is so much happening at once, so much water and so little land, and not much that looks like the diagrams in meteorology texts.

Six years later TIROS had evolved into an operational system of two cartwheeling satellites in near-polar orbits, flying about 850 miles (1,350 km) above the planet. Their two orbits were separated so that the satellites bracketed local noon. On each southward pass over the turning surface of the Earth, one crossed the Equator at 9 A.M. local time, the other at 3 P.M., times that coincided with the observational routines of meteorology. Although they comprised an American system, the twin satellites served meteorologists around the world as part of a World Weather Watch proclaimed by the World Meteorological Organization of the United Nations. Anyone with a proper receiver could bring down images of regional weather from passing spacecraft. The meteorological world grew smaller.

THE RIGHT ORBIT

That same year, 1966, NASA launched the first Applications Technology Satellite—ATS-1—into a very different kind of orbit, one that would provide a continuous view of Earth. This new spacecraft applied one of the rules of thumb of celestial mechanics: an object injected at sufficient speed in the right direction can be orbited at any altitude above the atmosphere; but, as the distance between satellite and planet increases, the speed required to maintain the orbit decreases.

To keep TIROS in its low orbit, the satellite needed to whip along at about 17,000 miles per hour (27,000 kph), completing one revolution about every 113 minutes. At an altitude of 22,300 miles (35,680 km), orbital speed drops to about 6,800 miles per hour (11,000 kph) and the period of this much larger orbit becomes 24 hours. If a satellite is injected into an orbit at this precise altitude, in the plane of the Equator, the craft will turn with the planet, always looking down onto the same point on the Equator—*geostationary,*

Earth synchronous, and *geosynchronous* are the terms used to describe such an orbit.

The technique had been used to good effect on civilian communications and some military spacecraft. ATS-1 pioneered the orbit's meteorological use. Now, for the first time, meteorologists could see the Earth as a blue disk of ocean striped here and there with free-forms of land, overlaid by a protean swirl of white clouds that seemed everywhere interlinked, all around the world. Only moonbound *Apollo* astronauts would have a better view of home than this.

Soon the ATS series were replaced by GOES, the Geostationary Operational Environmental Satellite, in the United States and by other mark-timing satellites like Europe's Meteosat, Russia's Geostationary Operational Meteorological Satellite (GOMS), India's Insat, and Japan's Geostationary Meteorological Satellite (GMS). Early sensors were replaced by devices that could watch the planet in a number of wavelengths in the visible and infrared spectra and sound the atmosphere below, using remote sensors to measure temperature, water vapor content, and other parameters.

At last, the atmosphere could be seen whole and seen continuously, day and night, with a resolution that discerned objects only 0.6 miles (1 km) across. Around the planet meteorological routines became choreographed into the simultaneous rhythms of a World Weather Watch. The atmosphere seemed finally to have come within the human grasp.

White-clad NASA technicians set the Geostationary Operational Environmental Satellite—GOES—inside its payload fairing atop a Delta rocket. Launched from Florida's Kennedy Space Center for NOAA, this GOES was used in a year-long global weather-gathering experiment that began in December 1978.

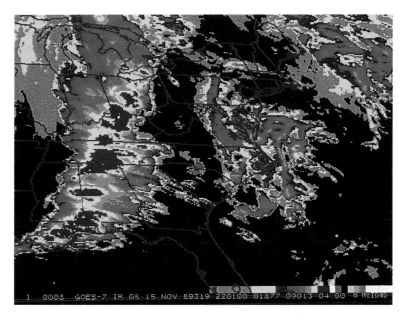

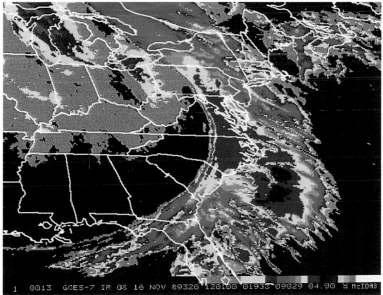

False-color images from the infrared sensors on a subsequent GOES reveal the structure of an intense, fast-moving cold front across the American Midwest in November 1993. The red areas represent the highest and coldest cloud-tops—the centers of maximum storm intensity.

The Road to Prophecy

That such massive inoculations of technology would reveal the present state of the atmosphere would not have been enough to justify the effort. Seeing weather as it occurs is only the tip of the meteorological iceberg—*prediction* is what this science is really about. Pilots are not greatly interested in present conditions at their destination thousands of miles away—they want to know what will greet them several hours hence. Generals need to know what the weather will be like on June 6, D-Day, not on May 30. A ship's captain needs to know where the storms will be in a week, a farmer the weather of a planting season, a mayor the severity of winters and summers yet to come. *Now-casting*, as determining the present state of the atmosphere is called, can be very useful in monitoring such short-fused events as thunderstorm formation; but *forecasting* is observational meteorology's professed reason for being. The relationship between the two has seemed crystal clear: perfect knowledge of present conditions should permit near-perfect predictions of how those conditions will change with time.

To Lewis Fry Richardson, it appeared that the necessary bridges between the atmospheric past, present,

British physicist Lewis Fry Richardson hypothesized in 1922 that global weather could be expressed by mathematical equations, which could be used to calculate how the atmosphere would evolve from that starting point. Without electronic computers, however, Richardson's technique could not keep up—it took three months' computation to predict weather just one day ahead.

and future could be built mathematically using the laws of fluid dynamics and Newtonian physics in combination with actual weather data. The Bjerkneses, father and son, and other Scandinavian pioneers in Bergen had dabbled with such things in developing their concept of fronts and cyclones, but no one had constructed the mathematical scaffolding needed to do the job. Richardson, as a British physicist in his early 30s, began exploring the problem in 1913 and kept at it even through a tour of ambulance duty during World War I. In 1922 he published the result: *Weather Prediction by Numerical Process*, the first detailed treatment of the thermal, compositional, and physical dynamics of the atmosphere—at least as it was understood at the time.

Richardson's computations imitated those used to compile the *Nautical Almanac*, the navigational tables showing the predicted positions of the Sun, moon, planets, and certain stars. But his work used the differential equations of calculus to develop tables from which future atmospheric conditions could be read. Given enough initial data, Richardson believed, the state of the atmosphere could be predicted mathematically. He even fantasized about how an operational numerical forecasting facility might look.

RICHARDSON'S AMAZING MODEL

"Imagine a large hall like a theatre," he wrote,

except that the circles and galleries go right round through the space usually occupied by the stage. The walls of this chamber are painted to form a map of the globe. The ceiling represents the north polar regions, England is in the gallery, the tropics in the upper circle, Australia on the dress circle and the Antarctic in the pit. In this imagined setting, 64,000 computers [human, for there were as yet no electronic ones] work on a small portion of the world's weather, one point on a vast grid. But each computer can see the results produced by adjacent colleagues. A higher-ranking official consolidates these individual efforts into regional predictions.

From the floor of the pit a tall pillar rises to half the height of the hall. It carries a large pulpit on its top. In this sits the man in charge of the whole theatre; he is surrounded by several assistants and messengers. One of his duties is to maintain a uniform speed of progress in all parts of the globe. In this respect he is like the conductor of an orchestra in which the instruments are slide-rules and calculating machines. But instead of waving a baton he turns a beam of rosy light upon any region that is running ahead of the rest, and a beam of blue light upon those who are behindhand.

Four senior clerks in the central pulpit are collecting the future weather as fast as it is being computed, and despatching it by pneumatic carrier to a quiet room. There it will be coded and telephoned to the radio transmitting station.

But even Richardson sensed that the operational heart of his elaborate fantasy was silly. "Perhaps some day in the dim future," he brooded, "it will be possible to advance the computations faster than the weather advances and at a cost less than the saving to mankind due to the information gained." One almost hears him sigh as he adds: "But that is a dream." It was indeed. Richardson needed three months of calculating to bridge from present weather conditions to predicted conditions 24 hours into the future.

Not that Richardson was regarded as less than serious. His meteorological research injected his surname into his science as the *Richardson number*—a fundamental quantity involving the way temperature and wind velocity change with distance. But he believed in the broader

powers of mathematics to solve human problems. In his later years—he died in 1953—he applied mathematics to foreign affairs in such works as *Statistics of Deadly Quarrels*. Ironically, it was just at the time of his death that experimenters at Princeton University demonstrated that Richardson's approach had been generally correct. Moreover, enough had been learned about the atmosphere's structure and dynamics since 1922 to improve the results of Richardsonian computations.

ELECTRONIC WEATHERCASTERS

The real difference in eras was that Richardson had lived in an age of slide rules and mechanical analog calculators. Such scholars as John von Neumann and Jule Charney of Princeton's Institute for Advanced Study were opening a new age of high-speed electronic computers. Early efforts suggested that the atmosphere might yield its future to the right set of equations and the right kind of weather data. But it would do so at a

An engineer scans the Cray-1 supercomputer for hot spots with an infrared scanner. With the ability to solve millions of computations every second, the powerful Cray has helped meteorologists make huge strides in weather modeling.

price. Even the simplest mathematical approximation of the atmosphere exceeded the capacity of any early computer. Numerical weather prediction, if possible at all, would require the largest computers human ingenuity could build and as much global weather data as it was possible to gather.

As weather forecasters, digital computers had to be given a way of expressing the complexities of the atmosphere in the simple binary language of yes and no, one and zero. They also had to be equipped with a mathematical point of view: that the atmosphere is deterministic at some scales of time and space. If it is deterministic, then, once set in motion, it should respond predictably to the unfolding sequence in accordance with known physical laws. Given sufficient accurate information on the initial state of the atmosphere, a large computer should be able to predict changes in atmospheric state at very large—or *synoptic*—scales and relatively small scales over certain periods of time. One difficulty is that the causes and effects of atmospheric determinism do not reveal themselves like religious dogma—they surface occasionally, perhaps randomly, and disappear, like the eddies and swirls in a swift, turbulent stream. One knows that they must be there because everything has a cause and every cause some effect; a rattle of leaves tells us there is wind, though no one can see it. Still, it is no mean thing to put such abstractions into numbers.

One Step at a Time

The other difficulty is that the computer comprehends not the atmosphere itself but a model of it—a model made of mathematical equations and functions that express physical laws and constraints intended to make the simulation more like the real atmosphere. The view is still a composite, not a continuous one. If the points are too far apart, the model loses coherence, like an enlarged newspaper photograph expanding into huge, meaningless dots. Set in motion, the computer begins to solve equations describing conditions for points—thousands of points—on several gridded, imaginary surfaces or layers. One layer represents the atmospheric boundary with the planet. The other layers are selected levels higher in the atmosphere. As the gigantic weather program is run, the computer generates its responses along one further dimension: time.

Atmospheric conditions are numerically described for each grid point on each surface, using the real-world data that comes in from stations around the globe. This provides a foundation for a subsequent response that moves the description forward one step in time. That becomes the basis for a second time step, which in turn becomes the basis for a third, and so on, into the future.

The model's physical appearance, if it can be said to have one, is vaguely reminiscent of some medieval cosmos—a tabernacle-shaped universe, perhaps. Until it is populated with mathematics and real observations the model is only a layered, gridded box. A typical model might use a three-dimensional coordinate system overlying a world map centered on the North Pole. Its horizontal grid system would be a mesh of squares forming some 10,000 grid points 31 miles (50 km) apart. If 10 layers are used, that comes to 30,000 grid points. Reality lives in the central portions of the model; along the edges weather sinks into numerical gibberish.

To the analog human mind, the atmospheric model is both simple and nightmarishly abstract. In the rushing unreality of these fragile, imaginary grids and layers, eddies may develop, slowing and finally destroying the deterministic path of prediction, driving the yes-no chatter into an unintelligible rant. Chaos tends to devour such predictive efforts. Gravity waves and other oscillations plague the models, shake them out of control—destroy them, as the mathematicians say. Worlds come and go, bloom and disappear, hurried from birth to maturity to death in minutes. Real life and death seem almost meaningless terms in this realm of hurrying electrons and imaginary weather.

Four global views created by the Cray X-MP supercomputer at the National Center for Atmospheric Research in Boulder, Colorado, show various levels of resolution for computer models of the atmosphere. NCAR's climate models use a grid (*top, near right*) on which points are separated by eight degrees, and a tighter, four-degree grid (*top, far right*) for weather research. A three-degree grid (*bottom, near right*) is the basis for NOAA's daily weather forecasts for the United States. A still-denser one-degree grid (*bottom, far right*) is used for computer modelers at the European Centre for Medium-Range Weather Forecasts.

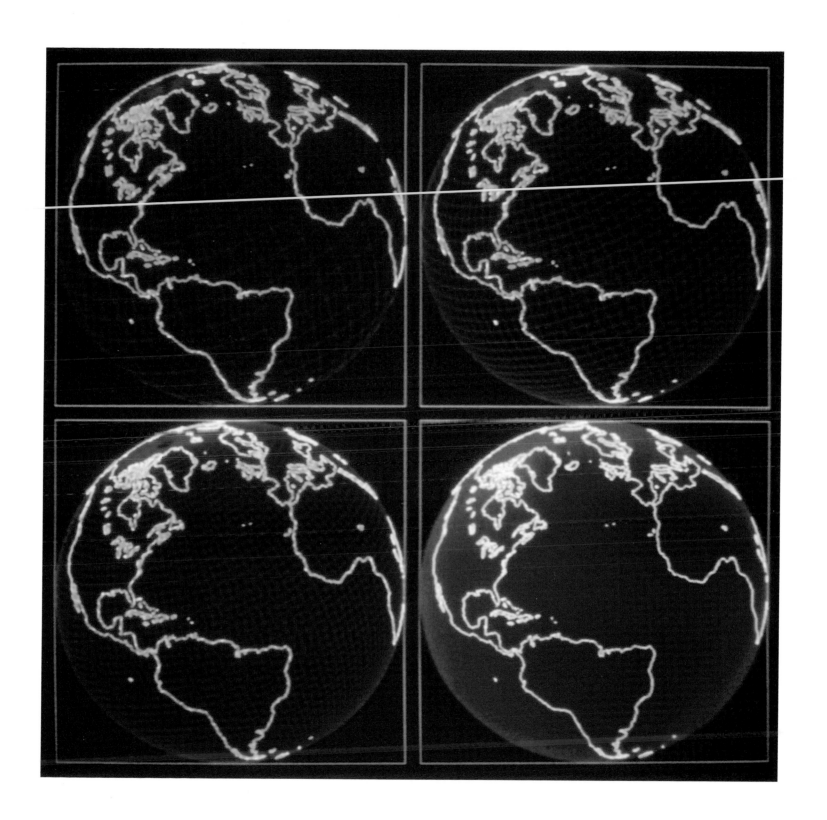

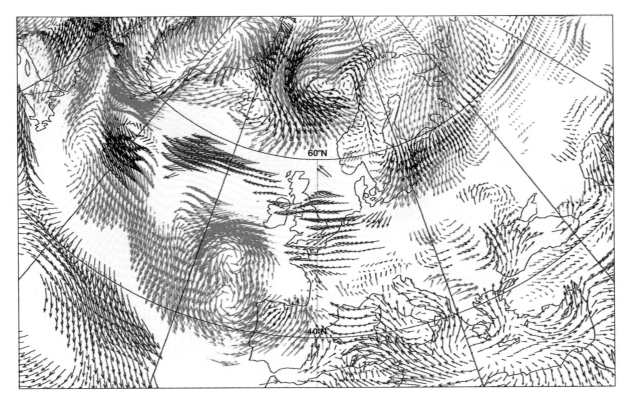

A computer analysis of wind fields over Europe shows the speed and direction of moving air about 100 feet (30 m) above the planet's surface at 12 A.M. Greenwich Time on May 13, 1994. Prepared by the European Centre for Medium-Range Weather Forecasts (ECMWF), the analysis uses colors from purple (above 10° C (50° F)) to cyan (below 4° C (39° F)) to indicate warmer or colder temperatures of air near the top of the boundary layer, about a mile (1,500 m) above the ground. Wind speeds are indicated by the lengths of arrows.

Prophetic Numbers

In fact, there is a powerful connection between this imaginary world and the actual realm of dangerous weather. The world's advanced weather services have reconstructed themselves around numerical prediction. Data flows in from all over the planet, but not to a human—it moves to a computer model and begins to take the atmosphere through its fluid dynamic paces. This predictive product is the backdrop on which weathercasters scan America's Midwest for potential tornadoes, where hydrologists in central England read future floods from heavy rainfall, where the hurricane and typhoon watchers of the world's tropical coastlines find their life-saving prophecies. These imaginary worlds tell futures to airline crews and crews afloat, to farmers and builders and a host of other specialized users of weather information. They tell us whether the roses should be burlapped, the air conditioner checked, the umbrella readied for the morning commute.

To the trained eye this comprehensive view is a tableau in which the unfamiliar, the anomaly, pops out—El Niño, for example, has emerged from this closely detailed view of the air and ocean. These human uses are all portals that link our lives to the alien world that floats in the circuitry of giant computers.

Nobody yet knows how far such prognostication can be pushed. Many scientists believe that deterministic numerical weather prediction can be extended reliably out to two weeks. Some experts think that the supposed determinism of the atmosphere turns very quickly into chaos and that there is little point in trying to predict chaos very far in advance. Others cling to the hope that ever-larger computers and more sophisticated mathematical models will make the atmospheric future as transparent as air itself.

A WORLDWIDE NETWORK

In the United States, laboratories operated by the National Oceanic and Atmospheric Administration and by a university

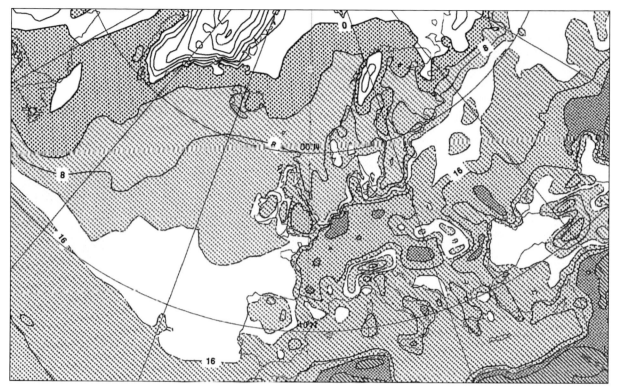

An ECMWF analysis depicts air temperatures, in degrees Celsius, at 12 A.M. Greenwich Time on May 13, 1994, virtually at ground level—about 6 feet (2 m) above the surface. Colors from purple to cyan are used within isotherms (contours of equal temperature) to indicate warmer or cooler temperatures.

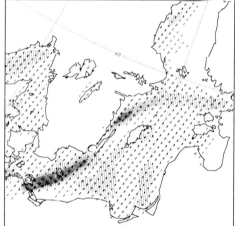

consortium that runs the National Center for Atmospheric Research lead the effort to mate numerical weather and the real thing more accurately over greater and greater intervals of time. But the world's most accomplished long-range forecasters are reputedly in Great Britain. At the British Meteorological Office at Bracknell, west of London, one of the world's most elaborate operational weather-forecasting models predicts weather by solving for a global array of grid points about 60 miles (100 km) apart over the entire surface of the planet in 19 horizontal layers stretching from the ground up to 22 miles (35 km) altitude. At the same time it celebrates the first hero of numerical weather prediction. When the Met Office model spins up on one of the two powerful supercomputers at Bracknell, it does so in what is called the Richardson Wing—named for the man who first believed that what is now done day in and day out at places like Bracknell, on computers located near Frankfurt, Washington, Moscow, and Melbourne, was possible.

HIRLAM—the European Centre's High-Resolution Limited Area Modeling—produces forecasts with astonishing detail. The HIRLAM forecast (*top right*) uses grid points separated by about 12 miles (20 km) to achieve such detail. The forecast shows cold air from the east forming over the Baltic Sea, with snow along the Swedish coast and the northern German border. At this high resolution, even the clouds forming over the small lakes in central Sweden and dissolving downwind of Gotland are predicted and appear on the corresponding satellite image (*bottom right*).

Aiding France's International Cooperation Centre for Agronomic Research for Development, ECMWF provided this analysis of low-level winds over the Mediterranean and northern Africa for mid-February 1993. The data was used not to forecast weather, but instead to predict the arrival of locusts in the Sahel and Magreb regions.

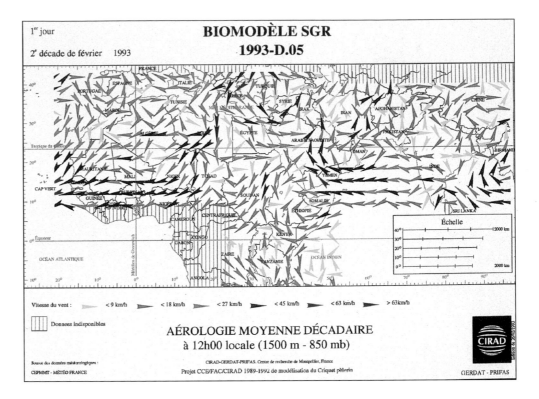

What is widely regarded among experts in the field as the best operational forecast in the world—"best" meaning the most accurate over the longest period of time—is prepared by a second facility located 11 miles (18 km) to the northwest of Bracknell, in Reading. Established in 1973 and now supported by 18 European states, the European Centre for Medium-Range Weather Forecasts employs a computer model of amazing complexity. Grid points 39 miles (62 km) apart cover the globe on 31 levels between the surface and 18 miles (29 km)—five layers are between the surface and 5,000 feet (1,500 m). Using data coming in from the real world, a supercomputer recalculates weather information—wind, humidity, temperature, and, at surface grid points, atmospheric pressure—every 15 minutes for each of the model's 128,800,900 grid points. Such numbers do not do the model justice, however. Also included in its mathematical world are factors such as terrain height, ground cover, precipitation, clouds, solar angle, surface roughness, incoming and outgoing radiation, evaporation, sensible and latent heat—among others. All told, more than 20 trillion computations go into each 10-day forecast issued by the Centre to Europe's national meteorological

services, which apply the forecast to their own shorter-fused predictions of regional weather.

Reading is also a center for research in numerical forecasting. Working with the weather services of its member nations, it is pioneering high-resolution modeling for Scandinavia, Spain, and France, using model grid points only 12 miles (19 km) apart. At the other end of the size spectrum, the supercomputer models the entire global atmosphere for university researchers. The beneficiaries of this more specialized work are obvious—offshore petroleum, agriculture, maritime commerce, aviation, and various other weather-sensitive industries. But there are less obvious ones, too. For example, the Centre modeled low-level wind, temperature, and humidity fields over the Mediterranean and Africa in 1992 and early 1993 for the French CIRAD—an international cooperative effort in agronomy research. But the ensuing prediction had little to do with weather—instead, it estimated the 10-day mean population of what those winds were expected to scatter over the Sahel and Magreb: locusts by the trillions.

TAKING THE ATMOSPHERIC MEASURE

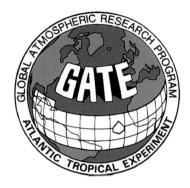

This instrumented DC-6 operated by the National Oceanic and Atmospheric Administration was one of 13 research aircraft contributed by the United States, Soviet Union, Britain, France, and other nations. The NOAA aircraft took data from near the air-sea boundary, sometimes flying just 50 feet (15 m) off the water—so low that the airplane's propeller wash left a wake.

Under the aegis of the Global Atmospheric Research Programme of the Geneva-based World Meteorological Organization—a technical agency of the United Nations—and the International Council of Scientific Unions in Paris, a series of ambitious international experiments have pieced together a broad mosaic of atmospheric closeups around the world. The first and grandest of these was staged in 1974: the Atlantic Tropical Experiment.

GATE, as the project was called, was the cooperative effort of 75 nations, which sent some 4,000 scientists to Dakar, Senegal, that summer, along with 38 research vessels, 13 instrumented weather research aircraft, and various automated air-sea sensors. The experiment effectively transformed a huge volume of atmosphere and ocean—a segment stretching from central Africa to South America and about 20 degrees of latitude across, reaching from 1 mile (1.8 km) beneath the ocean's surface to an altitude of 20 miles (36 km)—into a vast outdoor laboratory.

As weather systems were spawned by the meteorological incubator of equatorial Africa, aircraft and satellites would monitor their progress across the continent's hot surface and out into the deep atmospheric current over the Atlantic—a current that runs westward for some 20,000 miles (36,000 km), all the way to the Indian Ocean. These disturbances take the form of U-shaped

kinks or waves in the easterly winds and have long been associated with torrential rains and hurricanes. GATE discovered that heat does not merely flow into the tropical atmosphere from a warm sea—it moves on explosions of vertical motion, the storm systems of the easterly wave.

A few years later, that knowledge had become part of the equipment of hurricane forecasters. And GATE had paved the way for similar experiments probing the Indian Ocean monsoon, the winter weather systems of the Alps, and the way air-sea interactions in the tropical Pacific influence global weather.

Snapshots into Film

It would seem at this point that the atmosphere has little left to reveal. Satellite cameras watch its every move, balloon and satellite soundings monitor its burden of water and heat and its chemistry. Grand experiments using fleets of ships and aircraft have explored regions that had suffered from meteorological neglect: the tropical Atlantic, the equatorial Pacific, the Alps, the Great Lakes, the Indian Ocean, Africa, the empty spaces south of the Aleutians, the Atlantic nursery of New England's famed nor'easters. Automated weather stations pour their surface data into the torrent of information converging on computerized world weather centers around the planet. And elaborate computer models stand by to churn all that data into a prediction of weather to come—to set this enormous atmospheric snapshot into motion.

Even so, the atmosphere keeps a few secrets. What happens down inside those towering cumulonimbus anvils? What do the wind and weather do between frames of this moving picture of the atmosphere? Even being able to see so much, meteorologists still sense that they see too little. Too much is still invisible, too much still concealed. If one believes in the determinism of the atmosphere, one has to believe that perfect vision will lead to perfect forecasts, especially in the middle range of sizes—the regional, thunderstorm size—where things happen fast and where computer models blur what are actually sharp dynamic distinctions.

MEASURING CHANGES

As it turns out, there is a way to see all this and more. It has its roots in a discovery made in 1842 by Christian Doppler, an Austrian mathematician with little interest in the atmosphere. He had observed that a sound changed pitch, or frequency, depending upon whether the sound's source was approaching or receding. Since sound travels in waves rippling through the air, Doppler concluded that the shift in frequency was caused by relative motion between the source and the receiver. The familiar example is a train whistle. As the train approaches the listener, sound waves from its whistle are shortened, causing the sound to rise in frequency and pitch; as the train recedes,

Austrian mathematician Christian Johann Doppler discovered in 1842 that the motion of a source and an observer relative to each other produces a shift in the frequency of electromagnetic and sound waves. Known as the *Doppler effect*, it has been applied to measuring the velocity of everything from highway traffic to distant galaxies. In meteorology, the Doppler effect has rendered visible the formerly invisible movement of raindrops and other particles inside clouds.

the sound waves are stretched, decreasing the pitch and frequency. While light waves are not the same as sound vibrations, Doppler thought they must behave similarly, and said so in a work that spoke to his real interest in the subject: *Concerning the Coloured Light of Double Stars.*

The *Doppler effect*—the shift of a signal's frequency, or wavelength, caused by the relative motion between the source and the listener—has since been used to define our universe. The elongated waves of light from distant stars, with spectra

A Doppler radar image profiles the dynamic interior of a super-cell thunderstorm in Franklin County, Pennsylvania, in May 1994. Colors ranging from yellow to red show windborne droplets moving away from the radar antenna at Sterling, Virginia; yellow to dark blue show movement toward the radar. Where contrasting colors are paired, the radar shows a rotary circulation.

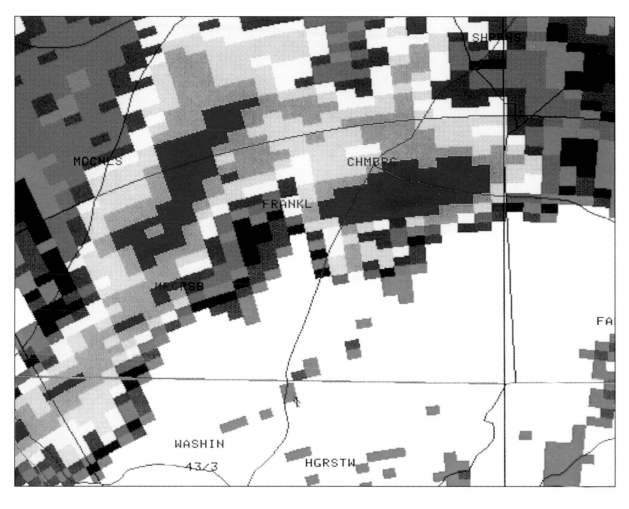

Doppler shifted toward red, indicate that the universe is expanding, most objects in it flying away from most other objects. Written on the photographic records of light spectra from the stars and galaxies, this red shift tells astronomers that the universe is about 15 billion years old; it also creates such mysteries as *quasars*, the impossibly brilliant points of light that may be blinking at us from the brink of time.

Finding the Doppler shift in the spectra of stars and galaxies is relatively simple if one has the huge telescopes, delicate spectrographic instruments, and endless patience to do it. If meteorologists coveted a measuring device as straightforward as the red shift, they were quiet about it—you could not apply it to phenomena that were changing faster than your measurements could be made. Besides, the really interesting motions were either inside clouds or invisible in clear air.

In the 1960s, however, it became clear that the phenomenon noted by Christian Doppler might have a meteorological application after all. When a radar beam probes a cloud, its echo is Doppler shifted by the motion of targets—water

droplets, ice crystals—in the cloud. A properly programmed computer could convert those shifts into a display that showed how fast the particles were moving relative to the radar. Storm researchers at a federal laboratory in Oklahoma eventually developed huge radars capable of reaching into severe storms and pulling out a digital display of the rotational wind shear around a birthing tornado, still hidden from view inside the storm cloud. Put aboard research aircraft, Doppler radars could peer at the powerful winds and torrential rains imbedded in the cylinder of a hurricane's eyewall. Indeed, Doppler radars are even found today at television stations, especially those in Tornado Alley, where in spring and summer the weather is the vital news of the day.

Reinventing Meteorology

In Boulder, Colorado, during the 1970s, a small cadre of government scientists who had spent their careers studying the propagation of radio waves put their experience—and Christian Doppler's discovery—to work on what seemed at first to be an impossible task. Using beams of radio energy, sound waves, and laser light, along with powerful computers programmed to read the complex shower of reflected echoes, they set about developing a broad range of remote sensors with which to search out the secret movements of the air. Their search turned out to be a 20-year odyssey of continuous technical innovation.

Without being handsomely funded, the team fielded a variety of lasers, radars, and atmospheric sonars mounted in military surplus trailers and radar dishes—aging devices that, gathered in one place, evoked the improvised, hay-wired vehicles in a postapocalyptic science-fiction film. But what the scientists were doing with this odd armada was unprecedented: they were developing real-time spectroscopy—the ability to observe the Doppler shift where and as it occurred. *Lidar*, the laser counterpart of radar, was adept at seeing the invisible motions of the air itself and its burden of suspended microscopic solids, or *aerosols*. Acoustic sounders could profile the vertical air column the way sonar probes the sea, sending back a cutaway of dense and less dense layers of air—a visual corollary of density that is read as air temperature. Microwave radars were brought into service

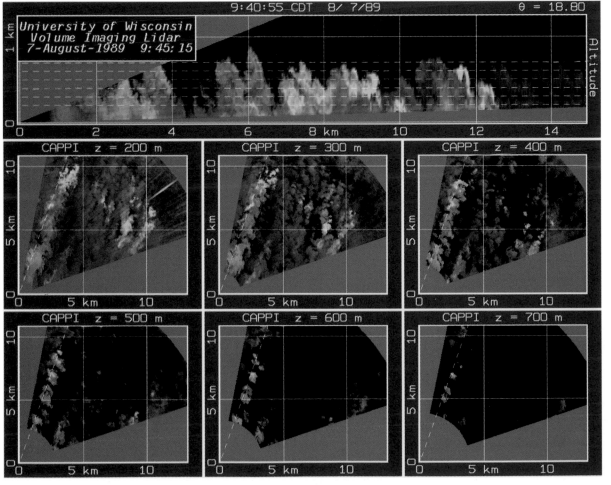

Invisible to radar or the human eye until its cargo of water vapor condenses into clouds, these rising castles of clear, sun-heated air (*top*) were seen by the University of Wisconsin's volume-imaging lidar—a device that operates on the echo-location principle of radar, but uses a beam of laser light instead of a radio signal. The lidar detects microscopic solid particles, or aerosols, which backscatter laser light. The top image is a single range-height scan by the lidar showing clear-air convection to an altitude of about 0.5 mile (1 km) and 9 miles (14 km) from the lidar; dashed lines denote the six pie-shaped cross-sections at left.

alongside their longer-wavelength cousins to discern the more detailed velocities of very small droplets in a cloud.

What these new devices promised was to make the invisible atmosphere continuously visible as events there unfolded. Instead of a radiosonde sounding two or three times a day, the vertical column of the local atmosphere could be sounded remotely at intervals of minutes. The harvest of weather data around the world would not ebb and flow with its traditional rhythms, in which observations are taken every few hours and passed to a central office for computation—it would become a river of information that brought the atmosphere to vivid, continuous life. It would make the simulations of computers virtually as detailed as the atmosphere itself. From the

standpoint of local forecast offices, the new tools meant a continuous, detailed view of their immediate domain—a system that was quicker than such fast-breaking trouble as a mountain flash flood or a tornadic thunderstorm.

During the 1990s, the fruits of this research began entering operational service. The men and women in Boulder had not just brought new techniques on line—they had reinvented meteorological observation.

Coincidentally, they had reinvented the meteorologist as well. As remote-sensing systems called *profilers* mark the arrival of the future, the steadfast old balloon may become a relic of the past. The meteorologists of the 21st century may not even know how to inflate and launch a weather balloon, and they will certainly not wish to be called balloon-blowers. Profilers, perhaps, or magicians.

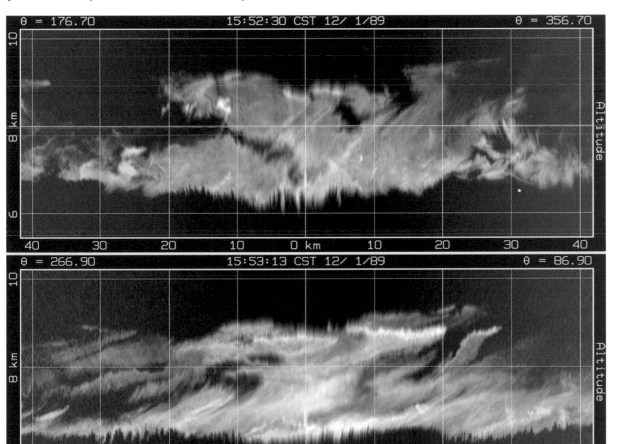

The fast-scanning University of Wisconsin lidar permits cross-sections of broad, flat cirrus clouds, which are effective tracers of upper-level air movement over a large area. This image represents the cloud as partially transparent and shows its fine structure, including vertical showers of ice crystals from the base. It is the product of successive lidar scans, integrated by a computer into a continuous, three-dimensional depiction of cirrus cloud structure from about 4 miles (6 km) to 6 miles (9 km) above the Earth, and 24 miles (40 km) on either side of the lidar.

Prospero's Magic

Not everyone finds the ability to see the atmosphere continuously and in detail, and to predict its slide toward chaos with fair accuracy a week or two in advance, to be magical enough. Some insist on taking a hand, or trying to, either as entrepreneurs or as scientists. Indeed, the idea of controlling atmospheric processes touches some Faustian nerve. Being the least possible of things, grasping the atmospheric levers is tantamount to magic.

> I have bedimm'd
> The noontide sun, call'd forth the mutinous winds,
> And 'twixt the green sea and the azur'd vault
> Set roaring war; to the dread rattling thunder
> Have I given fire, and rifted Jove's stout oak
> With his own bolt…

That is Prospero, Shakespeare's great magician in *The Tempest*, presenting his impressive credentials. In his vast repertoire of dark powers, one proves omnipotence: the power to regulate the atmosphere can be nothing less than magic.

RAINMAKERS…

In the technical world, tinkering with the atmosphere is called *weather modification*. But in the world at large, weather modifiers tend to be grouped generically neither as scientists nor magicians, but under the faintly pejorative heading of "rainmaker." The word evokes charlatans trouping across an arid plain, often towing some outlandish apparatus capable of generating sparks, or steam, or sound—anything, in fact, but rain. Starbuck, the title character in N. Richard Nash's 1955 play *The Rainmaker,* is just what the word suggests.

"I get out my big wheel and my rolling drum and my yella hat with the three little feathers in it!" he explains to skeptical clients.

I look up at the sky and I say: 'Cumulus!' I say: 'Cumulo-nimbus! Nimbulo-cumulus!' And pretty soon way up there—there's a teeny little cloud the size of a mare's tail—and then over there—there's another cloud lookin' like a white-washed chicken house! And then I look up and all of a sudden there's a herd of white buffalo stampedin' across the sky! And then, sister-of-all-good-people, down comes the rain!

Meteorologists with a hankering to modify the weather have always known that nature would require more than a rolling drum and yellow hat to produce rain. If the sky was clear of clouds, it was not going to rain, no matter what people did on the ground. But it seemed to many that clouds that were already charged with water but not quite ready to release their moisture as rain or snow or hail might be coaxed into releasing a little bit more or a little bit less.

The idea that clouds could be made to precipitate was discovered accidentally in 1946 by Vincent Schaefer, a scientist at the General Electric Company in Schenectady, New York. Adding dry ice (frozen carbon dioxide) to a deep-freeze full of supercooled fog quickly caused the droplets to freeze and fall as snow. Silver iodide, whose crystalline structure fosters the freezing of supercooled water, produced a similar effect. Both substances triggered freezing, the dry ice by lowering the temperature enough for supercooled water to freeze without a nucleus, silver iodide by providing a nucleus for supercooled water to freeze on. In no time at all researchers were flying above New England's winter stratus clouds, carving holes in the cloud deck with salvos of silver iodide—they even carved a big *GE* in the clouds. Seeding became a tool for clearing cold fog off airport runways. To many it looked like the beginning of a new age of human manipulation of the weather. Seeding might reduce the worst winds in hurricanes or augment snowpack in mountain areas or suppress crop-damaging hail. The military also had a sizable interest: the weather—what a weapon!

…AND CLOUD-SEEDERS

The arid American Midwest quickly attracted a small legion of rainmakers, some of them airborne Starbucks trying to extract a living from the hopes of stricken farmers, some of them serious, well-intended entrepreneurs. Seeding clouds, they argued, would cause that leftover supercooled water to freeze,

A wing-mounted burner on this Twin Comanche spews a smoke of silver iodide into the updrafts feeding potential hailclouds over the North Dakota plains. One of the few weather-modification projects in North America, this work, paid for by farmers, is intended to make the clouds produce rain instead of crop-damaging hail.

triggering or at the very least reinforcing the rainmaking process. By tapping the cloud's reservoir of water, seeding might also short-circuit the hail-formation process inside the cloud, causing thunderstorms that might have dropped destructively large hailstones to produce small stones or even rain instead. In the United States, government scientists toyed with seeding hurricanes, hoping to use one of the effects of seeding—the release of latent heat as supercooled water was induced to freeze—to cause disorganization within the huge storms. Scientists seeded winter cloud decks flowing over Lake Erie, trying to make them drop their burden over the lake instead of burying Buffalo and other downwind cities in deep snow. Others took seeding to tropical cumuli, reasoning that rainfall would be enhanced if the clouds were made to grow and converge through seeding—again, by the triggered

release of latent heat. Secret missions over Vietnam added silver iodide smoke from canisters slung under the wings of Phantom jets in the hope that the stimulated tropical cumuli would rain the jungle trails into lakes.

Most of these attempts produced tantalizing results. Hurricane winds in one storm dropped about 20 percent after seeding, and other seeded hurricanes seemed to falter briefly before revving back up to full strength. The Russians reported that firing antiaircraft shells bearing silver iodide into storm clouds was reducing hail by 60 to 90 percent. A cloud-seeding program in North Dakota that was funded by farmers seemed to be reducing crop damage that was caused by hail. Entrepreneurs claimed success in wringing rain from summer cumulus clouds over the Midwest. In the high Rockies, seeding appeared to increase snowfall—and the resulting snowpack, a crucial water resource—by some 18 percent. Lake Erie lake-effect clouds obligingly dumped their snow into the water after seeding. In Florida seeding cumulus clouds was reliably accompanied by increased rainfall. In Israel seeded clouds over the Sea of Galilee watershed yielded 20 percent more rain.

Observing radar images of growing cumuli targeted by the North Dakota hail suppression project, a meteorologist on the ground guides cloud-seeding airplanes toward their quarry.

Despite such signs of success, the human signal—the clear trace of what seeding, not nature, had done—remained obscured by the chaotic complexity of the experimental subject and the inherent messiness of the natural laboratory. The atmosphere's variability successfully masked any such small changes that seeding might have introduced. Hurricanes were seen to rev up and down naturally just as much as they had when seeded. Commercial rainmakers were diminishing, not increasing, the rain that was falling from Missouri clouds. Increased snowfall occurred in years when snowfall increased everywhere. Enhanced rainfall in tropical cumuli coincided with rainier days in general. Researchers in North America and in Switzerland were unable to verify Russian claims for hail suppression.

The problem was that the effect of seeding could not be verified absolutely—it had to be indicated statistically by a consistent pattern of cause and effect in a large sample of experiments. Few of the projects were able to provide a sample large enough to support that statistical case. In fact, only the Israeli project was able to demonstrate a statistically real increase in rainfall from seeded clouds.

What the statisticians began, the government money people finished; with no success in sight, public funds dried up with Dust Bowl alacrity. In the United States of the 1990s, only the farmers of North Dakota were paying to have cumulus clouds seeded every summer to suppress damaging hail. They were the sole believers, and even their support, as one cloud-seeder put it, was soluble in rainwater.

The weather modification business is no place for anyone but believers—there is no accommodation for vaporous agnostics and doubting statisticians. Spending all those hours bucking through budding thunderheads and hurricanes adds layers of consciousness to the meteorological mind—some researchers develop almost a sixth sense about randomized "blind" experiments, for example. Many of the scientists who labored to change weather still believe that what they sensed, what they thought they saw, was real—that their seeding had really done what they had hoped: killed winds, increased precipitation, suppressed hail.

Most governments have abandoned weather modification research, and some of the most talented practitioners have followed their hearts. You encounter them around the world now, in Israel and Morocco and tropical Asia, running cloud-seeding operations of their own for local clients. They have become what they once shunned: rainmakers. But there are important differences between them and Starbuck—they understand the atmosphere, and they may be the real thing.

The Atmospheric China Shop

Where weather is concerned, the human hand has demonstrated its greatest potency where it has slipped. It inadvertently changes the quality and clarity of air, diverts its thermal patterns, alters its chemistry, all with the surgical precision of the proverbial china-shop bull. Like the bull's, our destructive activity has no malice in it—it arises from ignorance of our surroundings. But what this ignorance of ours does to the atmosphere unintentionally may exceed the wildest imaginings of any fictional magician.

No one doubts that the human hand has fallen heavily upon the natural atmosphere from time to time. One need only listen to Charles Dickens open *Bleak House* with that most pervasive form of condensation, the legendary pea-soup London fog:

Fog everywhere. Fog up the river, where it flows among green aits and meadows; fog down the river, where it rolls defiled among the tiers of shipping, and the waterside pollutions of a great (and dirty) city. Fog on the Essex marshes, fog on the Kentish heights. Fog creeping into the cabooses of collier-brigs; fog lying out on the yards, and hovering in the rigging of great ships; fog drooping on the gunwales of barges and small boats. Fog in the eyes and throats of ancient Greenwich pensioners, wheezing by the firesides of their wards; fog in the stem and bowl of the afternoon pipe of the wrathful skipper, down in his close cabin; fog cruelly pinching the toes and fingers of his shivering little 'prentice boy on deck. Chance people on the bridges peeping over the parapets into a nether sky of fog, with fog all round them, as if they were up in a balloon, and hanging in the misty clouds.

Such foggy days in London-town are quite rare today and have been for decades. They were less something that crept in from the sea than the result of inadvertent seeding of the moisture-laden English skies—seeding with ash from the smoky coal with which the British formerly made themselves comfortably warm and industrialized. The old black fog of London was actually legislated out of existence after World War II, when a smokeless coal was forced into common use.

Fog engulfs downtown London on a typical winter day in January 1947. About this time, England began to enact pollution control laws that have greatly reduced the amount of fog the city sees now.

Now the English sky is blue, when one can see it, and the fogs that swirl now in those narrow old streets are gray, penetrable, and temporary.

SMOKE AND SMOG

Not every city has been so lucky. The gathering of pollutants from people and traffic in the thin, high-altitude air over Mexico City is legend, as is the ochre cloud that fills the Los Angeles basin for days on end and drifts out through notches in the coastal ranges to tinge the clear blue skies over Nevada

A Belleglade, Florida, sugar mill belches smoke into the tropical sky—and evokes the difficult choices to be made between jobs and environmental quality.

and Arizona. We look with apprehension at the annual dry-season rite of rain forest burning in Bolivia and Brazil, when smoke obscures the sky with the ashes of once stately jungle trees. Visitors to the Grand Canyon often note a faint haze muting the magnificent colors of the canyon's rocks—haze that comes sometimes from Los Angeles and the stacks of huge coal-burning power plants around Four Corners, where Arizona, New Mexico, Colorado, and Utah meet. Industrialization in the Third World and in the teeming nations of Asia has produced huge swatches of polluted atmosphere. The collapse of communism in Europe is commemorated by a chemical pall that will not soon go away.

Some of this is curable. After a rain the rinsed sky over Los Angeles still glows as it did in the 1930s, reminding the visitor why so many people live there in the first place. The wet season cleanses the tropical skies of rain forest ash. It may be that in time these obvious sinks for civilization's exhaust products will be cleaned up, as the sky above London has been. Regulating the emission of various sulfur compounds has already begun to ease the problem of acid rain in North

A bronze horse in St. Marks Basilica in Venice exhibits green discolorations caused by acid rain—a corrosive brew of water and sulfuric and nitric acids from automobile exhausts, industry, and such natural sources as volcanoes and forest fires.

America and can no doubt do the same for eastern Europe and the industrial pockets of Asia. Obvious pollution offers an equation, after all, in which eliminating the cause makes the problem go away.

The sky above this patch of Brazilian rain forest fills with smoke during the 1990 dry season, a seasonal return to the traditional methods of slash and burn used to bring the modern world to the ancient ecosystem of the tropical forest. Many observers believe that humanity will pay dearly for the destruction of rain forests by reducing species diversity and by adding greenhouse gases such as carbon dioxide to the atmosphere, possibly creating an intolerably warmer planet.

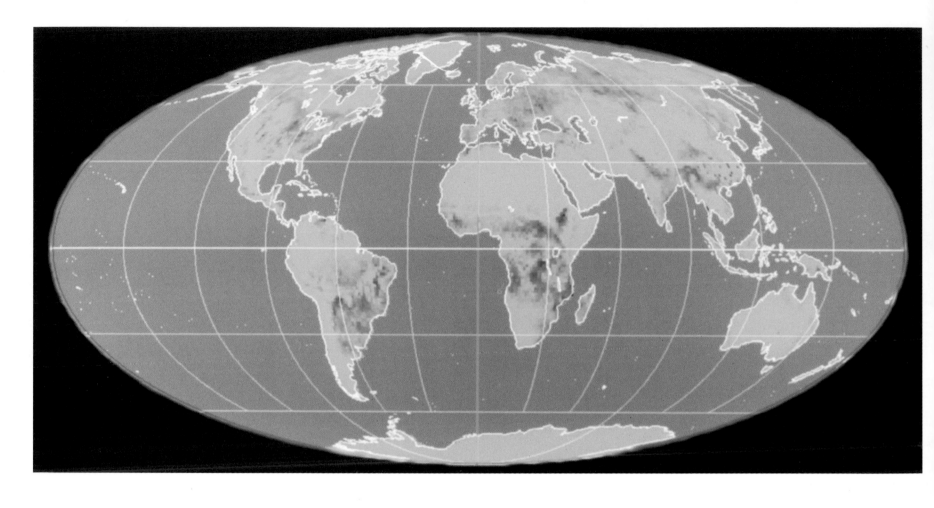

The Sweltering Sky

Most people who worry about what humans are doing to the atmosphere fret less about urban pollution, which appears to be straightforwardly a matter of what goes in and what comes out of the air, than about damage on the global scale, which is linked to two structural and chemical peculiarities of the atmosphere. One of these is the curious fact that air everywhere is laced with a whiff of carbon dioxide—a tenth to a hundredth of one percent; the other is a relatively dense, but still very thin, stratum of triatomic oxygen, or *ozone*, in the stratosphere. Both are crucial to the way the planet handles solar radiation and both have come into the general consciousness as major problems.

The Earth seems to breathe in this computer-generated rendering by NASA of the planet during a typical June. Green areas denote the uptake, or fixing, of carbon by plants; red areas show the release of carbon dioxide into the atmosphere from the microbial decomposition of plant matter in the soil. Because carbon dioxide causes the lower atmosphere to retain heat—the so-called greenhouse effect that makes the Earth habitable—a 10-percent carbon dioxide increase over the past century is seen by some as the harbinger of global warming.

Solar radiation not reflected back into space reaches the Earth's surface unimpeded—incoming radiation finds the atmosphere nearly transparent—and is absorbed by air, water, rocks, soil, and everything that does not reflect it. Absorbed, it becomes heat that would eventually be reradiated back into space but for the presence of carbon dioxide, which absorbs infrared radiation. By trapping outgoing infrared, the radiation of heat energy, carbon dioxide—aided by such other infrared absorbers as methane and water vapor—keeps the planet's surface tolerably warm. Although carbon dioxide is a selective filter, not merely a pane of glass, this carefully balanced process is called the *greenhouse effect*—apt, perhaps, because the life it sustains would perish outside its protection.

In a world without people the concentration of carbon dioxide would wax and wane seasonally, diminishing in spring when plants revive and begin taking up carbon from the air for photosynthesis. On average, global concentrations would be about 275 parts per million, the amount of carbon dioxide estimated to have been in the atmosphere at the beginning of the 19th century's Industrial Revolution. As early as 1896, Swedish chemist Svante Arrhenius noted that increased concentrations of carbon dioxide should be accompanied by rising temperatures in the lower atmosphere. Doubling the concentration, he estimated, would raise global temperatures by about 9 Fahrenheit degrees (5 Celsius degrees). During the 1930s scientists discerned a slight warming trend over a 60-year period and thought that it might be traceable to the rising use of fossil fuels, combustion of which exhausts carbon dioxide waste into the atmosphere.

CO₂ WATCH

It was not until the 1950s that Charles David Keeling, aided by researchers in the American weather service, began keeping a close watch on atmospheric CO_2. Following preliminary measurements in the pristine Antarctic environment, Keeling began a long-term study from an observatory 11,000 feet (3,300 m) up the flank of Hawaii's Mauna Loa, which juts into the clean air flowing eastward over the Pacific. Measurements made in 1958 put carbon dioxide at 315 parts per million,

A researcher at Scripps Institute of Oceanography in San Diego, California, works at a carbon dioxide extraction rack, where the trace gas is frozen or pumped out of air samples collected at various locations and altitudes around the world and sent to Scripps in spherical flasks for analysis.

a 14-percent rise over the pre–Industrial Revolution concentration. Only 30 years later it had increased another 11 percent, to 350 parts per million. These measurements suggested that human activity was changing the chemistry of the atmosphere and that the rate of change was also increasing.

Carbon dioxide was not the problem. Its role as a greenhouse gas was. Too much carbon dioxide meant a warmer Earth and dire consequences. Some observers pointed with alarm to the possibility that the polar ice caps could melt, raising sea level some tens of feet. Some nodded toward Venus, where a runaway greenhouse effect has created an 800° F (425° C) sauna. There were indications of a rise in methane in the terrestrial atmosphere, added mainly from such odd places as tropical termite colonies, organic decomposition, and the intestines of cattle. Nitrous oxides, which are more efficient than carbon dioxide as infrared absorbers, were contributed by the increased combustion of nitrogen-based fuels. Industrial compounds called *chlorofluorocarbons* absorb thousands of times more infrared per molecule than carbon dioxide and for a time were poured into the atmosphere. And *ozone,* an infrared-absorbing pollutant created by interactions of sunlight and other pollutants, was also on the increase.

Clearly, people were doing something ghastly to the atmospheric greenhouse. Indeed, many think that the human signal here is as clear as it is in the exhaust-choked air of Los Angeles or Tokyo or the smoky dry-season sky of Brazil. But it is not. As with deliberate weather modification, our inadvertent alterations of the atmosphere leave a very faint, ambiguous trail. Only half the carbon dioxide generated by humanity and nature finds its way into the atmosphere. No one knows where the other half goes, although it is probably taken up by the sea. As carbon dioxide increases, will the ocean take up more? No one knows. Moreover, the presumed effect—a steady increase in global temperatures—has not been verified. Although a slight increase has been recorded, the record is not long enough to show a link with an intensified greenhouse effect. The atmosphere varies so widely over so many scales of time and space that any existing record could be just an anomalous detail. While the planet is littered with literal smoking guns, no one can prove there has been a crime.

Cracks in the Shield

Whether the Earth grows warmer or colder may be irrelevant, in the view of some observers, to people living under a lethal barrage of unfiltered solar ultraviolet radiation. They refer to the destruction of what has come to be known as the *ozone layer,* an ultraviolet-absorbing shield of this highly active form of oxygen in the high stratosphere. In fact, the so-called layer is a thin smoke of ozone, reckoned in a few parts per million, drifting on the high-level winds of an atmosphere about as dense as the near-vacuum covering Mars. Most of this ozone is created about 150,000 feet (45,000 m) above the tropics by incoming ultraviolet radiation in the 0.29- to 0.32-micrometer range out of oxygen molecules, which split into atoms and recombine as ozone. The average lifetime of an ozone molecule in this cradle is a matter of minutes. But some ozone sinks to lower levels, where it is protected from incoming radiation, and may endure for years, wafted across the globe by stratospheric winds.

In the early 1970s atmospheric chemists became excited about a chemical that would permit them to trace mixing between the troposphere and stratosphere. The substance was a family of industrial molecules called chlorofluorocarbons, designed to be chemically inert—they reacted with nothing, which made them perfect as refrigerants, cleaners, and foam blowers. Because they were inert, they would slowly migrate from the lower atmosphere into the stratosphere and help researchers trace the subtle interchange between those atmospheric layers.

By 1974, however, it had become apparent that this perfect tracer had a down side. When it rose into the stratosphere above the protective screen of ozone, it was ripped apart by the same ultraviolet radiation that ozone absorbed. And the sundered chlorofluorocarbon molecule would release atoms of one of ozone's myriad chemical enemies—chlorine—into the stratosphere. All this was just theory until scientists began sampling the stratosphere directly with balloons and instrumented aircraft. Sure enough, chlorofluorocarbons were about constant all the way to the midstratosphere, where they fell off sharply—presumably destroyed by solar ultraviolet. Further measurements found chlorine in large quantities in the stratosphere—strong circumstantial evidence that the theory was correct. But, for a time at least, there seemed to be no diminution of the amount of ozone in the global stratosphere.

PUZZLING EVIDENCE

In 1985 British scientists in Antarctica reported what has since come into the language as an *ozone hole*—a continent-sized area over their station in which as much as 50 percent of the stratospheric ozone was missing. Further studies suggested that the depletion had been caused by chlorine, and the presumption was that the chlorine had come from fragmented chlorofluorocarbon molecules. The ensuing alarm led to agreement among 24 nations meeting in Montreal in 1987 to phase out production of chlorofluorocarbons. In 1990 they agreed to cease production and use by 2000. Incredibly, the scientists had convinced industry that stratospheric ozone was at such risk, and the consequences of ozone depletion were so dire, that this multibillion-dollar adjustment was in order.

Perhaps it was. But the devastating barrage of ultraviolet radiation (UV) that was supposed to accompany ozone depletion has not yet been discerned, and little support has gone into measuring it. Most of the evidence for increased UV has been anecdotal: Patagonian sheep with cataracts, for example.

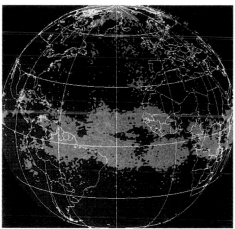

The March 1986 eruption of Mount Augustine (*left*) spews ash and sulfur compounds into the atmosphere above Alaska's Cook Inlet—and into the high-altitude wind belts that girdle the planet. A false-color image (*above*) produced by NASA from the Total Ozone Mapping Spectrometer aboard the Nimbus satellite shows how volcanic effluent from the 1991 Mount Pinatubo eruption spreads across the world.

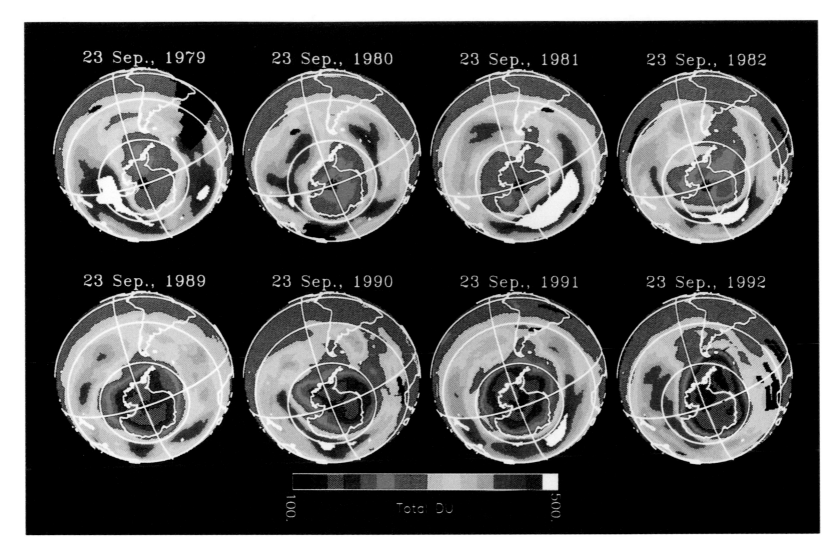

A continent-sized dearth of stratospheric ozone—an ozone hole—opens over Antarctica in this sequence of images based on sensings from Nimbus 7. Showing ozone between the satellite and Earth for eight years on September 23—the beginning of the Austral spring—the images indicate a steady trend toward less and less ozone over the pole. Warm colors indicate higher ozone concentrations, cool colors, lower concentrations. The observed depletion appears to be caused by chlorine freed in the stratosphere when inert industrial compounds called *chlorofluorocarbons* are broken up by solar ultraviolet radiation.

The extinction of some frog species has been attributed to a thinning of the ozone shield, although some of the vanished species live in the deep rain forest where sunlight, let alone the easily blocked ultraviolet, seldom penetrates. Some biological studies indicate, with huge uncertainties, a deleterious effect on plankton in the ocean off Antarctica. The effect of increased ultraviolet on trees and plants seems negative, although many adapt quickly to such environmental changes. The picture has been further complicated by a rash of large volcanic explosions, whose debris may accelerate the ozone-destroying activities of chlorine already in the atmosphere.

Scientists working on such complex problems can be as testy about competing theories as they can be clamorous in raising the alarms that stimulate, among other things, the flow of money for additional research. Still, there is a good deal of dissent. While most scientists accept that the depletion of stratospheric ozone seen over the Antarctic was caused by chlorine from chlorofluorocarbons, some believe that something like the Antarctic ozone hole would have occurred on a planet where there were neither people nor a chemical industry. These heretics point to powerful correlations between the blooming and fading of the El Niño, for example, and the rise

Probing the polar darkness, scientists prepare to launch chemical-sensing instruments with a pair of large, high-altitude research balloons from a site near Kiruna, Sweden, in January 1986. Such probes of the Arctic stratosphere looked for—but did not find—northern counterparts to the ozone "hole" detected over the Antarctic, although ozone-destroying chlorine was found to be abnormally abundant.

and fall of ozone over Antarctica. Indeed, a global decrease in ozone amounting to several percentage points that began in the late 1970s may very well be linked to contemporary changes in wind patterns in the Southern Hemisphere.

A Mystery Forever

Global warming there may be, and perhaps the thinning ozone will admit an intolerable blast of ultraviolet radiation after all. Certainly there are other human signals still to be decoded. But such questions are like the atmosphere in which their answers must be found: everything connects to everything else. Ozone is not just a shield against radiation—it is a greenhouse gas, part of the global warming puzzle, and an urban pollutant causing great concern. The burning of rain forests may add carbon dioxide enough to melt the polar ice caps and destroy species; but it also, some researchers say, releases bromines into the atmosphere that eventually attack stratospheric ozone, suggesting a kind of cosmic punishment for burning down the rain forests. Doubled carbon dioxide may intoxicate plants into runaway growth and oxygen production—unless they are retarded by the radiation let in by a thinned ozone layer. No one knows where humanity ends and the atmosphere begins, but here is an extreme hypothesis: suppose we are adding carbon dioxide to the atmosphere because, somewhere down in our vestigial memories, we sense the coming of another ice age and need to make our planet warmer. No one knows.

In the face of all this interconnected complexity, we may never fully comprehend what our actions mean to the ocean of air or find a reliable way to change it or confidently predict what it is going to do a week, a season, or a year into the future. The only certainty we have is that the sky will not fall; that, for as long as the planet has enough gravity to hold onto it and the Sun does not explode and burn it all away, the atmosphere will stay in place. It will also continue to ignore us as it grandly whirls and eddies, flows and arcs through its unending, magnificent exhibitions of chaos. We can only watch. But watch we should. ☁

Like warring giants standing on thick pedestals of rain, thunderstorms bring sweet rain and relief from the African sun above the Loita Hills of Kenya.

TOOLS OF THE
METEOROLOGICAL
TRADE

I n trying to predict what the atmosphere will do, meteorologists around the world begin with a detailed global view of the entire atmosphere, probed by sensors on satellites, ships, aircraft, balloons, and ground-based remote sensing devices. The forecaster's task is to use that data to predict local and regional weather. This may be the straight-forwardly seasonal flow of the monsoon, bringing weather charged with Indian Ocean moisture to the arid Indian subcontinent and western plains of Africa, or the vast cold fogs that shut down commercial aviation over much of western Europe. In North Africa forecasters look toward the region's complement of dessicating winds and in China the seemingly endless rains that repeatedly flood the vast, crowded nation.

Since the beginning of meteorology, the signals of weather to come have been converted into coded forms. Cloud types, grouped into low, middle, high, and vertical, are part of the data taken at each of thousands of weather stations at frequent intervals. These symbols, taken together, comprise an artifact that is universally familiar to television viewers today: a map showing the large patterns of pressure at the surface, over-lying a mosaic of weather data from individual stations.

On the pages that follow, a sequence of atmospheric events is illus-trated by a dictionary of meteorological symbols, and a demonstration—in March 1993's "Storm of the Century"—of how weather moves across a weather map. Such displays may represent the past, however. Modern meteorology is turning to the exotic products of sensors and computers to reproduce and forecast atmospheric behavior. Accordingly, beyond the weather maps, this section presents some of the research products that will evolve into the highly rendered weather maps of the new century.

Meteorology's Universal Shorthand

Since the early days of meteorology, the weather has been recorded on maps, with data from each meteorological station written in the appropriate location on the chart. This was once a simple matter of jotting down atmospheric pressure, temperature, relative humidity, surface winds, and the like, received from relatively small networks. But nowadays, in the meteorological services of most countries, the number of stations has multiplied explosively—there are hundreds on any continent today—and the data itself has expanded for added detail. Now, at intervals of a few hours, the thousands of weather stations around the globe spew out their latest summary of conditions—temperature, humidity, dewpoint, cloud cover,

FRONTS

Fronts are shown on surface weather maps by the symbols below. (Arrows—not shown on maps—indicate direction of motion of front.)

 Cold front (surface)

 Warm front (surface)

 Occluded front (surface)

 Stationary front (surface)

 Warm front (aloft)

 Cold front (aloft)

AIR PRESSURE TENDENCY

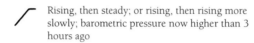 Rising, then falling; same as or higher than 3 hours ago

Rising, then steady; or rising, then rising more slowly; barometric pressure now higher than 3 hours ago

Rising steadily, or unsteadily; barometric pressure now higher than 3 hours ago

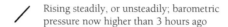 Falling or steady, then rising; or rising, then rising more rapidly; barometric pressure now higher than 3 hours ago

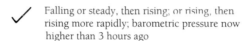 Steady; same as 3 hours ago

Falling, then rising; same as or lower than 3 hours ago

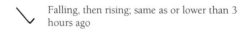 Falling, then steady; or falling, then falling more slowly; barometric pressure now lower than 3 hours ago

Falling steadily, or unsteadily; barometric pressure now lower than 3 hours ago

 Steady or rising, then falling; or falling, then falling more rapidly; barometric pressure now lower than 3 hours ago

WIND SPEED

	Knots	Miles per hour	Kilometers per hour
	Calm	Calm	Calm
	1–2	1–2	1–3
	3–7	3–8	4–13
	8–12	9–14	14–19
	13–17	15–20	20–32
	18–22	21–25	33–40
	23–27	26–31	41–50
	28–32	32–37	51–60
	33–37	38–43	61–69
	38–42	44–49	70–79
	43–47	50–54	80–87
	48–52	55–60	88–96
	53–57	61–66	97–106
	58–62	67–71	107–114
	63–67	72–77	115–124
	68–72	78–83	125–134
	73–77	84–89	135–143
	103–107	119–123	192–198

precipitation, atmospheric pressure, winds—in a string of numbers, which, in turn, must be entered on maps. The meteorological shorthand developed by the world's weather services to do this has evolved into the single, international code shown on the following pages. These symbols are the hieroglyphics of modern meteorology—a way of describing the weather of a day in a space the size of a small coin.

CLOUD TYPES

 Cumulus of fair weather, little vertical development and seemingly flattened

 Cumulus of considerable development, generally towering, with or without other cumulus or stratocumulus bases all at same level

 Cumulonimbus with tops lacking clearcut outlines, but distinctly not cirriform or anvil shaped; with or without cumulus, stratocumulus, or stratus

 Stratocumulus formed by spreading out of cumulus; cumulus often present also

 Stratocumulus not formed by spreading out of cumulus

 Stratus or stratofractus, but not stratofractus of bad weather

 Stratofractus and/or cumulofractus of bad weather (scud)

 Cumulus and stratocumulus (not formed by spreading out of cumulus) with bases at different levels

 Cumulonimbus having a clearly fibrous (cirriform) top, often anvil shaped, with or without cumulus, stratocumulus, stratus, or scud

 Thin altostratus (most of cloud layer semitransparent)

 Thick altostratus, greater part sufficiently dense to hide sun (or moon), or nimbostratus

 Thin altocumulus, mostly semitransparent, cloud elements not changing much and at a single level

 Thin altocumulus in patches; cloud elements continually changing and/or occurring at more than one level

 Thin altocumulus in bands or in a layer gradually spreading over sky and usually thickening as a whole

 Altocumulus formed by the spreading out of cumulus or cumulonimbus

 Double-layered altocumulus, or a thick layer of altocumulus, not increasing; or altocumulus with altostratus and/or nimbostratus

 Altocumulus in the form of cumulus-shaped tufts or altocumulus with turrets

 Altocumulus of a chaotic sky, usually at different levels; patches of dense cirrus usually present also

 Filaments of cirrus, or "mares' tails," scattered and not increasing

 Dense cirrus in patches or twisted sheaves, usually not increasing, sometimes like remains of cumulonimbus; or towers or tufts

 Dense cirrus, often anvil shaped, derived from or associated with cumulonimbus

 Cirrus, often hook shaped, gradually spreading over the sky and usually thickening as a whole

 Cirrus and cirrostratus, often in converging bands, or cirrostratus alone; generally overspreading and growing denser; the continuous layer not reaching 45° altitude

 Cirrus and cirrostratus, often in converging bands, or cirrostratus alone; generally overspreading and growing denser; the continuous layer exceeding 45° altitude

 Veil of cirrostratus covering the entire sky

 Cirrostratus not increasing and not covering entire sky

 Cirrocumulus alone or cirrocumulus with some cirrus or cirrostratus, but the cirrocumulus being the main cirriform cloud

CLOUD COVER

 No clouds

 One tenth or less

 Two tenths or three tenths

 Four tenths

 Five tenths

 Six tenths

 Seven tenths or eight tenths

 Nine tenths or overcast with openings

 Completely overcast (ten tenths)

Sky obscured

PRESENT WEATHER

Cloud development NOT observed or NOT observable during past hour

Clouds generally dissolving or becoming less developed during past hour

State of sky on the whole unchanged during past hour

Clouds generally forming or developing during past hour

Visibility reduced by smoke

Light fog (mist)

Patches of shallow fog at station, NOT deeper than 6 feet (2 meters) on land

More or less continuous shallow fog at station, NOT deeper than 6 feet (2 meters) on land

Lightning visible, no thunder heard

Precipitation within sight, but NOT reaching the ground

Drizzle (NOT freezing) or snow grains (NOT falling as showers) during past hour, but NOT at time of observation

Rain (NOT freezing and NOT falling as showers) during past hour, but NOT at time of observation

Snow (NOT falling as showers) during past hour, but NOT at time of observation

Rain and snow or ice pellets (NOT falling as showers) during past hour, but NOT at time of observation

Freezing drizzle or freezing rain (NOT falling as showers) during past hour, but NOT at time of observation

Slight or moderate dust storm or sandstorm, has decreased during past hour

Slight or moderate dust storm or sandstorm, no appreciable change during past hour

Slight or moderate dust storm or sandstorm has begun or increased during past hour

Severe dust storm or sandstorm, has decreased during past hour

Severe dust storm or sandstorm, no appreciable change during past hour

Fog or ice fog at distance at time of observation, but NOT at station during past hour

Fog or ice fog in patches

Fog or ice fog, sky discernible, has become thinner during past hour

Fog or ice fog, sky NOT discernible, has become thinner during past hour

Fog or ice fog, sky discernible, no appreciable change during past hour

Intermittent drizzle (NOT freezing), slight at time of observation

Continuous drizzle (NOT freezing), slight at time of observation

Intermittent drizzle (NOT freezing), moderate at time of observation

Continuous drizzle (NOT freezing), moderate at time of observation

Intermittent drizzle (NOT freezing), heavy at time of observation

Intermittent rain (NOT freezing), slight at time of observation

Continuous rain (NOT freezing), slight at time of observation

Intermittent rain (NOT freezing), moderate at time of observation

Continuous rain (NOT freezing), moderate at time of observation

Intermittent rain (NOT freezing), heavy at time of observation

Intermittent fall of snowflakes, slight at time of observation

Continuous fall of snowflakes, slight at time of observation

Intermittent fall of snowflakes, moderate at time of observation

Continuous fall of snowflakes, moderate at time of observation

Intermittent fall of snowflakes, heavy at time of observation

Slight rain shower(s)

Moderate or heavy rain shower(s)

Violent rain shower(s)

Slight shower(s) of rain and snow mixed

Moderate or heavy shower(s) of rain and snow mixed

Moderate or heavy shower(s) of hail, with or without rain, or rain and snow mixed, not associated with thunder

Slight rain at time of observation; thunderstorm during past hour, but NOT at time of observation

Moderate or heavy rain at time of observation; thunderstorm during past hour, but NOT at time of observation

Slight snow, or rain and snow mixed, or hail at time of observation; thunderstorm during past hour, but NOT at time of observation

Moderate or heavy snow, or rain and snow mixed, or hail at time of observation; thunderstorm during past hour, but NOT at time of observation

(∞)	Haze
S	Widespread dust in suspension in the air, NOT raised by wind, at time of observation
(dust/sand symbol)	Dust or sand raised by wind at time of observation
(dust whirl symbol)	Well-developed dust whirl(s) within past hour
(-S→)	Dust storm or sandstorm within sight of or at station during past hour
)•(	Precipitation within sight, reaching the ground but distant from station
(•)	Precipitation within sight, reaching the ground, near to but NOT at station
(thunderstorm symbol)	Thunderstorm, but no precipitation at the station
∇	Squall(s) within sight during past hour or at time of observation
)(	Funnel cloud(s) within sight of station at time of observation
(shower symbol)	Showers of rain during past hour, but NOT at time of observation
(snow shower symbol)	Showers of snow, or of rain and snow, during past hour, but NOT at time of observation
(hail shower symbol)	Showers of hail, or of hail and rain, during past hour, but NOT at time of observation
=]	Fog during past hour, but NOT at time of observation
(thunderstorm symbol)	Thunderstorm (with or without precipitation) during past hour, but NOT at time of observation
(severe dust storm symbol)	Severe dust storm or sandstorm has begun or increased during past hour
(drifting snow symbol)	Slight or moderate drifting snow, generally low (less than 6 ft or 2 m)
(heavy drifting snow symbol)	Heavy drifting snow, generally low
(blowing snow symbol)	Slight or moderate blowing snow, generally high (more than 6 ft or 2 m)
(heavy blowing snow symbol)	Heavy blowing snow, generally high
≡	Fog or ice fog, sky NOT discernible, no appreciable change during past hour
|− −	Fog or ice fog, sky discernible, has begun or become thicker during past hour
|≡	Fog or ice fog, sky NOT discernible, has begun or become thicker during past hour
(rime fog symbol)	Fog depositing rime, sky discernible
(rime fog symbol)	Fog depositing rime, sky NOT discernible
,,	Continuous drizzle (NOT freezing), heavy at time of observation
(∿)	Slight freezing drizzle
(∿)	Moderate or heavy freezing drizzle
•,	Drizzle and rain, slight
•,	Drizzle and rain, moderate or heavy
•••	Continuous rain (NOT freezing), heavy at time of observation
(●∿)	Slight freezing rain
(●∿●)	Moderate or heavy freezing rain
•*	Rain or drizzle and snow, slight
•*•*	Rain or drizzle and snow, moderate or heavy
***	Continuous fall of snowflakes, heavy at time of observation
←→	Ice prisms (with or without fog)
—△	Snow grains (with or without fog)
—*—	Isolated starlike snow crystals (with or without fog)
△	Ice pellets or snow pellets
*∇	Slight snow shower(s)
*∇	Moderate or heavy snow shower(s)
△∇	Slight shower(s) of snow pellets, or ice pellets with or without rain, or rain and snow mixed
△∇	Moderate or heavy shower(s) of snow pellets or ice pellets, or ice pellets with or without rain or rain and snow mixed
▲∇	Slight shower(s) of hail, with or without rain or rain and snow mixed, not associated with thunder
(thunderstorm symbol)	Slight or moderate thunderstorm without hail, but with rain and/or snow at time of observation
(thunderstorm symbol)	Slight or moderate thunderstorm, with hail at time of observation
(thunderstorm symbol)	Heavy thunderstorm, without hail, but with rain and/or snow at time of observation
(thunderstorm symbol)	Thunderstorm combined with dust storm or sandstorm at time of observation
(thunderstorm symbol)	Heavy thunderstorm with hail at time of observation

The Daily Weather Maps

Plotted on maps like the one shown here, the data from hundreds of stations becomes an intelligible mosaic of information—what weathercasters call a surface analysis. These maps are usually in rough form, intended for forecasters. National meteorological services preserve such data as a history of weather. Perhaps the best example of these archival maps is the one produced by the United States, which has such a varied sampling of meteorology from day to day.

This cartographic snapshot shows surface weather conditions at 7 A.M. EST over the United States. Contours of equal pressure—isobars—show the invisible terrain that will guide the flow of winds, with a dotted line marking the southward extent of freezing temperatures. The movement of well-defined low-pressure systems, or cyclones—the source of most noteworthy weather—is marked by a chain of arrows, with white crosses indicating where the low was 6, 12, and 18 hours earlier. Shaded areas denote precipitation; north of the freeze line, this would be ice or snow. The three maps displayed in this series show three days in March 1993, when, with the country locked in subfreezing temperatures, a low-pressure system spins up in the Gulf of Mexico—and becomes the eastern seaboard's Storm of the Century.

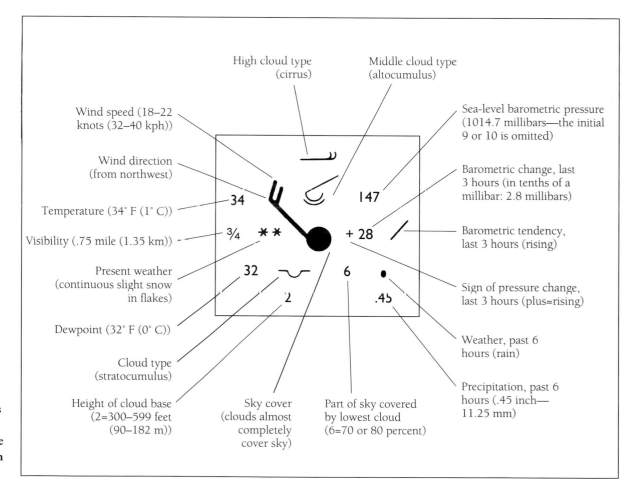

A TYPICAL WEATHER STATION ENTRY
Weather symbols were not the only thing standardized—so was their method of presentation. For each of the thousands of weather-reporting stations around the world, they must be presented in a certain way, as in this example.

High cloud type (cirrus)

Middle cloud type (altocumulus)

Wind speed (18–22 knots (32–40 kph))

Sea-level barometric pressure (1014.7 millibars—the initial 9 or 10 is omitted)

Wind direction (from northwest)

Barometric change, last 3 hours (in tenths of a millibar: 2.8 millibars)

Temperature (34° F (1° C))

Visibility (.75 mile (1.35 km))

Barometric tendency, last 3 hours (rising)

Present weather (continuous slight snow in flakes)

Sign of pressure change, last 3 hours (plus=rising)

Dewpoint (32° F (0° C))

Weather, past 6 hours (rain)

Cloud type (stratocumulus)

Precipitation, past 6 hours (.45 inch—11.25 mm)

Height of cloud base (2=300–599 feet (90–182 m))

Sky cover (clouds almost completely cover sky)

Part of sky covered by lowest cloud (6=70 or 80 percent)

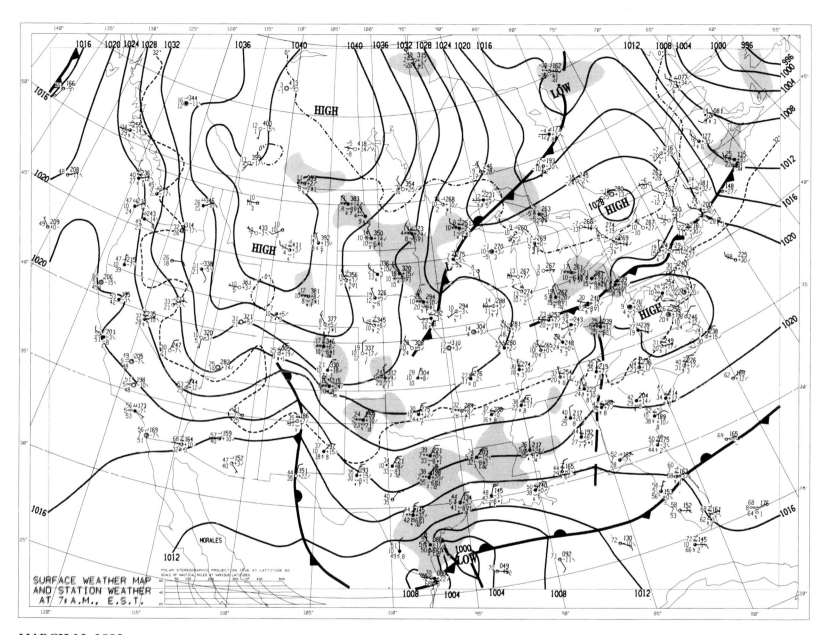

MARCH 12, 1993

Although still steeped in cold air—the freeze line extends well into Texas—the country begins to clear as high pressure dominates the central and western states. But off the Gulf Coast of northern Mexico, a low-pressure system coalesces, energized by the relatively warm waters of the Gulf of Mexico—the seed of what forecasters will call the Storm of the Century.

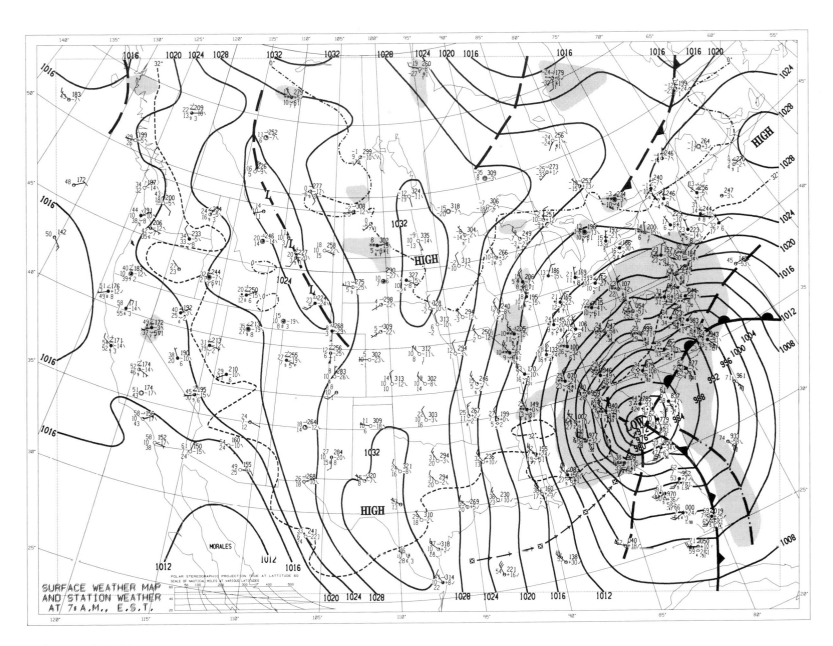

MARCH 13, 1993

Like the strands of a spiderweb, isobars from the deep, highly
organized cyclone radiate out from a center over Georgia after
crossing the northern Gulf of Mexico. The freeze line has dipped
farther south, almost to the Gulf Coast. The rest of the nation
shivers in subfreezing temperatures. But most of the action in the
American atmosphere is concentrated in this single cyclone.

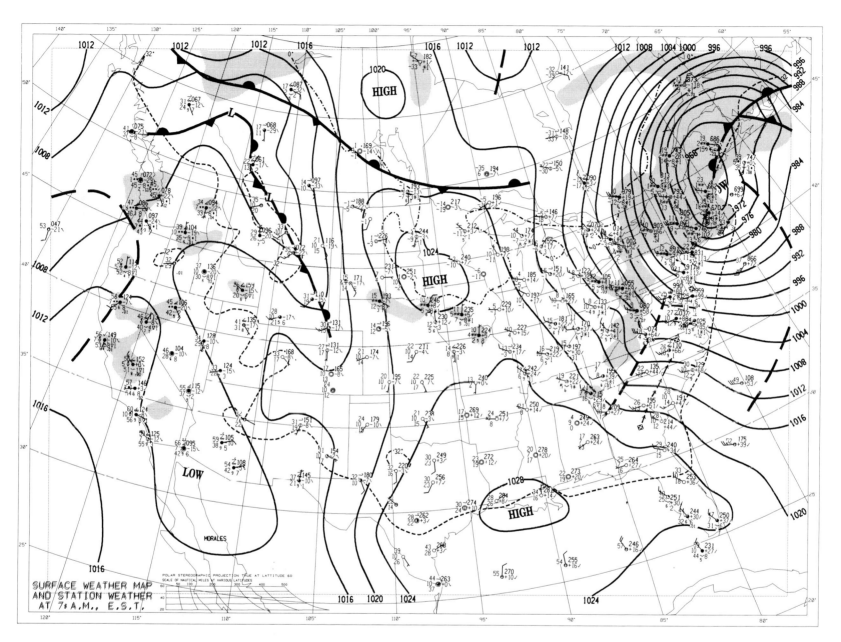

MARCH 14, 1993

The fast-moving low travels more than 800 miles (1,500 km) overnight and by morning is centered over northern New England. Counterclockwise nor'easter circulation around the low shunts vast quantities of Atlantic moisture inland and southward toward Maryland and Virginia. In the wake of the storm, cities from Atlanta to Boston lie paralyzed under heavy mounds of ice and snow.

Weather Map: A.D. 2000

Instrument-bearing satellites and giant computers are changing the way in which the world's weather is mapped. While conventional surface charts are still prepared, they are being rapidly overtaken by the more comprehensive, real-time renderings available from space and some of the world's top meteorological research facilities.

The GOES (Geostationary Operational Environmental Satellite) image offers a case in point. Unlike the coiling isobars of the conventional weather map, the composite image shown below combines data from the American GOES and the European Meteosat to construct a view of weather over the Atlantic from the Gulf of Mexico to western Africa—an invaluable vantage point from which to catch the early signs of hurricane formation in the tropical easterlies.

At right, a computer-assembled mosaic of images from the American polar-orbiting NOAA (National Oceanic and Atmospheric Administration) satellites provides a vast panorama of weather from the Indian subcontinent to the western North Pacific, and from the steppes of Central Asia to the East Indian archipelago.

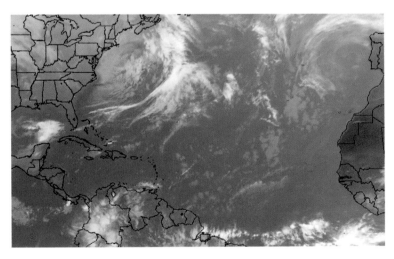

Joint European-American satellite view of weather over the Atlantic Ocean.

Composite of storm systems (*right*) over Eurasian continent.

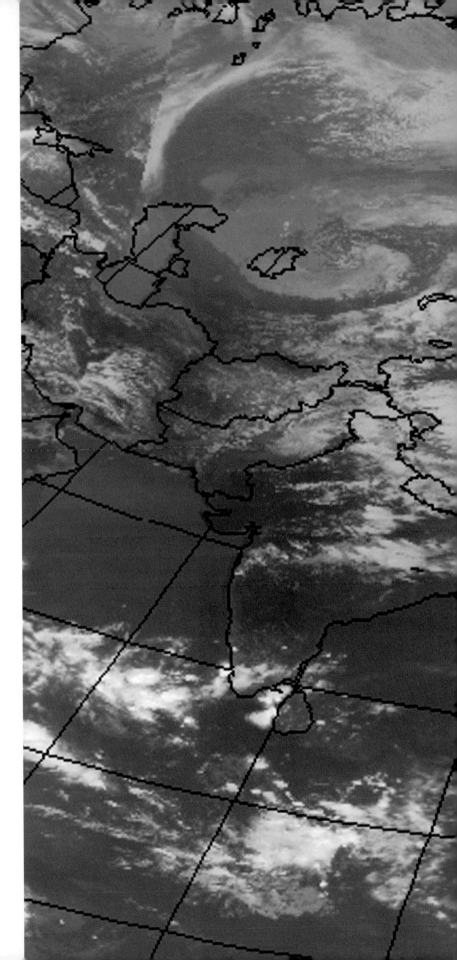

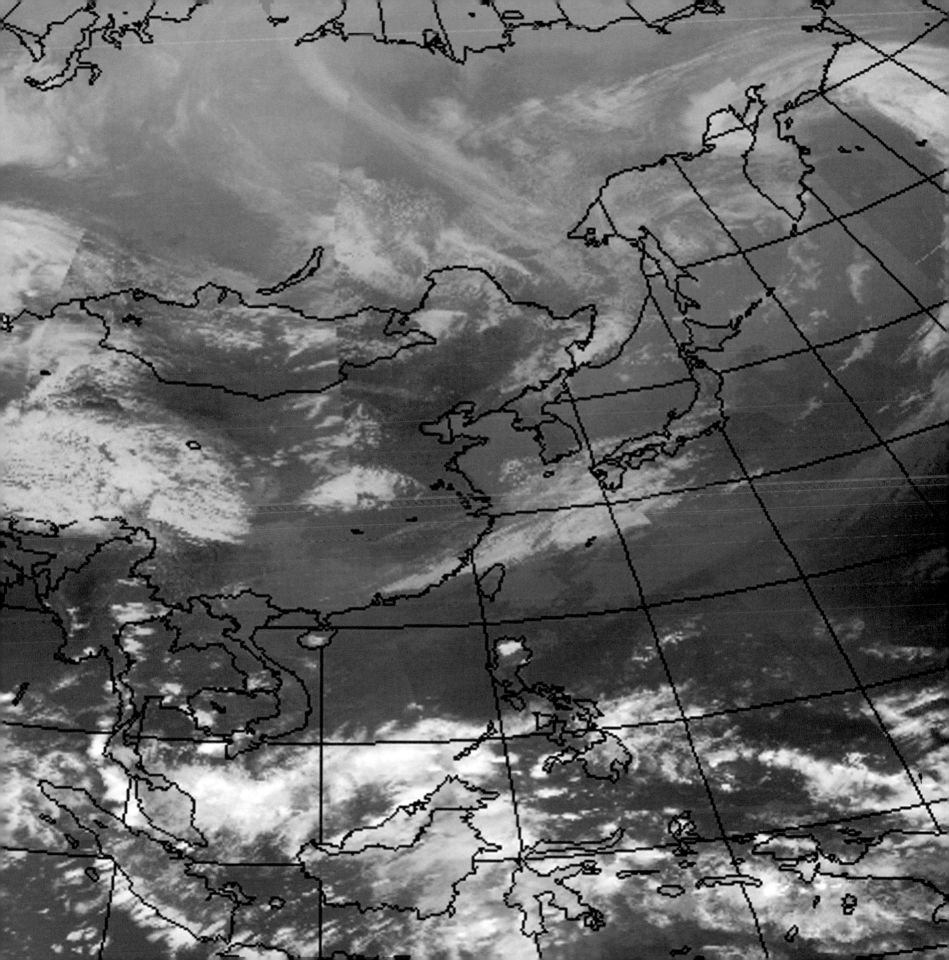

A Dynamic New Perspective

Using radar, satellite, and other data gathered and disseminated by the National Oceanic and Atmospheric Administration, a large family of innovative, real-time computerized displays has been developed. One product: a winter storm mosaic (*below*) that combines radar data from numerous stations into a map color coded to show where precipitation will be snow, mixed ice and water, and rain during a major March 1994 storm that brought mid-Atlantic cities to an icy standstill. Weather stations in the area are denoted by their three-letter code names—usually the same as corresponding airport designations.

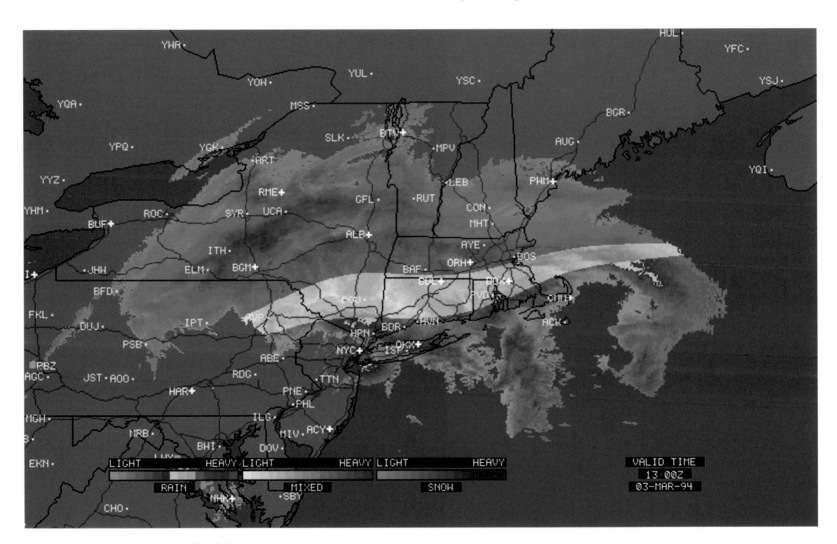

Computerized radar picture of mid-Atlantic winter storm.

But weather will not be the only thing on the weather maps of the future. Modern instruments can see a good deal of what used to be invisible. For example, a Doppler radar operating in its clear-air mode—some 2,000 times more sensitive than its precipitation mode—can detect the movement of clear air by sensing echoes from the tiny airborne particles called aerosols that are always present. In the image below, the movement of aerosols becomes a map of clear-air motions between 10,000 and 12,000 feet (3,000 and 3,600 m) above the Sterling, Virginia, radar. Colors warmer than light orange denote movement away from the radar; cooler colors indicate movement toward the radar.

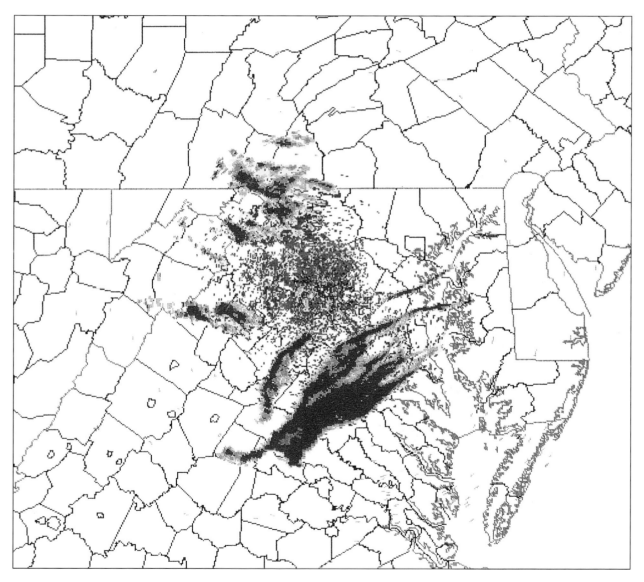

Radar image of clear-air movement above northern Virginia.

A Global View

Because clouds are such crucial indicators of atmospheric conditions, scientists are developing new ways of extracting detailed information from the global view of satellites. Using archival data taken by polar-orbiting NOAA satellites on a typical July day in 1979, NASA and Jet Propulsion Laboratory researchers assembled the image of global cloud cover seen below. Red indicates extensive cover, green moderate cover, and blue little or no cloudiness.

At the European Centre for Medium-Range Weather Forecasts, new satellite products made from Meteosat data include computer presentations of cloud-top heights (*right*),

Global cloud cover from combined satellite images.

an indication of cloud temperatures and weather. In this depiction, cloud tops above about 2 miles (3.2 km) are color coded at 1-mile (1.6-km) intervals, going from cooler colors near the surface to warmer ones at altitude. Red indicates cloud tops higher than 8 miles (13 km) and shows strong vertical cloud development over large regions of southern Africa, a sign of powerful thunderstorms. A similar procedure yields heights for winds derived from cloud motions.

MIXING AIR AND SEA

Research during the latter half of the 20th century has confirmed the inextricable link between events in the atmosphere

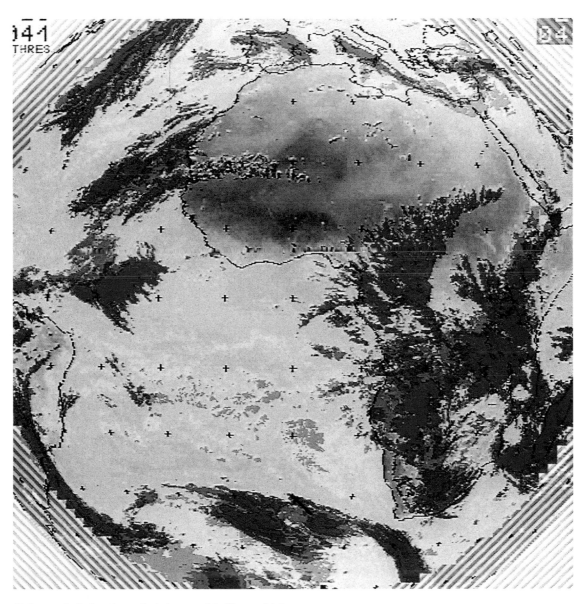

Color-coded cloud-top heights: red indicates highest.

and events in the world ocean. Heat energy, water vapor, and precipitation are key elements in that interaction.

Scientists at NASA and the Jet Propulsion Laboratory have used data from instruments aboard NOAA polar orbiters to construct a global snapshot of temperature (*below*), which averages surface temperatures for June 1988. Colors from blue to yellow to red show the surface heating up, ranging from about -22° F (-30° C) in the far south, where it is winter, to 104° F (40° C)—where the subtropical deserts of Africa, North America, and Asia are in summer.

Similar data went into another NASA product: global views of winter and summer rainfall (*top right*). Offering clues

to the transport of heat energy by precipitation and to the hydrologic cycle itself, the images show total rainfall for December 1987 through February 1988, and for June through August 1988. Colors range from hot colors for little rainfall, to blues for heavy rains—for example, the rainy monsoon area in the Indian Ocean is a large, blue free-form in the summer map.

A research product from the European Centre for Medium-Range Weather Forecasts looks at water vapor in the atmosphere over Europe and North Africa (*bottom right*). Contours are in kilograms per square meter of precipitable water vapor—the amount of water the vapor would produce if it condensed and fell as rain.

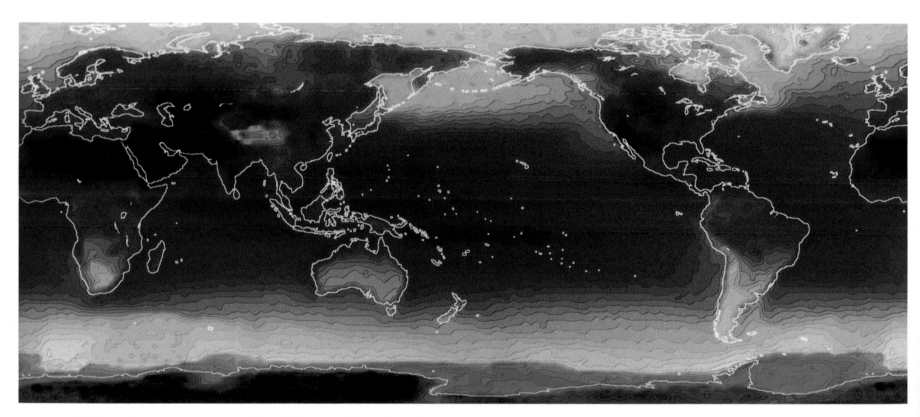

Global surface temperature map: blue indicates cold southern winter.

Global rainfall map for winter (*top*) and summer (*bottom*), 1988.

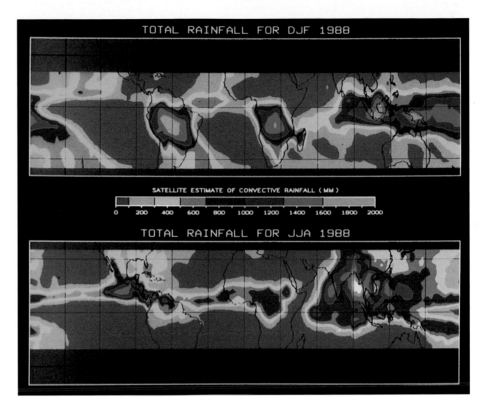

Water vapor in the atmosphere over Europe and North Africa (*below*).

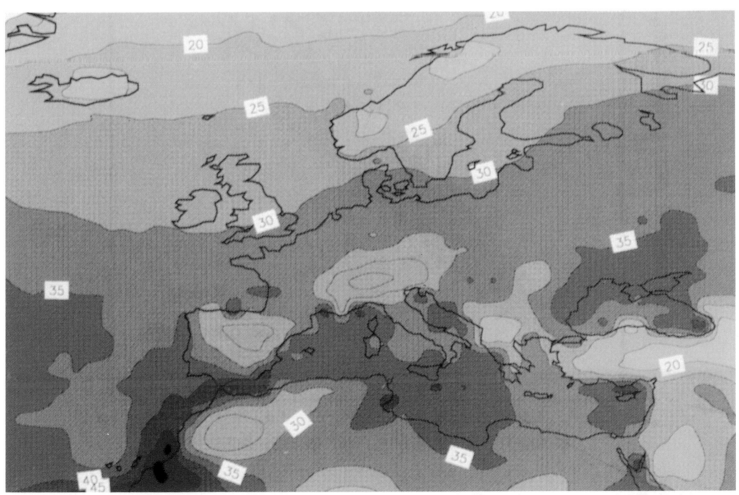

SEASONAL SEA LEVELS

Over the seasons, the global ocean—the flywheel of the air-sea heat engine—actually alters its shape as the water warms and cools, expanding and contracting as it does. In 1993 the Jet Propulsion Laboratory produced the first long-term analysis drawn from its TOPEX/Poseidon satellite, a joint mission of NASA and France's space agency, the Centre National d'Etudes Spatiales, or CNES. Using data from the satellite's precise radar altimeter, scientists constructed these four views of the seasons of the global ocean, from October 1992 to October 1993.

At temperate latitudes in both northern and southern hemispheres, sea-level changes from one season to another are

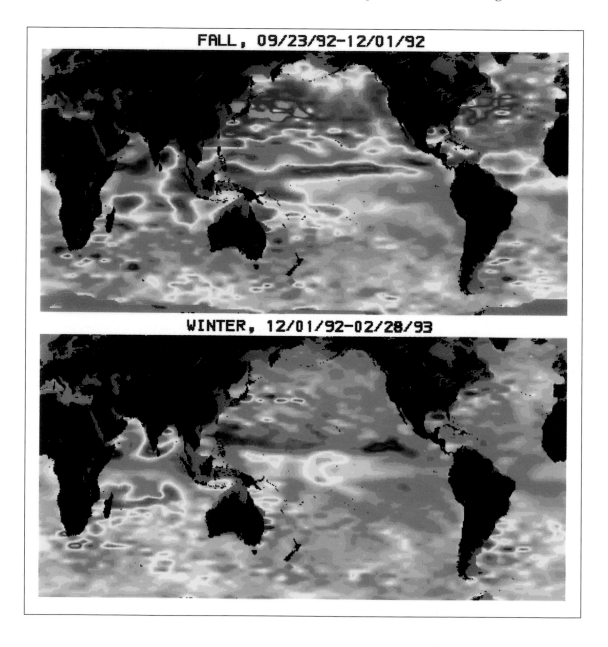

dominated by the heating and cooling of the upper levels of the ocean. In the tropics, where sea level is mainly controlled by the winds, bands of alternating high and low sea level move across the Atlantic and Pacific oceans, in step with the seasonal strengthening and weakening of the easterly trade winds. Sea-level changes in the Indian Ocean, however, march to a different drummer: the regular cycle of the monsoon. The resulting topography of the worldwide ocean does more than show how winds and sea currents will flow—it also provides a way of watching such anomalous events as El Niño, which produces a characteristic tongue of relatively high sea level (warmer water) across the equatorial Pacific.

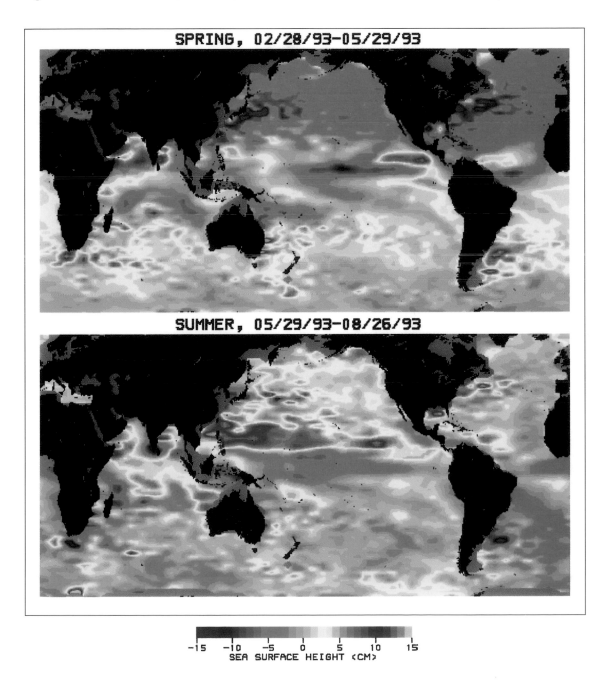

SPRING, 02/28/93-05/29/93

SUMMER, 05/29/93-08/26/93

-15 -10 -5 0 5 10 15
SEA SURFACE HEIGHT (CM)

Cloud Atlas

Clouds are weather rendered visible, atmospheric messengers that are both the heralds and historians of what the vast sea of air has done and is about to do. With rare exceptions they drift on the winds of the troposphere, traveling thousands of miles horizontally, but no more than about 10 miles vertically, and are always changing, as atmospheric water vapor condenses into visibility, or evaporates and disappears, or freezes. Their height, shape, and movement are primary clues to the atmosphere's intentions.

THE LOW CLOUDS

Found between the surface and about 6,500 feet (2,000 m), these are variants of stratus (St), a low-lying gray cloud layer with a uniform base, producing drizzle, ice prisms, or snow grains. They are often opaque enough to mask the Sun and are sometimes formed by the gradual lifting of a fog layer—which is a stratus cloud at ground level.

Nimbostratus (Ns) is darker and thick enough to blot out the Sun, producing continuous rain or snow but without electrical activity, and is found in both the low and middle levels of the troposphere. Stratocumulus (Sc) clouds are gray and whitish layers with dark patches formed of rounded masses and rolls, with larger elements than normal stratus layers. They are composed of water droplets.

STRATUS in a thin ground layer—fog—turns a river bridge into a celestial crossing.

NIMBOSTRATUS veils the Sun, its dark hue hinting at a potential for drizzle or light snow.

STRATOCUMULUS deck shows a circular hole, possibly created by a stream of descending, drying air.

STRATOCUMULUS (*left*) ruffles the lower layers, topped by a higher layer of ALTOCUMULUS—both indicators of unsettled conditions.

STRATOCUMULUS advances like a dark wing across the sky, a harbinger of possible unsettled weather.

STRATOCUMULUS spreads like smoke before the Sun, its puffy cumulus mounds suggesting mild vertical motion.

THE MIDDLE CLOUDS

At the Equator, where the troposphere is deepest, middle clouds are found from 6,500 to 25,000 feet (2,000–7,500 m) but they reach only to about 13,000 feet (4,000 m) at the poles, where the tropopause is lower. Altostratus (As) is a grayish or bluish cloud sheet that may be striated, fibrous, or of uniform appearance, covering part or all of the sky, and is composed of water droplets, ice crystals, raindrops, and snowflakes. It is thin enough to reveal the Sun vaguely, as though viewed through ground glass. Altocumulus (Ac) is most often seen as extensive sheets of regularly arranged cloudlets, white and gray and somewhat rounded. Sometimes these take the form of parallel rolls separated by cloud-free lanes or, rarely, a honeycomb of ragged holes alternating with cloudlets. They are mostly water droplets, although they may contain ice at very low temperatures.

ALTOSTRATUS (*above*) **in a thin gauze covers the sky, its water droplets veiling but not obscuring the Sun.**

ALTOSTRATUS lenticular clouds (*left*) rounded and moulded into glassy teardrops by the wind indicate smooth air motion at middle altitudes.

ALTOSTRATUS orographic clouds are created as winds lift air over a mountain barrier, causing its water to condense.

ALTOSTRATUS lenticular, or lens-shaped, cloud shows wave motion in the winds above a low STRATOCUMULUS layer.

ALTOCUMULUS boil up in a disorganized manner, suggesting unstable conditions in the middle troposphere.

ALTOCUMULUS form a curved street of clouds, some of which may develop vertically into thunderheads.

ALTOCUMULUS sail flotilla-like against the Sun, suggesting faintly unsettled atmospheric conditions.

ALTOCUMULUS arrayed in a fishbone pattern, sculpted by the rise and fall of short wind waves at middle altitudes.

THE HIGH CLOUDS

Seen from 20,000 to 60,000 feet (6,000–18,000 m) over the Equator—and from 10,000 to 25,000 feet (3,000–7,500 m) at the poles—high clouds are composed mainly of ice crystals. Cirrus (Ci) appear as detached wisps of clouds, sometimes hairlike and formed of delicate filaments, patches, or narrow bands. They take their name from the Latin for "a lock of hair" or "a tuft of horse hair." Cirrostratus (Cs) is a transparent, whitish veil that can be either fibrous or smooth, covering part or all of the sky The optical properties of its ice crystals produce various halo phenomena. Cirrocumulus (Cc) is a thin, white, grainy or rippled patch, sheet, or layer showing very slight vertical development in the form of turrets and shallow towers.

CIRRUS clouds, in wisps of ice crystals, spread on strong, high-level winds high in the troposphere.

CIRRUS ice crystals act as prisms, creating this rainbow glow in the upper troposphere.

CIRRUS in mares' tails flick across the upper troposphere, often an early sign that a warm front is coming.

CIRROSTRATUS ice crystals refract light to create this symmetrical halo around the winter Sun.

CIRROCUMULUS form a herringbone pattern, caused by undulating rising and falling winds at high altitude.

THE VERTICAL CLOUDS

Signs of instability, these clouds break the stratified rule of the atmosphere, building from low levels to and sometimes beyond the tropopause and releasing vast amounts of latent heat as the cloud's cargo of water droplets freezes into ice crystals at high altitudes. Cumulus (Cu) clouds are detached, dense, and sharply outlined and develop as rising mounds, domes, or towers, brilliant white in sunlight, ascending from a dark and nearly horizontal base. They take their name from the Latin for a "heap" or "pile." Cumulonimbus (Cb) is a heavy, dense cloud of great vertical extent, reaching to 40,000 feet (12,000 m) or more, and containing the powerful engine of the thunderstorm at its core. Seen in the shape of a mountain or immense tower, the clouds are usually smooth in the upper part, often drawn into an anvil shape by high-level winds. They are composed of water droplets in the lower layers and mainly of ice at higher altitude and produce such dangerous phenomena as tornadoes, hail, torrential rains, destructive winds, and lightning.

CUMULUS thunderhead towers above surrounding clouds, its cap sculpted from the rising airflow over its domed top.

CUMULUS build-up (*right*) causes one cloud to tower, drawing energy from its smaller cousins and from the surrounding atmosphere.

CUMULONIMBUS towers above a dark lower layer and a shaft of rain, with high CIRRUS covering part of the background sky.

CUMULONIMBUS explodes into a huge anvil, with feeder lines of STRATOCUMULUS spiraling in around its base.

CUMULUS turret boils upward, powered by rising air currents and the release of its water's latent heat.

CUMULONIMBUS cloud base exhibits the duglike protrusions called mammatus, a sign of violent thunderstorm activity.

CLOUDS ABOVE THE TROPOSPHERE

Close to the poles, at very high altitudes reckoned in kilometers and miles rather than meters and feet, an exotic type of cloud is sometimes seen. Polar stratospheric clouds, or PSCs, form within the vortex of winds that surround and isolate the poles in winter. The wispy clouds coalesce at altitudes between about 12 and 18 miles (21–32 km), but only when winter temperatures are abnormally low. PSCs have been implicated in the severe depletion of stratospheric ozone observed over the Antarctic: evidently, reactive chlorine uses the surface of the clouds' ice crystals as a kind of frozen crucible for the catalytic destruction of ozone.

Noctilucent clouds are seen in brilliant fibrous bands linked by waves and form between about 50 and 65 miles (90 and 115 km), moving at hundreds of miles per hour across the sky, usually from the northeast or east. More the creations of ions and radiation fields than the atmosphere, these clouds are believed to be composed of fine cosmic dust.

NOCTILUCENT CLOUDS spread like luminous veins across the sky near the horizon in Finland.

POLAR STRATOSPHERIC CLOUDS (*right*) photographed from a high-flying research aircraft over Antarctica.

Glossary

ABSOLUTE HUMIDITY A measurement of the amount of water vapor in a defined volume of air.

ACID PRECIPITATION Rain with a pH lower than 5.6 because of the presence of air-borne pollutants such as sulfuric acid.

ACRE FOOT The amount of water required to cover an acre of land to a depth of one foot.

ADIABATIC Without direct heating. In an adiabatic process, the temperature in an air mass increases or decreases because of changes in pressure.

ADVECTION The process by which heat and humidity are transported by horizontal air movement.

ADVECTION FOG Fog that is created when warm, humid air moves over a cooler surface.

AERONOMY The science of studying the upper atmosphere.

AEROSOLS Minute particles suspended in a gas.

AIR MASS A large area of air that has nearly uniform characteristics, such as water vapor concentration and temperature, within any given altitude.

AIR-MASS THUNDERSTORM A thunderstorm that develops within an unstable mass of warm, moist air.

AIR PRESSURE The force exerted on a surface by the air.

AIRGLOW A faint luminosity caused by energy emissions from atoms and molecules in the ionosphere.

ALBEDO The amount of radiation reflected by a surface, usually expressed as a percentage.

ALTIMETER A type of aneroid barometer that is used to measure altitude.

ALTOCUMULUS A middle-altitude cloud characterized by multiple puffs that create a wavy pattern.

ALTOSTRATUS A middle-altitude cloud characterized by thin layers that create a relatively uniform sheet.

ANEMOMETER A device used to determine wind speed.

ANEROID BAROMETER A device used to measure air pressure. The aneroid is a flexible metal part that reacts to changes in air pressure by contracting or expanding.

ANTICYCLONE An area of high atmospheric pressure surrounded by wind.

ANTICYCLONIC FLOW The direction in which the wind blows in an anticyclone; that is, clockwise in the Northern Hemisphere and counterclockwise in the Southern Hemisphere.

ARCTIC SEA SMOKE A steam fog that occurs over the ocean in high-latitude regions.

ATMOSPHERE The gaseous layer surrounding the Earth.

ATMOSPHERIC PRESSURE The force that a given unit of air exerts because of the weight of the atmosphere directly above it.

AURORA AUSTRALIS Glowing lights in the night sky of the Southern Hemisphere caused by electromagnetic activity in the upper atmosphere.

AURORA BOREALIS Glowing lights in the night sky of the Northern Hemisphere caused by electromagnetic activity in the upper atmosphere; also known as the northern lights.

BACK DOOR COLD FRONT A cold front in the eastern United States that comes from the northeast rather than the north or northwest.

BACKING WIND SHIFT A counterclockwise shift in wind direction.

BAROGRAPH An instrument used to record atmospheric pressure.

BAROMETER An instrument used to measure atmospheric pressure.

BLIZZARD An extended period of heavy snowfall accompanied by winds over 35 mph (56 kph).

BLOCKING HIGH A stationary high-pressure system that temporarily impedes the usual eastward progression of weather systems.

BUYS BALLOT'S LAW A law describing the correlation of wind direction to air pressure. If a person stands with his or her back to the wind in the Northern Hemisphere, the air pressure will be lower to the left than to the right; the reverse is true in the Southern Hemisphere.

CELSIUS SCALE A system of measuring temperature based on 0° as the freezing point of water at sea level and 100° as the boiling point.

CHAOS THEORY The theory that some systems are finally unpredictable because of the effects of unforeseeable, small-scale occurrences.

CHLOROFLUOROCARBONS (CFCs) Inert synthetic compounds containing atoms of chlorine, fluorine, and carbon used in air conditioners and in many industrial applications.

CIRROCUMULUS A high-altitude ice-crystal cloud characterized by small white patches in a wavy pattern.

CIRROSTRATUS A high-altitude ice-crystal cloud characterized by a smooth appearance similar to a veil; often forms a halo.

CIRRUS A high-altitude cloud ice-crystal characterized by a thin, wispy appearance.

CLIMATE A description of weather for a given region based on the average of various conditions, such as rainfall, temperature, and humidity levels, over a long period of time.

CLOUD A visible body of suspended water droplets or ice crystals.

COLD FRONT The boundary where an advancing mass of cold air meets a mass of warm air.

COLD WAVE A swift and dramatic drop in temperature that matches or exceeds a prescribed number of degrees and reaches a prescribed minimum in a 24-hour period.

CONDENSATION The transforming of a gas or vapor to a liquid.

CONDENSATION NUCLEI Minute particles on which water vapor condenses.

CONDUCTION The transfer of heat within an object or between objects by molecular activity.

CONTINENTAL AIR MASS An air mass that develops over land.

CONTINENTAL CLIMATE A climate that is not affected by maritime weather.

CONTRAIL A long, thin, cloudlike formation caused by vapor from the engine exhaust of flying airplanes.

CONVECTION The transfer of heat by the movement of a fluid or gas, or the motion of air caused by heating.

CONVECTIVE STORM A storm caused by a large mass of rapidly rising warm air.

CONVERGENCE The horizontal compression of air within a given atmospheric region that results in a net inflow of air into that region.

CORIOLIS FORCE The curved deflection of the ground path of objects moving over the Earth's surface caused by the planet's rotation.

CORONA A bright disk that is centered on the Sun or the moon; the image is caused by diffraction when either object is behind a thin cloud. Also, the Sun's atmosphere.

CORONA DISCHARGE Discharges from electrified surfaces such as ships' masts and airplane wings; also called St. Elmo's Fire.

CUMULONIMBUS A low-altitude cloud characterized by a thick, vertical mass, produces thunderstorms.

CUMULUS A low-altitude cloud characterized by billowy masses.

CYCLOGENESIS The process by which a cyclone develops.

CYCLONE An area of low atmospheric pressure.

CYCLONIC FLOW The direction of the wind in a cyclone; that is, counterclockwise in the Northern Hemisphere and clockwise in the Southern Hemisphere.

DEPRESSION An area of low atmospheric pressure.

DEW A type of condensation characterized by small drops of water.

DEW POINT The temperature to which air must be cooled before its water vapor condenses.

DIFFRACTION The slight bending of light as it passes the edge of an object.

DIURNAL Recurring daily.

DIVERGENCE The condition in which the wind distribution pattern in an area results in a net outflow of air from that same area.

DOPPLER SHIFT The change in a signal's frequency, or wavelength, caused by the motion of either the source or the receiver.

DOWNBURST An intense downdraft, or descending air, from a thunderstorm.

DROUGHT A prolonged period of abnormally dry weather for a given region.

DRY ADIABATIC LAPSE RATE The rate of change in temperature with change in height as unsaturated air sinks or rises—about 5.5° F per 1,000 feet (10° C per 100 m) of uplift.

DRY LINE The boundary between warm, dry air and warm, moist air.

EL NIÑO The periodic warming of the surface water in the central and eastern Pacific Ocean, which can affect global weather.

ELECTROMAGNETIC RADIATION The energy that is emitted and absorbed by all objects and that travels through space at the speed of light.

ENTRAINMENT The mixing of cool, dry air from the surrounding environment into the downdraft of a cumulus cloud.

EQUINOX The moment when the Sun crosses the Equator.

EVAPORATION The process by which a liquid transforms into a gas.

EXOSPHERE The outermost layer of the atmosphere, found about 311 miles (500 km) above the Earth's surface.

EXTRATROPICAL CYCLONE A massive weather system that originates outside the tropics and has a low-pressure center.

EYE The roughly circular calm center of a hurricane or typhoon.

EYE WALL The area of cumulonimbus clouds and intense winds surrounding the eye of a hurricane or typhoon.

FAHRENHEIT SCALE A system of measuring temperature based on 32° as the freezing point of water at sea level and 212° as the boiling point.

FLASH The electrical discharge of lightning that is seen as a burst of light.

FLASH FLOOD Flooding characterized by rapidly rising water.

FOG A cloud with its base at the ground.

FORECASTING Determining the probable future course of a weather system based on analysis of existing conditions.

FREEZING The process by which a liquid transforms into a solid.

FREEZING NUCLEI Small particles in the air that serve as cores for the formation of ice.

FREEZING RAIN Supercooled raindrops that freeze when they come into contact with a cold surface.

FRONT The boundary between air masses with differing temperatures and/or water vapor concentrations.

FROST Water vapor that turns to ice crystals on an exposed surface.

FUNNEL CLOUD A revolving column of air descending from a cloud.

GEOSTATIONARY SATELLITE A satellite that orbits in the plane of the Equator at the same angular speed as the Earth's rotation; also known as a geosynchronous satellite.

GEOSTROPHIC WIND Horizontal wind that blows in a relatively straight path because of the balancing effect of the Coriolis force and the horizontal pressure gradient.

GLAZE A thin layer of supercooled water that freezes on a surface.

GOES Geostationary Operational Environmental Satellite, an American weather satellite positioned over the Equator.

GRAUPEL Ice crystals coated by supercooled water droplets.

GREENHOUSE EFFECT The warming of the Earth's atmosphere caused by the selective transmission of radiation by carbon dioxide, which admits incoming short-wave radiation but absorbs outgoing long-wave radiation.

GROUND FOG Fog that forms when the ground cools.

GULF STREAM A warm ocean current that moves from the Gulf of Mexico to western Europe; it is a major factor in moderating the temperature in the North Atlantic.

GUST FRONT The wind at the leading edge of a thunderstorm.

HADLEY CELL A system of air circulation in tropical and subtropical latitudes that has a convective cell in each hemisphere.

HAIL Balls or chunks of ice that fall during a thunderstorm.

HALO A ring around the moon or Sun caused by refraction when either body is seen through clouds of ice crystals.

HEAT LIGHTNING A flash of light in the clouds caused by reflection of lightning from very distant thunderstorms.

HIGH An area of high atmospheric pressure; the same as anticyclone.

HUMIDITY Water vapor in the air.

HURRICANE A cyclonic storm that originates in the tropics and has winds over 74 miles per hour (119 kph); called a typhoon in the western Pacific Ocean; see also typhoon.

HYDROLOGIC CYCLE The continuous recirculation of water from the ocean to the air to the land and back to the ocean.

HYDROSPHERE The watery environment of the Earth.

HYDROSTATIC BALANCE The equilibrium of the upward pressure gradient force and the downward force of gravity.

HYGROMETER An instrument used for measuring relative humidity.

HYGROSCOPIC NUCLEI Small particles of matter on which water begins condensing even before the air is saturated.

ICE PELLETS Frozen raindrops; sleet.

INSOLATION Incoming solar radiation; the radiation that is received by the Earth.

INTERTROPICAL CONVERGENCE ZONE (ITCZ) The belt near the Equator where the trade winds of the Northern and Southern hemispheres converge.

INVERSION An atmospheric condition in which the temperature rises with altitude.

IONIZE To cause an atom or group of atoms to lose or gain one or more electrons, thereby providing it with a net electrical positive or negative charge.

IONOSPHERE High layers of the atmosphere characterized by ionized atoms and molecules and strong electrical currents.

ISOBAR A line drawn through points of equal pressure, similar to contour lines on a topographic map.

ISOTHERM Lines on a weather map drawn through points with the same air temperature.

JET STREAM A strong high-altitude wind in the troposphere that flows in a narrow, irregular band around the planet.

KATABATIC WIND The flow of cold, dense air downslope caused by gravity.

KELVIN SCALE A Celsius-based system for measuring temperature that begins at absolute zero.

KINETIC ENERGY The energy of motion.

KNOT A measurement of speed equivalent to one nautical mile (1.15 statute miles or 2.07 km) per hour.

LA NIÑA The periodic cooling of surface water in the central and eastern Pacific Ocean

LAKE-EFFECT SNOW Usually localized snowfall from clouds travelling over a large upwind body of water.

LAND BREEZE A nocturnal coastal wind blowing from the land toward the sea.

LAPSE RATE The drop of temperature with increasing height in the troposphere.

LATENT HEAT The heat or energy absorbed or released when matter changes state, as from a solid to a liquid, or from a liquid to a gas.

LEADER The channel of electrically charged air that begins the formation of a lightning stroke. A step leader is the preliminary path of electrical discharge in a lightning flash.

LIDAR An optical (laser) radar.

LIGHTNING One or more sudden streaks of light caused by a discharge of electricity from a cloud, between clouds, or between a cloud and the ground.

LOW An area of low atmospheric pressure.

MAGNETIC FIELD The line of force around a magnetic body.

MARITIME AIR MASS Moist air mass that originates over an ocean.

MELTING The process by which a solid transforms into a liquid.

MERCURIAL BAROMETER A mercury-filled vacuum tube used for measuring air pressure.

MESOCYCLONE A column of intense wind within an intense thunderstorm.

MESOPAUSE The transitional zone between the mesosphere and the thermosphere.

MESOSPHERE The layer of the upper atmosphere beyond the stratosphere.

METEOROGRAPH An instrument that can measure many variables of weather at the same time, such as temperature, relative humidity, air pressure, and wind speed.

MICROBURST A thunderstorm downburst less than 2.5 miles (4 km) wide.

MILLIBAR (mb) A unit of measurement for air pressure.

MOIST ADIABATIC LAPSE RATE The rate of temperature change in saturated rising or sinking air.

MONSOON A wind that changes direction seasonally; that is, it blows from land to ocean in the winter, from ocean to land in the summer.

MOUNTAIN WAVES The motion pattern of the air downwind of a mountain.

NAUTICAL MILE A measure of distance equivalent to 6,111 feet (1,852 m) based on the length of a minute of arc of a great circle of the Earth.

NEWTON A unit used to measure force; it is equivalent to the amount of force required to accelerate 1 kg (2.2 pounds) of mass 1 m (39.6 inches) per second^2.

NIMBOSTRATUS A low-altitude cloud characterized by thick gray layers.

NOWCASTING Determining the existing state of the atmosphere.

NUMERICAL FORECASTING The prediction of weather using mathematical calculations; also known as numerical weather prediction.

OCCLUDED FRONT The boundary that is formed when a cold front overtakes a warm front.

OROGRAPHIC LIFTING The forced upward flow of air over mountains.

OVERRUNNING Warm air rising over a wedge of cooler, denser air.

OZONE An oxygen molecule containing three oxygen atoms.

OZONE HOLE A severe depletion of ozone in the stratosphere.

PARHELIA Bright spots of light on either side of the Sun caused by refraction by ice crystals in the air.

pH SCALE The system for measuring the acidity or alkalinity of a substance.

PHASE CHANGES The transformation of matter from one state to another, as from solid to liquid, liquid to gas, or the reverse.

PHOTOSYNTHESIS The process by which plants create nutrients from sunlight, water, and atmospheric carbon dioxide. One of the by-products of this process is oxygen.

PILOT BALLOONS Small balloons, 30 inches (75 cm) in diameter, used to trace wind patterns in the lower troposphere.

POLAR AIR MASS A cold air mass that has developed at a high latitude.

POLAR-ORBITING SATELLITE A satellite that has a low-altitude orbit over the Earth's poles.

PRECIPITATION FOG Fog produced by precipitation falling through a layer of cold air.

PREFRONTAL SQUALL LINES Bands of thunderstorm activity that precede an advancing cold front.

PRESSURE GRADIENT The rate of change in pressure in a given distance.

PRESSURE GRADIENT FORCE The force that results from differences in pressure in the atmosphere.

PRESSURE TENDENCY The change in air pressure over a period of hours; used for short-term weather forecasting.

PROFILERS Remote sensing systems used for continuous collection of atmospheric data in a vertical column from the Earth's surface to the tropopause.

PSYCHROMETER An instrument consisting of two thermometers used for measuring relative humidity.

RADAR From "radio detection and ranging," a system for detecting the location of an object by using reflection of sound waves from the object.

RADIATION The process by which energy is transmitted through space as electromagnetic waves.

RADIATION FOG Ground-level fog produced by nighttime radiational cooling of humid air; that is, cooling induced by infrared radiation.

RADIOSONDE A set of instruments sent aloft on a balloon together with a radio to track and transmit data on the atmosphere. A rawinsonde is a radiosonde that is monitored from the ground by tracking antennae.

RAIN Drops of water with diameters greater than 0.02 inch (0.5 mm).

RAINBOW An arc of colors created by refraction and reflection of sunlight by a layer of water droplets.

REFRACTION The bending of light as it passes from one transparent medium to another.

RELATIVE HUMIDITY The ratio, expressed as a percentage, of the amount of water vapor in the air compared to the maximum amount that the air can hold at its current temperature.

RIDGE An elongated area of relatively high atmospheric pressure.

RIME An opaque layer of ice that forms when supercooled water freezes on contact with a cold surface.

ROSSBY WAVES The long wave pattern of air in the upper atmosphere.

SATURATED ADIABATIC LAPSE RATE The drop in temperature with height as saturated air rises in the adiabatic process.

SATURATED AIR Air that holds the maximum amount of water vapor for its current temperature.

SEA BREEZE A cool, daytime breeze blowing from the sea toward land.

SEA SMOKE Visible, steamlike evaporation from a warm body of water into cold air; also called steam fog.

SEVERE THUNDERSTORM A thunderstorm in which winds that are faster than 57 mph (91.2 kph) are accompanied by hail 0.75 inch (18.75 mm) or wider.

SHORT WAVE A wave in the pattern of wind flow, usually hundreds of miles long, in the upper atmosphere.

SHOWER Sporadic rain or snowfall occurring over a short duration.

SLEET Frozen or partially frozen rain.

SMOG Fog containing large amounts of air pollutants.

SNOW A type of precipitation consisting of ice crystals.

SOLSTICE The moment when the Sun is farthest north or south of the Equator, when the longest or shortest day of the year occurs.

SQUALL LINE A band of numerous intense thunderstorms.

STABLE AIR Air that has a fairly uniform vertical moisture and temperature profile, thus resisting displacement.

STATIONARY FRONT The boundary where a cold air mass and warm air meet, with neither advancing.

STEAM FOG Visible, steamlike evaporation from a warm body of water into cold air; also called sea smoke.

STORM SURGE A marked rise of the height of the sea along the shoreline caused by intense winds.

STORM TRACKS The patterns of movement that storms typically take.

STRATOCUMULUS A low-altitude cloud characterized by large puffy or rolled masses that fuse into an irregular sheet.

STRATOPAUSE The transitional zone between the stratosphere and the mesosphere.

STRATOSPHERE A layer of the atmosphere, found 7 to 30 miles (11–50 km) above the Earth's surface.

STRATUS A low-altitude cloud characterized by gray layers.

STROKE A component of a lightning flash; a single perceived flash usually consists of several closely spaced strokes.

SUBLIMATION The process by which a solid changes to a gas, or the reverse, without passing through a liquid phase.

SUBSIDENCE The gradual sinking of air over a large area.

SUPERCELL A violent thunderstorm that lasts several hours.

SUPERCOOLING The process by which water is cooled well below its freezing point without its solidifying.

SUPERSATURATION The state in which the relative humidity of the air exceeds 100 hundred percent.

THERMAL LOW A low pressure region formed by abnormal solar heating of the ground.

THERMOSPHERE An upper layer of the atmosphere.

THUNDER The sound that a lightning discharge produces as a result of air expanding along the path of the discharge.

THUNDERSTORM A usually brief, localized storm accompanied by strong winds, lightning, thunder, and heavy rain, hail, or snow.

TIROS Television Infrared Observation Satellite.

TORNADO An intense, whirling column of air extending from the base of a cumulonimbus cloud to the ground.

TRADE WINDS Two bands of easterly surface winds located in tropical latitudes.

TRANSPIRATION The process by which water vapor is released by plants to the atmosphere.

TROPICAL AIR MASS A warm air mass originating in the subtropics.

TROPICAL CYCLONE A low-pressure system in which the center is warmer than the air around it.

TROPICAL DEPRESSION A tropical cyclone having winds at least 23 miles per hour (37 kph) but less than 39 miles per hour (63 kph).

TROPICAL DISTURBANCE An area with a low-pressure center and marked convective activity.

TROPICAL STORM A tropical cyclone having winds between 38 and 74 miles per hour (63–119 kph).

TROPOPAUSE The transitional zone that is found between the troposphere and the stratosphere.

TROPOSPHERE The lowest layer of the atmosphere.

TROUGH An elongated area of relatively low atmospheric pressure.

TYPHOON A cyclonic storm in the western Pacific that originates in the tropics and has winds over 74 miles per hour (119 kph); see also hurricane.

ULTRAVIOLET RADIATION Electromagnetic energy from the Sun with wavelengths of 0.2 to 0.4 micrometer.

UNSTABLE AIR An air layer in which the air moves up and down in altitude.

URBAN HEAT ISLAND The higher temperature found in a city relative to the surrounding countryside.

VAN ALLEN BELTS Bands of high-energy particles in the upper atmosphere that are trapped by the Earth's magnetic field.

VAPOR PRESSURE The force exerted by water vapor in a given air sample.

VEERING WIND SHIFT A clockwise shift in wind direction.

VIRGA Streaks of rain or snow that evaporate before they reach the ground.

VISIBILITY The maximum distance at which an object can be seen by the unaided eye.

VISIBLE LIGHT The part of electromagnetic radiation that can be seen, having a wavelength from 0.4 to 0.7 micrometer.

WARM FRONT The boundary where an advancing mass of warm air meets a retreating mass of cold air.

WATER VAPOR Water in gaseous form.

WATERSPOUT A column of rotating air extending from the base of a cumulonimbus cloud to a large body of water; a tornado over water.

WEATHER MODIFICATION Human attempts to influence physically the outcome of weather, such as dropping silver iodide particles by aircraft into clouds to induce rain.

WILLY-WILLY The Australian Aboriginal term for a hurricane in the Indian Ocean.

WIND CHILL The wind's cooling power on the still temperature of the air as felt by the human body.

WIND SHEAR An abrupt change in wind speed or direction.

INDEX

Boldface indicates photo.

CREDITS

Front Cover: Summer lightning in Manitoba, Canada, by Eastcott and Momatiuk/Woodfin Camp, Inc.

Illustration for the Reader's Digest Living Earth logo by Jerry Dadds, Eucalyptus Tree.

Back Cover: National Aeronautics and Space Administration.

An Ocean of Air
6-7 Clouds over Wisconsin farmland, Richard Hamilton Smith; 8-9 Dust devil, Washington wheat farm, Will Landon/Allstock; 10-11 River of clouds, Harald Sund.

Thinner Than an Onion Skin
12 Illustration by David S. Merrill; 12-13 Thunderstorms over Western Africa, National Aeronautics and Space Administration; 14 Illustrations by David S. Merrill; 15 C. Allan Morgan; 16 Illustration by David S. Merrill; 17 Illustration by David S. Merrill; 18 (left) Illustration by David S. Merrill; 18 (right) National Aeronautics and Space Administration; 19 (top) Tom Soucek/AlaskaStock; 19 (middle) Clark James Mishler/AlaskaStock; 19 (bottom) Randy Brandon/AlaskaStock; 20-21 Illustrations by David S. Merrill; 22-23 Lynn M. Stone; 24 Tom McHugh/Photo Researchers, Inc.; 24-25 Jim Brandenburg/Minden Pictures; 26 Kevin Schafer/Peter Arnold, Inc.; 27 James L. Amos/Peter Arnold, Inc.; 27 (inset) James L. Amos/Peter Arnold, Inc.; 28 Robert Holmes; 28-29 Frans Lanting/Minden Pictures; 30 National Aeronautics and Space Administration; 31 Illustration by David S. Merrill; 32 National Aeronautics and Space Administration; 33 Heintz, J., "Panoramic View of Venice," Alinari/Art Resource, NY; 34 Leonardo, "A Study of Water," The Royal Collection © 1994 Her majesty Queen Elizabeth II; 35 (both) University of Bergen, Picture Collection; 36 Gary Braasch/Woodfin Camp, Inc.; 37 National Aeronautics and Space Administration; 38-39 Illustration by David S. Merrill; 40-41 Robert Madden/Folio.

Gift From the Sea
42-43 Fishing boat in stormy sea, William McCloskey; 44 J. W. Sherriff/Tony Stone Worldwide; 45 Joseph Mallord William Turner, "Snowstorm, Steamboat Off a Harbour's Mouth," Clore Collection, Tate Gallery, London/Art Resource, NY; 46 (both) National Aeronautics and Space Administration; 47 Richard Olsenius; 48 Illustration by Nicholas Fasciano; 49 (top both) Hans Pfletschinger/Peter Arnold, Inc.; 49 (bottom) Wolfgang Kaehler; 50 Woodward Payne/Photo 20-20; 51 (left) Mark E. Gibson; 51 (right) Richard Olsenius; 52-53 Frans Lanting/Minden Pictures; 53 Kirk Schlea/Picture Perfect USA; 54 (left top) Paul Skelcher/Rainbow; 54 (left bottom) Steven C. Kaufman/Peter Arnold, Inc.; 54-55 Roberto Soncin Gerometta/Photo 20-20; 55 Clyde H. Smith/Peter Arnold, Inc.; 56 (top) Eastcott and Momatiuk/Woodfin Camp, Inc.; 56 (bottom) Robert S. Walch; 57 Francois Gohier; 58 Mark E. Gibson; 59 Z. Roberts/Allstock; 60 Maxwell Mackenzie/Tony Stone Worldwide; 60-61 Jon Brenneis/Photo 20-20; 61 (top) Arvil A. Daniels, Science Source/Photo Researchers, Inc.; 61 (bottom) Noah Satat/Earth Scenes; 62 NOAA/Everett C. Johnson/Folio; 62 (inset) Sheila Beougher/Liaison International; 63 R. F. Head/Earth Scenes; 64 (top) Henebry Photography; 64 (bottom) Kenneth Garrett/Woodfin Camp, Inc.; 65 NASA/Science Source/Photo Researchers, Inc.; 66 Gregory J. Tripoli, Department of Atmospheric and Oceanic Sciences, University of Wisconsin, Madison; 67 (top left) C. J. Walker/Sygma; 67 (top right and bottom) Cameron Davidson/COMSTOCK, Inc.; 68-69 National Oceanic and Atmospheric Administration Satellite Photos; 70 Tom Nebbia; 71 Illustrations by David S. Merrill; 72 (top) Tom Nebbia; 72 (bottom) David Austen/Woodfin Camp, Inc.; 73 O.G.S./Picture Perfect USA; 74-75 Christopher Arnesen/Allstock.

The Atmosphere Electric
76-77 Lightning storm, Grand Junction, Colorado, Valrie Massey/Photo 20-20; 78-79 Tr. No.3730–Painting on wood of Thunderbird and Killer Whale, Nootka Indians (Photo by K. Perkins and J. Beckett) American Museum of Natural History; 79 Zeus, 5th century. B.C., at the National Museum, Athens /C. M. Dixon; 80 Shahadin, "Krishna Lifting Mount Govardhana," Copyright British Museum; 81 Ken Kanowsky/Creative Illustrations; 83 Thomas Ives; 84 Culver Pictures, Inc.; 85 Culver Pictures, Inc.; 86-87 National Center for Supercomputing Applications, Champaign, Illinois; 88 Robert Frerck/Odyssey Productions; 88-89 Eastcott and Momatiuk/Woodfin Camp, Inc.; 90 (left) Thomas Ives; 90 (right) P. Hubert/Langmuir Laboratory, New Mexico Tech; 91 Thomas Ives; 92-93 Illustration by David S. Merrill; 94 (left) Hank Morgan/Rainbow; 94 (right) Capt. T. J. Smith; 95 From an article by Richard E. Orville and Ronald W. Henderson in *Monthly Weather Review*, December, 1986, courtesy of American Meteorological Society; 96-97 Thomas Ives; 98 National Aeronautics and Space Administration; 99 National Oceanic and Atmospheric Administration; 100 Dan McCoy/Rainbow; 101 (both) National Aeronautics and Space Administration; 102 E. R. Degginger/Earth Scenes; 103 National Aeronautics and Space Administration; 104-105 Johnny Johnson/AlaskaStock.

Going to Extremes
106-107 Storm clouds, rural Minnesota, Richard Hamilton Smith; 108 R. W. Tolbert/Photo 20-20; 109 Kim Kulish/Sygma; 110-111 Robert S. Walch; 112 (top) Jim Brandenburg/Minden Pictures; 112 (bottom) Wolfgang Kaehler; 113 Sabine Weiss/Photo Researchers, Inc.; 114 Frans Lanting/Minden Pictures; 115 (top) Illustration by David S. Merrill; 115 (bottom) Serguel Fedorov/Woodfin Camp, Inc.; 116 Johnny Johnson/AlaskaStock; 117 Tim Riley/Art Wolfe Incorporated; 118 Francois Gohier; 119 Galen Rowell; 120-121 Richard Hamilton Smith; 122 Illustration by David S. Merrill; 123 (top) Jim Brandenburg/Minden Pictures; 123 (bottom) Mark Wexler/Woodfin Camp, Inc.; 124 Richard Hamilton Smith; 125 UPI/Bettman; 126 (both) Frans Lanting/Minden Pictures; 127 (left) Frans Lanting/Minden Pictures; 127 (right) Wolfgang Kaehler; 129 John Gerlach/Earth Scenes; 130 Richard Hamilton Smith; 131 Gary Braasch/Allstock; 132 National Aeronautics and Space Administration; 133 National Oceanic and Atmospheric Administration; 134 Steve Schneider/Richard Hamilton Smith Stock; 135 (both) Lake County (IL) Museum, Curt Teich Postcard Archives; 137 UPI/Bettmann; 138-139 Wade Balzer/Sygma.

Prophets and Magicians
140-141 Clouds at sunset, Wolfgang Kaehler; 142 Fletcher & Baylis/Photo Researchers, Inc.; 143 William McCloskey; 144 Brown Brothers; 145 Library of Congress; 146 Courtesy, Kenneth W. Howard; 147 Library of Congress; 148 Steven C. Kaufman; 149 Courtesy, Kenneth W. Howard; 150 (left) Archive Photos; 150 (right) National Meteorological Library and Archive, Bracknell, U.K.; 151 National Meteorological Library

and Archive, Bracknell, U.K.; 152 (left) Library of Congress; 152 (inset) Archive Photos; 153 Archive Photos; 154 From *Photography from the V-2 Rocket at Altitudes Ranging up to 160 Kilometers*, by T. A. Bergstralh, Naval Research Laboratory, 1947/courtesy of Kenneth W. Howard; 154-155 National Aeronautics and Space Administration; 157 (left) National Aeronautics and Space Administration; 157 (right both) National Oceanic and Atmospheric Administration; 158 National Meteorological Library, Bracknell, U.K.; 159 Hank Morgan/Rainbow; 161 National Center for Atmospheric Research (NCAR); 162-163 (all) European Centre for Medium-Range Weather Forecasts, Reading, U.K.; 164 European Centre for Medium-Range Weather Forecasts, Reading, U.K.; 165 (both) National Oceanic and Atmospheric Administration; 166 American Institute of Physics/Emilio Segre Visual Archives; 167 National Weather Service, Sterling, VA/National Oceanic and Atmospheric Administration; 168-169 (both) Lidar images provided by Ed Eloranta, Senior Scientist and Director of the University of Wisconsin-Madison Lidar Research Program. Graphics created by Dan Forrest; 171 Jim Brandenburg/Minden Pictures; 172 Jim Brandenburg/Minden Pictures; 173 Brown Brothers; 174 (left top) Kevin Fleming; 174 (right top) Vic Cox/Peter Arnold, Inc.; 175 L. McIntyre/Woodfin Camp, Inc.; 176 National Aeronautics and Space Administration; 177 Hank Morgan/Rainbow; 179(left) Steven C. Kaufman; 179(right) National Aeronautics and Space Administration; 180 National Aeronautics and Space Administration; 181 P. Bourseiller/Sygma; 182-183 Yann Arthus-Bertrand/Peter Arnold, Inc.

Tools of the Meteorological Trade
184 Analysis of total global ozone content in atmosphere, by The European Centre for Medium-

Range Weather Forecasts, Reading, U.K.; 185 Satellite imagery of hurricane, compliments of WSI Corporation, Billerica, MA; 186-189 National Oceanic and Atmospheric Administration; 190-193 National Meteorological Center, National Weather Service, NOAA; 194-195 (both) WSI Corporation, Billerica, MA; 196 WSI Corporation, Billerica, MA; 197 National Weather Service, NOAA; 198 National Aeronautics and Space Administration; 199 The European Centre for Medium-Range Weather Forecasts, Reading, U.K.; 200 National Aeronautics and Space Administration; 201 (top) National Aeronautics and Space Administration; 201(bottom) The European Centre for Medium-Range Weather Forecasts, Reading, U.K.; 202-203 National Aeronautics and Space Administration; 204 (left) Ron Holle; 204 (right top) Kevin Fleming; 204 (right bottom) Mickey Pfleger/Photo 20-20; 205 (left) Galen Rowell; 205 (right top) Thomas Ives; 205 (right bottom) Jeffrey E. Blackman; 206 (left) Ron Holle; 206-207 Wolfgang Kaehler; 207 (right top) Ron Holle; 207 (right bottom) Galen Rowell; 208 (left) Mark E. Gibson; 208 (right top) Ron Holle; 208 (middle bottom) Wolfgang Kaehler; 208 (right bottom) David C. Fritts/Earth Scenes; 209 (left top) Patrick Morrow; 209 (left bottom) Thomas Ives; 209 (right) Gary Braasch/Woodfin Camp, Inc.; 210 (left) Jeffrey Alford/Asia Access; 210 (right) Thomas Ives; 211 (left) Ron Holle; 211 (right) C. Allan Morgan; 212 (left) Thomas Ives; 212 (right top) Thomas Ives; 212 (right middle) Thomas Ives; 212 (right bottom) Gary Braasch/Woodfin Camp, Inc.; 213 (top) Pekka Parviainen/Science Photo Library/Photo Researchers, Inc.; 213 (bottom) National Aeronautics and Space Administration.

Produced for
Reader's Digest by

REDEFINITION

President
Edward Brash

Editor
Rebecca Hirsh

Design Director
Edwina Smith

*Finance, Administration,
and Production Director*
Glenn Smeds

Text Editor
Debra Greinke

Production Assistant
Catherine Rawson

Writer/Researchers
Susi Lill
Zachary Dorsey

Picture Researchers
Susi Lill
Zachary Dorsey

Color Separation
Colourscan Overseas
Co. Pte. Ltd.,
Singapore

For Reader's Digest

Executive Editor
James Wagenvoord

Editorial Director
Elizabeth Simon

Design Director
Michele Italiano-Perla

Managing Editors
Diane Shanley and
Christine Moltzen

Editorial Associate
Daniela Marchetti

Carl A. Posey, an award-winning science writer, formerly directed public information for the National Oceanic and Atmospheric Administration's environmental research laboratories and for the National Optical Astronomy Observatories, which operates major telescope facilities in the United States and Chile. He is the author of five novels, an illustrator and cartoonist, and a private pilot.

The editors wish to thank Thomas W. Schlatter who acted as general consultant for *Wind & Weather*. For other editorial contributions, the editors wish to thank Greg Edmondson, Margaret Higgins, Linda Kosarin, Brian Miller, and many knowledgeable and helpful people at the National Oceanic and Atmospheric Administration. The index for this book was prepared by Jeanne C. Moody.

Further Reading

Lockhart, Gary, *The Weather Companion: An Album of Meteorological History, Science, Legend, and Folklore*. New York: Wiley Science Editions, John Wiley & Sons, Inc. 1988.

Schaefer, Vincent J. and John A. Day, *A Field Guide to the Atmosphere*. Boston: Houghton Mifflin Company, 1981.

Scorer, Richard and Arjen Verkaik, *Spacious Skies*. London: David & Charles Publishing Co., 1989.

Trefil, James, *A Scientist Looks at the Sky*. New York: Charles Scribner's Sons, 1987.

Watson, Lyall, *Heaven's Breath: A Natural History of the Wind*. New York: Willaim Morrow and Co., 1984.

Williams, Jack, *The Weather Book*. New York: Vintage Books, A Division of Random House, Inc., 1992.